# THE ARCHAEOLOGY OF
# AIRFIELDS

# THE ARCHAEOLOGY OF
# AIRFIELDS

BOB CLARKE

First published in 2008 by Tempus Publishing

Reprinted in 2009 by
The History Press
The Mill, Brimscombe Port,
Stroud, Gloucestershire, GL5 2QG
www.thehistorypress.co.uk

British Library Cataloguing in Publication Data.
A catalogue record for this book is available from the British Library.

ISBN 978 0 7524 4401 7

Typesetting and origination by
The History Press
Printed in Great Britain

# CONTENTS

# ACKNOWLEDGEMENTS

As is customary with projects of this type, work carried out by previous archaeologists, historians and members of the public features heavily here; I hope they are happy with my attempt to complement that. Help, especially with discussing the project, must go to the Defence Estates Conservation Team, especially Guy Hagg, Richard Osgood, Phil Eley and colleagues; Pete Cooper, the staff of the Public Record Office, Jeff Nelson and Mike Stone of Boscombe Down Conservation Group; Ministry of Defence Copyright Team at Abbey Wood, especially Nicola Hunt and Sue Farmer for permission to publish the Boscombe Down pictures and help with other copyright issues; David Mackie of the Orkney Library & Archive for assistance and permission to publish the splendid Caldale Airship Station pictures; Don Todd at Upper Heyford, Adrian Robins, Kev Taylor, David Struthers, Frank Watt, Aldon Ferguson, Mike Digby, David Bullock and all my fellow enthusiasts who have dropped in useful leads. A special mention goes to Amy Rigg at Tempus for continuing to support my work, Barry Huntingford for covering the text and Malcolm Holland for information in advance of his own publication. Finally to Sarah who over the last few months has come to realise that a small detour 'to look at a site' actually indicates a four- to five-hour trek, and has asked for little other than a good holiday at the end in return!

# PREFACE

The story of aviation is populated with visionaries and entrepreneurs, Icarus, Eilmer, da Vinci, George Caley to name but a few. However, the ability to fly, rather than glide in a heavier than air machine, had to wait until the twentieth century to reach fruition when, on 17 December 1903, Orville Wright flew for 12 seconds using a powered aircraft, the Wright Flyer. Within a few years many pioneer aviators around the globe had made their first faltering, and sometimes fatal, 'steps' into the air. By October 1908 Samuel Cody had conducted the first controlled flight from British soil. Developments continued a pace until just forty years later jet aircraft were close to breaking the sound barrier. All this information is well documented and can be found in any one of the myriad of books published on aviation, as can books covering the history of individual bases or, as is the fashion now, county-wide surveys, but very few books cover airfield structures and even fewer investigate the geography or archaeology of the subject.

A few years ago I wrote a book covering the Cold War and Britain's part in it. Having spent most of my working life on or around aerodromes it came as a bit of a surprise that the questions I asked of airfields were nothing like those of my colleagues. It is probably one of the hazards of being an archaeologist but I wanted to know why the airfield was where it was: what decisions had driven airfield constructors to build where they had? The answer may sound obvious, but investigating a little deeper it is clear that lots of different criteria dictate how the network of British airfields developed.

As an example, in the 1950s the British Government embarked on an ambitious plan to build a country-wide air defence network – The ROTOR Project. When I looked into this I discovered that it was possible to see, through the archaeology of the bases, what the 1950s thinking was on nuclear warfare. Sites down the east coast were invariably underground, well protected and hidden where possible. Those on the west coast were unprotected and often just brick and Seco hutting. Defence thinking clearly considered the Soviet threat, at the time of construction bombers not missiles, would not reach the west coast of Britain, presumably being shot down long before that. Other early Cold War sites conformed to this thinking. A cursory look at airfields demonstrated a similar thought pattern.

This, naturally is dangerous territory; aviation is a discipline 'littered' with experts; the mass of publications pays credence to that. It is with that knowledge that I have embarked on this project, stating here and now that this work does not cover every airfield the British Isles has contained, nor is it a squadron or 'mission history'. Units will naturally be placed in historical context. It is impossible to mention RAF Scampton without reference to 617 Squadron or the Dam Buster raids, although the famous Lancaster squadron becomes almost irrelevant when considering Scampton's construction and location in the landscape, and when one considers Scampton's origins as a Home Defence Station called Brattleby in 1916 then it becomes immediately apparent why squadrons and missions play little part in this work.

This book investigates the landscape archaeology of British military airfields, how they came to be where they are, what the thinking of the period was and why they have the layout they do. It follows construction from the earliest site at Larkhill on Salisbury Plain through to the rebuilding of RAF Leeming in the mid-1980s. It is a book of trends and one which, I hope, demonstrates the subject from landscape and political point of view.

one

# GENESIS

The birth place of British aviation would appear to be Scarborough, or at least a small village a few miles outside the Yorkshire seaside town. George Caley, through a number of experimental gliders, discovered the effects of aerodynamic lift and drag, along with ways to control an aircraft in flight. These discoveries were published in 1810 in a paper entitled 'On Aerial Navigation'. Of course, no airfield was used. Some models were tested from the cliffs at Scarborough, whilst the first manned glides were undertaken on his estate at Brompton-by-Sawdon, a few miles to the west. These were piloted by his coachman who promptly resigned after the event!

The first true powered controlled flight in Britain came when Samuel Cody flew his British Army Aeroplane No.1 on three flights in 1908. He achieved 304ft on 29 September and by 16 October he had flown 1,390ft. Unfortunately, whilst attempting a turn the wingtip touched the ground, crashing the aircraft. These flights were undertaken at Farnborough, a station that was to become synonymous with British aircraft research throughout the twentieth century.

From here the story becomes infinitely more complex. The early years of aviation are often difficult to decipher, and pinpointing the start of the airfields is no different. However, the sites from which powered fix wing aircraft first operated fall into two broad categories – those with military patronage and those set up privately.

*The Balloon Factory*
Balloons were first employed on active service in the Sudan in 1885 and were later used in the Boer War at Kimberly and Lombard's Kop. These first balloons were manufactured at Woolwich Arsenal in 1878, cementing the use of flight with the artillery and provide the first clue as to why flying fields developed where they did. By 1890 the first Balloon Section of the British Army had been formed and the following year it and the manufacturing unit, by now containing the School of Ballooning, were relocated to Aldershot. It was at this time that aviation pioneer Samuel Cody joins the story.

Cody had been in Britain since 1901 with his travelling Wild West show, however, popularity had waned in the venture and he had fallen back on his other talent – kite manufacture. By 1903 Cody had displayed a variety of kites at Alexandra Palace and had been demonstrating man-lifting devices to the Admiralty. In 1905, Cody built his first glider kite and on 5 October 1907 the first military airship, *Nulli Secundus*, designed by Col. J.E. Capper RE and Cody, made a world record-breaking flight of 3 hours 25 minutes from Aldershot to London. That same year, Cody turned his attention to powered flight. It is here that the origins of Farnborough appear.

The Balloon Factory quickly outgrew its site at Aldershot and another location was sought. Just a mile to the north lay Farnborough Common, a wide open space covered by light heath and scrub, and during the winter of 1904–05 the Balloon Factory was relocated to the Common. Cody was employed as 'Instructor of Kiting' by the factory in 1907 and a year later, with War Office backing, he made Britain's first powered and controlled flight from Farnborough Common.

This official patronage was to be out lived. In 1909 Cody and Lieutenant J.W. Dunne were sacked from the Balloon Factory for being 'not properly scientific' by the Secretary of State for War, R.B. Haldane. They were replaced by Mervyn O'Gorman, a consulting engineer, who headed up the newly formed Army Aircraft Factory. It was Haldane's view that 'Science should come first' when developing aircraft for war. Others such as the Admiralty thought otherwise and continued to allow individual pilot/designers freedom in development.

### Larkhill

Larkhill and substantial areas of Salisbury Plain had been acquired by the War Office Committee from 1897 as the need for better training facilities was recognised. With advancements in artillery it had become increasingly difficult to fire live ammunition in Britain and by 1860 only two areas were considered safe – Plumstead Marshes at Woolwich and Shoeburyness. By 1900 over 22,000 acres had been secured for military use on Larkhill and West Down. Balloons were in use on the newly acquired ranges soon afterward. By 1902 records at Larkhill demonstrate that they were used for both observation and as targets having been transported from Aldershot for the summer season. Then, in June 1909, Horatio Barber rented a small piece of land from the Ministry and built a shed on it. A few days later the first aircraft to be stationed at Larkhill arrived.

Barber was one of a number of individuals who started building their own aircraft, inspired by the Wrights, Cody and a number of French aviators. Naturally if the War Office (WO) could be tempted then lucrative contracts could materialise, hence Larkhill as first choice. The WO was indeed tempted and erected a further shed for use by The Hon. Charles Stewart Rolls in the instruction of army pilots. Unfortunately Rolls, as the *Daily Journal and Tribune* in America reported, 'became the twelfth victim of the science of aviation' when he was killed at Bournemouth in July 1910. The shed was then rented to Captain Fulton, the owner of a Blériot. Three more military sponsored sheds appeared early in 1910, one rented by G.B. Cockburn, and in June a three-bay hangar was erected by the British and Colonial Aircraft Co. (BCAC) of Bristol. BCAC soon extended their operation with the construction of a further two-bay hangar to house the new flying school they had established.

British and Colonial Aircraft Company Hangars, Larkhill, in 2007. This group is one of the earliest examples of military involvement in aviation.

The British and Colonial Aircraft Co. was the enterprise of Sir George White, owner of the Bristol Tramway a vast coach building firm, and an aviation enthusiast. He was a shrewd businessman, saving many transport firms from the edge of bankruptcy, building a large, European-wide empire in the process. Importantly he opened a number of flight training schools – other than Larkhill – at Filton, Brooklands and Shellbeach. Initially the company built Boxkites based on the French design, the first being demonstrated at Durdham Down near Bristol, but went on to produce a range of aircraft by the outbreak of the First World War.

On 28 February 1911 the Government took the first step towards the creation of an independent air force when it decreed the formation of the Air Battalion of the Royal Engineers. From 1 April fourteen officers and 150 other ranks were employed in the field of aviation. The BCAC now came into its own as anyone within the Air Battalion or who wished to join as a pilot had to finance their own Royal Aero Club licence before an application would be considered. Naturally, the pilot was reimbursed £75 to cover costs on successful application. The Air Battalion comprised two companies: No.1, which operated balloons and kites, based at Farnborough, and No.2, primarily interested in powered, fixed wing aircraft formed at Larkhill.

## Royal Flying Corps

The Royal Flying Corps (RFC) was formed by Royal Warrant on 13 April 1912 and assumed control of the Air Battalion of the Royal Engineers on 13 May 1912. Initially it comprised a military wing, a naval wing and a new Central Flying School at Upavon. The first commander of the new force was Captain Frederick H. Sykes of the 15th Hussars, demonstrating that the RFC was in fact a department of the Army. The Army Aircraft Factory, as the Balloon Factory had become, was renamed the Royal Aircraft Factory, remaining at Farnborough.

Contrary to how it may appear the Royal Flying Corps was not formed to provide a single fighting force, rather it was designed to address issues surrounding training and supply of new equipment. The Army wing was administered by the War Office whilst the Admiralty was initially to control the naval flyers. In reality the Admiralty smarted as the majority of control was exercised by the Army. Complaints to the Committee for Imperial Defence, the only governmental body acting on behalf of both services, came to nothing. Soon the 'senior service' was training its own pilots at the Eastchurch Airfield and within two years of formation the RFC lost the naval wing altogether as the Admiralty set up the Royal Naval Air Service on 1 July 1914, with the patronage of one Winston Churchill, then First Sea Lord.

For twenty-five days in August 1912 the War Office held trials at Larkhill to discover which of the aircraft types already in existence would be suitable for use by the fledgling RFC. Competitors from all nations were welcome to compete for the prize of £4,000 and the possibility of a lucrative military contract. To accommodate the trials a further twenty temporary aircraft sheds were erected on the site, later these structures were transported to Farnborough. Although the eventual winner was one Samuel Cody, the construction contract was actually awarded to George White for his Bristol Tractor Biplane.

## Upavon

The Central Flying School was formed on 19 June 1912. The site was chosen because of its location on Salisbury Plain and flying distance to Larkhill. However, other drivers focused attention on this particular piece of downland. Prior to construction the landing area had been laid out as gallops and the area was fairly remote. It was this remoteness that attracted the Ministry. Flight tests at Larkhill had been drawing crowds from the local villages for a number of years. In May 1912 an aircraft crashed into the crowd killing one young lad from Amesbury outright and injuring two others. With the increase in flying the hazards due to spectators became worse and eventually the decision was taken to exclude the public. Upavon was then the ideal site, remote from large settlement, on an ideal piece of ground and elevated.

Upavon was also an attempt to contain the growing rift between the Army and Navy, with the Committee for Imperial Defence using the school to unify both services. Subsequently the aerodrome was based on army land but its first Commander was Captain Godfrey Paine of the Royal Navy. The school was not concerned with training of pilots from scratch, rather the honing of airmanship skills ready for combat. Accordingly pilots already holding Royal Aero Club certificates were those accepted on the course. After receiving a grant covering their flying fees students were introduced to a number of aircraft types. Course Number One graduated on 5 December 1912.

Records for this very early period are sparse; nonetheless, what does survive gives a valuable insight into the organisation and expansion of the school. The Second Annual Report on the Central Flying School 1913 (Air 1/2310/217) states:

Central Flying School, Upavon, late 1913. The first course graduated on 5 December 1912. (Courtesy of Phil Eley)

During the year the temporary Officers' Mess has been enlarged considerably, and two new Barrack rooms have been added to the School.

4 more Aeroplane Sheds will have been added, making a total of 9 double sheds.

The Quartermaster's Store and the Engine Shop have been enlarged considerably.

The School was finally in possession of B6 Aeroplanes.

The reason for this 'considerable' enlargement becomes apparent when course numbers are investigated:

The number of Officers taken during the year was:–

Naval 34, Military 78. Of these, 28 Naval and 69 Military Officers passed. One Officer resigned and one was unfortunately killed as the result of an Aeroplane accident.

20 N.C.Os. and men were sent to the School for instruction in flying. Of these 14 were graded 2nd Class Fliers. The remainder failed to pass during the course.

Approval was given in August for an increase in the Establishment of 13 N.C.Os. and 20 men.

(Second Annual Report on the Central Flying School, 1913 (Air 1/2310/217))

The fatality was one Major Merrick in October in a Shorts biplane. The record is also a valuable social statement as the following extract demonstrates:

Servants

As a provisional arrangement approval was given for a pool of 14 ex-sailors or soldier servants for Officers on the Staff and under instruction at the rate of 1 to every 3 Officers. This allowance to be in lieu of granting individual allowances in lieu of servants to Officers on the Staff. In addition this assumes that of the approximate numbers of 48 Officers at the School, 6 of the Regular Officers under instruction will bring their own soldier servants. If more than 8 Officers bring soldier servants, then the number of civilians must be adjusted accordingly.

(Second Annual Report on the Central Flying School, 1913 (Air 1/2310/217))

This expansion was but a drop in the ocean when compared to the war period training; however, it demonstrates a clear commitment to the enlargement of the flying capacity. During 1913 aircraft from Upavon flew an incredible 170,000 miles.

## Netheravon

By the end of 1912 accommodation at Larkhill had reached crisis point; officers were billeted at the Bustard Inn, and many others, including other ranks, were dispersed across army camps on Salisbury Plain. The War Office subsequently surveyed land to the east of the River Avon, identifying a flat plateau above Netheravon. Due to its elevated position it was considered ideal for flying. A tented camp quickly appeared and personnel were billeted there before Christmas 1912. In June 1913 No.3 Squadron flew in from Larkhill and a few days later they were joined by No.4 Squadron which had been formed at Farnborough by the Royal Flying Corps.

## Cradle of Military Aviation

Larkhill, then, can claim to be the earliest military flying field in the country. The arrival of Fulton, Barber and Cockburn firmly established flying at Larkhill and led directly to the establishment of the BCAC flying school for training Army pilots. The BCAC offices were set up in June 1910, four months after those at Brooklands, but crucially Larkhill was the only military establishment of the first four sites. The decision to base No.2 Company at Larkhill on formation of the Air Battalion assured the airfield's place in aviation history and was the start of military airfields in Britain. By mid-1913 the Avon Valley between Upavon and Amesbury contained the three primary military airfields in Britain. The area is naturally packed with pioneering aviation history. The Central Flying School at Upavon and flying fields at Netheravon and Larkhill form the earliest military bases, the former two still open at the time of this research. Further No.3 Squadron, which moved from Larkhill in 1913, was the first to be equipped with powered aircraft and thus is the oldest operational squadron in Britain. The Central Flying School set up at Upavon is the oldest military flying school still operational anywhere in the world.

So why are they where they are? Quite simply, the reason flying took place from Larkhill was due to the entrepreneurial skills of the early pioneers. Barber, who incidentally went on to open a factory at Hendon, intended to demonstrate that the aeroplane was much more versatile than the observation balloon. The best way to do this was to be close to the new training ground on Salisbury Plain. The choice of location for Upavon was an interesting one, appearing to be driven, in part, by its remoteness to settlement and

A Henry Farman HF 20 parked outside the hangars at Larkhill, *c.*1914. The group of hangars in the distance are those in the picture on page 11.

therefore the public. Netheravon also conforms, in part, to this. The key driver for the location of each aerodrome can be traced back simply to the decision to open Larkhill as a gunnery range for the Royal Artillery. Upavon and Netheravon survive today, but unfortunately for Larkhill, events in Europe soon forced the flying field to close. From here on in the landscape history of British military airfields becomes infinitely more complex and widespread.

# two

# THE FIRST WORLD WAR

On 28 June 1914, Archduke Franz Ferdinand, heir to the Austrian throne, was assassinated in Sarajevo. The shooting was carried out by a member of a Serbian nationalist group known locally as Black Hand. Austria-Hungary was so stunned by the assassination that it took nearly three weeks before they reacted, but when they did a complex mixture of alliances and pacts were activated, plunging Europe into the bloodiest conflict then experienced.

The Austro-Hungarian Empire issued Serbia with an ultimatum demanding the assassins be brought to justice or face reprisals. Serbia looked to its alliance with Russia as a means of protecting itself whilst the Austro-Hungarian government sought assurances that Germany would intervene should Russia declare war on them. Germany, eager to demonstrate its recent rearmament, readily agreed. Austria-Hungary declared war on Serbia on 28 July 1914 forcing the Russians, bound by treaty, to mobilise. Subsequently Germany, allied to Austria-Hungary, declared war on Russia on 1 August. France, bound by treaty to Russia, responded by declaring war against Germany and Austria-Hungary two days later. On 4 August Germany invaded neutral Belgium in an attempt to quickly reach Paris. This prompted Britain, allied to Belgium, to declared war on Germany the same day. By the end of the month the majority of northern Europe had been sucked into the conflict.

*Deployment*

Naturally, when the British Expeditionary Force left for France the Squadrons of the Royal Flying Corps were not far behind. On 13 August Nos 2 and 3 Squadrons flew to Amiens and Nos 4 and 5 Squadrons followed a few days later. Bases in Britain were virtually deserted with only a handful of men and machines left and nowhere near enough to generate replacements for losses or substantial reinforcements, should they be needed. It was not long before the short decisive conflict against the Germans became a war of attrition, swallowing up men and machines at an alarming rate.

The removal of almost the entire air fleet from British shores also left the mainland open to Zeppelin attacks. It was well known that Germany had been testing airships in an offensive role before the war and, whilst they were still small in number, it was

Royal Flying Corps Morane-Saulnier Type N 1915. This French type, known as the 'Bullet', demonstrates the precarious environment early pilots experienced.

only a matter of time before the craft were used against Britain. The newly 'officialised' Royal Naval Air Service (RNAS) was subsequently tasked with attacking the Zeppelins if they raided Britain. In reality the service had actually been unofficially running from Eastchurch in Kent for a year, using the British and Colonial Aeroplane Company school, along with aircraft built by the enterprising Shorts Bros.

## RNAS Airship Stations

As early as 1912 Churchill had proposed the naval wing of the Royal Flying Corps should be responsible for home defence. The idea was to open a chain of stations along the entire east coast of Britain, facing the Continent across the North Sea and English Channel. Throughout the war the RNAS operated four types of base, land-based aircraft, seaplanes, balloon stations and airship stations.

Airships were to perform a number of roles throughout the war including Home Fleet liaison and submarine spotting. As the conflict marched steadily on, a myriad of airship designs were to be pressed into service, constructed by companies such as Vickers, Armstrong-Whitworth and Messrs Airship Ltd. Naturally as the RNAS airship fleet expanded so did the requirement for stations and therein lies the problem – how many stations, did they all perform similar functions and is there a discernable pattern to their distribution? Firstly we need to consider the types of craft concerned and the roles they played.

## Building the Airship Fleet

At the outbreak of war the RNAS had few stations: Farnborough, the still to be completed site at Kingsnorth, Kent and Wormwood Scrubs in London. The total air fleet was not much better; it comprised seven craft of which only three were operational. Two of these escorted the British Expeditionary Force across the Channel from 12 August, and sporadic North Sea patrols were undertaken throughout the winter. By 1915 the situation had changed dramatically as all sides dug in for the long haul. When it became clear that the war was not going to be over before Christmas the German navy embarked upon a highly aggressive submarine campaign. If Britain could be starved of supplies from its Empire then maybe it would pull out of Europe. On 4 February Germany extended its declaration of war to the waters around the British Isles. Now U-boats could sink any ship without warning and rapidly began to do so.

To counter this the Submarine Scout, or SS, airship was developed. Approval for the type was given on 28 February 1915 and with construction of the non-ridged airship came an immediate need for bases. In March 1915 Kingsnorth, by now complete, became the headquarters of the RNAS airship fleet as Farnborough was given over to the newly formed Royal Aircraft Factory and expanding RFC squadrons. Spring saw a greatly accelerated construction programme as stations were sited around the coast. It is difficult to ascertain the true reason for the selection of each station; however, they do display some logical positioning.

## Coastal, C-Star and North Sea

Towards the end of 1915 the RNAS turned its attention to the development of a craft that had greater range, ceiling and speed than the SS type. Thus the Coastal and later C-Star airships were designed and built. The Coastal operated predominantly from the south-west and north-east coasts with a duration of over 10 hours; however one craft spent over 24 hours on patrol, a record at the time. By the end of 1917 the Coastals were due for refit; consequently the RNAS replaced the majority with the C-Star. In 1916 the RNAS embarked on a programme to introduce a massive non-rigid airship for long duration flights. Classed the 'North Sea', using the experience gathered from operating the Coastal and SS types, this was a ship capable of 48 hours' operation with a speed of up to 60 knots carrying a double crew.

## The Rigids

Britain was far behind the Germans in airship technology at the outbreak of the war. The navy had worked with Vickers Ltd to build the first rigid type in this country, known as the Mayfly, whose maiden flight was on 22 May 1911. On 24 September it broke its back and was later scrapped, along with any further work on rigid craft whilst the RNAS was pulled into the Royal Flying Corps. It was not until March 1914 that the United Kingdom embarked on the construction of another rigid type and by then the Germans had opened up an impressive lead in the subject. It was not until 1916 that the Vickers-built craft was inflated, the second flight, after serious modification, being in March 1917. It left the Barrow-in-Furness construction site for active duties that same month. Ships were also constructed by Beardmore & Co., Glasgow and Armstrong, and Whitworth & Co., Selby, in this period.

Caldale Royal Naval Air Station 1917. The domestic site can be seen in the foreground with the hangars behind. (Copyright Orkney Library & Archive)

The war, as is so often the case, rapidly accelerated the science of aviation and airships were no exception. In fact the production of airships, itself a minor technological miracle in the early years of the war, had outstripped the capacity to build airship stations by 1916. By the time of the Armistice 103 craft were in operational commission and over 200 had been constructed. However, technological advances were to cause other problems, not least of which being one of size.

The non-rigid types increased dramatically in size over the four years of the conflict. An early SS type would have a length of around 140ft and a height of around 46ft, whilst the Coastal broke the 200ft length barrier and the North Sea types were in excess of 260ft long by 69ft high. This was nothing when compared to the rigid types. The first design, the Mayfly, was a staggering 500ft long but only 46ft high and by the end of the war craft had well exceeded 630ft. One of the biggest problems faced by the RNAS was where to moor such vessels, especially as they were, by necessity, required to fly over the sea.

## Constructing the Airship Stations

Tracking down the exact number of stations involved in airship operations is difficult. As with all early aviation, records are, at best, thin and more often than not inaccurate, leading to in-depth and sometimes protracted discussion. Recently English Heritage conducted a survey of aviation sites as part of the Thematic Listing Programme (2000 and 2003). They suggest that there were sixty airship stations in the United Kingdom by November 1918 and in work published in 1997 Ces Mowthorpe notes twenty-eight sites, of which twelve were RNAS Airship Stations on mainland Britain, the rest sub-stations/mooring-out sites, including four on the Irish mainland. Research for this publication offers a different number again, especially when considering all stations – permanent or not. A paper written by George Whale in 1919 sheds some light on the matter:

> Shortage of steel and timber for shed building, and the lack of labour to erect these materials had they been available, rendered other methods necessary. It was resolved to try the experiment of mooring airships in clearings cut into belts of trees or small woods.

> A suitable site was selected and the trees were felled by service labour. The ships were then taken into the gaps thus formed and were moored by steel wires to the adjacent trees. Screens of brushwood were then built up between the trees, and the whole scheme proved so successful even in winter, when the trees were stripped of their foliage, airships rode out gales of over 60 miles per hour. The personnel were housed in either tents or billeted in cottages or houses in the neighbourhood, and gas was supplied in tubes [cylinders?] as in the early days of the stations before the gas plants had been erected.

> (George Whale, *British Airships: Past, Present and Future*, 1919)

Clearly some distinction between airship stations, sub-stations and mooring sites should be possible and taking into account Whale's comments it is indeed likely; the most useful archaeological evidence being the types of construction utilised on all the various sites.

Other station types should also be introduced at this point; these include the Training Stations at Wormwood Scrubs, otherwise known as HMS *President*, and Cranwell, HMS *Daedalus*. Both these establishments operated as training flights and, on occasion, supplied operational craft and crews. From early 1915 Wormwood Scrubs was a storage depot for the Royal Naval Air Service; it also performed airship construction duties. A number of non-rigid airships including SS and Coastal types were manufactured and inflated here. Cranwell was an enormous establishment. It comprised a North and South aerodrome whose combined area covered a staggering 2,466 acres. From the north aerodrome personnel were trained in kite and free balloon techniques, on the south an airship training centre was established in March 1916, supported by boy apprentices for both RNAS and RFC.

Construction sites are also spread across the country. Alongside the station at Wormwood Scrubs, opened in 1910, are the site at Armstrong Whitworth & Co. at Barlow, Yorkshire, two sites for Vickers Ltd at Barrow-in-Furness, Shorts Bros at Cardington, Bedfordshire, the official Balloon factory at Farnborough, Hampshire, and Beardmore & Co. at Inchinnan, near Glasgow. One further site at Creekmouth in Essex is noted but it appears construction of the craft, known as the MacMechan, was cancelled and the purpose-built shed became a store for the RNAS. Mowthorpe proposes four bases down the east coast of Ireland: Ballyliffin, Larne, Malahide and Killeagh. However, Killeagh was not completed and two further stations at Lough Neagh and Killarney never got off the drawing board. One further station at Wexford was utilised by the United States Navy from 1918. It would appear eight stations proposed for the British mainland also failed to materialise; these include Cromer, Cramlington, Moreton and Flookburgh. All this leaves just one more site on the Scilly Isles. It would appear that a permanent station was proposed for St Mary's, probably the site of the current airfield; however, again, this never went beyond proposal. The Scilly Isles are ideally placed and what records that do survive suggest that airship involvement more likely occurred at Tresco, this becoming a mooring out station for Mullion. The site must have been in existence in 1917 as SSZ.14, assembled at Mullion on 28 July that year, carried out trial landings at the site on 25 August.

In summarising the total number of stations involved in the operation of 'lighter-than-air' craft we can now consider the following: there were thirteen RNAS airship stations around the United Kingdom by 1918; these were supported by seventeen sub-stations with minimal or light infrastructure. Manufacturing units covered seven sites, with two being sponsored by the Government and a further eight stations were proposed but never completed. This brings the considered total up to forty-five locations, including partially built stations, across the British Isles.

## Station Infrastructure

Airship stations were no different to their aerodrome counterparts. A standard station such as Longside or Howden could have up to 500 personnel at any one time and naturally the domestic site contained everything needed to billet them. Messing arrangements followed the traditional three-tier system, as did site entertainment, often in the form of an institute with services provided by a religious society or the YMCA. Guardrooms, jails, coal stores and transport yards were similarly constructed to service the site.

There were operational peculiarities. Airships, to become lighter than air, used hydrogen and this needed to be supplied in vast quantities. In the early days only Kingsnorth and a reduced site at Farnborough were capable of producing hydrogen, the rest were supplied commercially via cylinders. As new stations were being equipped, small portable silicol plants were installed, capable of producing around 2,500cu.ft per hour. Later, larger capacity gas producing sites were built, taking the hourly production up to 10,000cu.ft per hour. The gas was stored in large gasometers and cylinders. Hydrogen, as many aircrew knew only too well, was extremely flammable. The same hazard beset personnel posted to 'Hydrogen Duties', as Lieutenant George Wildman and another rating discovered on 19 April 1917 when the silicol gas plant at Pulham exploded. Both men were blown through the side of the gas house and killed; several others suffered burns and other injuries. Surprisingly, as Mowthorpe notes in 'Battlebags', there are no other recorded ground crew fatalities during the production of hydrogen. Gas for the sub-stations and landing out grounds was provided by the parent unit by cylinder and transportation between sites became very important. Accordingly a large motor transport yard was provided, sometimes populated by steam-driven lorries. Airship stations also, not unsurprisingly, had large fire stations and water storage sites; however, a fire around hydrogen quickly became an unmanageable situation. On 16 August 1918 a fire started by an electrical fault destroyed four ships hangared at Howden. The blaze was so intense it warped the structure of the massive building.

Airships by their very nature are big craft and being 'lighter-than-air' required lots of manpower to ensure they did not disappear off into the distance with the slightest breeze. Any work carried out on their structure required covered space, and by the time of the

AIRSHIP SHEDS FROM S.E.     CALDALE AIR STATION, ORKNEY.     T.KENT

Caldale Royal Naval Air Station, 1917. Winds whilst bringing out the airship could spell disaster, subsequently large wind breaks were constructed at either end of the sheds. (Copyright Orkney Library & Archive)

rigid craft this space needed to be over 700ft long and in excess of 100ft high. Howden opened in 1916 and by 1918 had four airship sheds. This was fairly unique but enables the distinction between rigid and non-rigid to be made. The two non-rigid sheds were just over 320ft long, 110ft wide and 80ft tall, which was enough space for six SS-type craft. The rigid sheds were altogether more massive. Howden had one single shed 703 x 148 x 100ft and a coupled shed 750 x 300 x 130ft, and this did not include wind breaks that were often the same length as the shed. The primary factor in determining how many sheds were built appears to be due to a chronic shortage of steel. Through a mixture of necessity and tactical awareness, a temporary or portable shed was designed for non-rigid types. This was erected on a number of sites relieving the pressure on scant resources.

## Distribution and Usage

As noted previously, when the RNAS took over the airship programme it was in a less than suitable state. The only permanent airship stations would appear to be Farnborough, Wormwood Scrubs and a partially completed Kingsnorth. The infrastructure around the Submarine Scouts developed as much through necessity as anything else. In early 1915 the major supply route was from the south-east coast to northern France, in support of the, by now, static front. Subsequently stations appeared at Capel-le-Ferne in May 1915 and Polegate in July. That same month Luce Bay Airship Station also opened, covering the critically important route from the Atlantic to the Irish Sea. The SS types were to patrol key routes looking for U-boats and mines and due to their limited duration – often just 6 to 8 hours – had to be based near their patrol area. As the war became more protracted so the U-boat and mine threat increased. To counter this further RNAS airship stations appeared throughout 1916, including Mullion, Howden, Pembroke, Pulham, Longside and East Fortune. Noticeably now every area of British coastal waters could be reached within 2 hours, SS types covering practically every port in the country.

By mid-1918 the coverage of airship stations had been increased to one every 50 miles or so along the south coast. Between the Wash and Moray Firth a similar distribution is evident and both entrances to the Irish Sea were covered. A clear concentration is evident in the north where Luce Bay Station is serviced by four sub-stations at Machrihanish, Larne, Ramsey and Ballyliffin. With America now in the war troop and supply ships were under constant threat from submarine attack, so much so that the Irish Sea became known as 'U-boat Alley'. It became so bad that the Walney Island construction station operated by Vickers was in the process of being moved inland to Flookburgh, away from attacks. The only thing that stopped construction was the critical shortage of steel and corresponding rising costs; by mid-1917 the station was estimated to have already cost over £800,000. It is probable that in the period 1916–18 a number of mooring out stations were cut into tree cover, interspaced between established sites. Some of those eventually became sub-stations, but the transient nature of such sites, probably only used in the winter months when bad weather forced some consideration as to cover, meant that those without permanent structures soon disappeared.

It is clear then that the majority of RNAS airship stations are located on or near the coast due to the role they played in anti-submarine and mine warfare. This can be further reduced down to three main areas of concern: the Irish Sea and the protection of freight and, later, troopships from America; the south coast and protection of shipping in the

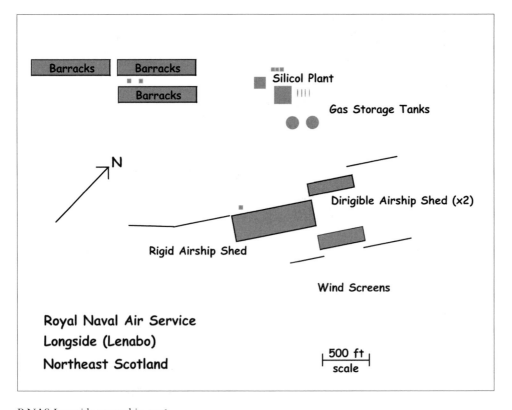

RNAS Longside opened in 1916.

English Channel; the east coast with its threat from the German navy to major industrial ports between Hull and Edinburgh. The construction sites are based where they are because they are simply on the manufactures' premises, whilst the training establishments were inland on sites that predated the outbreak of the war. It has to be remembered that airships, and balloons for that matter, were considered ideal for Army use, so basing them on the coast, exposed to all that weather, was, initially, far from the planner's thoughts.

Archaeologically airship stations are the rarest type of military airfields in the British Isles. As I noted earlier the jury is still out on the actual number of sites that were constructed to operate these majestic monsters from the early days of aviation. What hinders interpretation is the transient nature of the majority, often just clearings in woods. Those that did have infrastructure survived the post-war closures. Howden, East Fortune and Pulham being the main three, but these only for a few years. Howden was closed in 1921 only to be leased to the Vickers construction team building the R100 a few years later. However, when the R101 – the Government-built sistership – crashed that was the end of the British airship programme. What remains of this incredible period is scant to say the least. Probably the most endearing monuments to these craft are the internationally important sheds at Cardington, originally a Short Bros airship construction site and later an RAF training establishment. One shed is an extended example in original location; the other was removed from Pulham and re-erected next

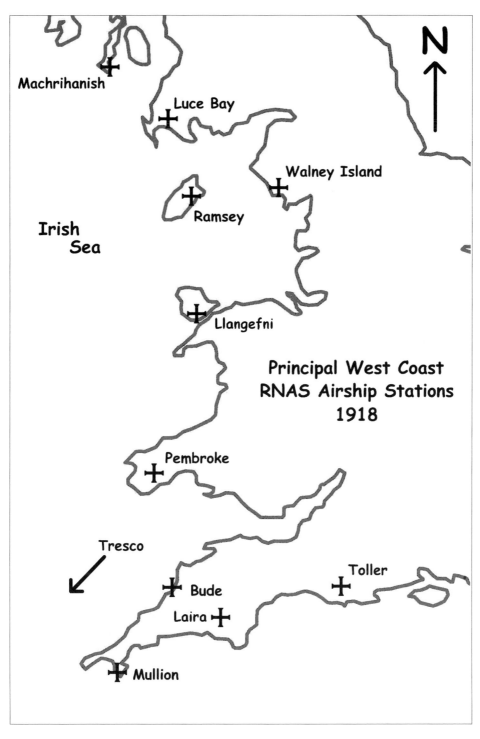

Distribution of RNAS Airship Stations around the Irish Sea.

Short Bros' Airship Station at Cardington, Bedfordshire, in 2007. Only the near structure originates from the site. The far one was bought from RNAS Pulham in 1928 to house work on the R100 airship.

to the Cardington original. Only Cranwell was to continue on; unfortunately all the stations built throughout the war have long since disappeared.

### Home Defence

Home Defence required dedicated infrastructure to operate effectively. Primary to the task was where to place aerodromes. Aircraft of the time needed to be close to the point of interception if they were to be effective. Subsequently a vast chain of Home Defence Stations and interspersed landing grounds were set up, predominantly, as one would expect, along the south and east coasts of England.

On 21 December 1914 a lone German FF29 seaplane dropped a single bomb in the sea near Dover. Three days later it was back, this time hitting the target. This was the first of many German raids into Britain using both fixed wing aircraft and airships. Six days earlier cruisers from the German navy bombarded Scarborough, Whitby and Hartlepool after sneaking through a gap in the minefield, killing and wounding nearly 100 in Scarborough alone. The Royal Naval Air Service was already fully committed to patrolling the North Sea in an attempt to stop further German naval incursions but was operating few aircraft at the time, relying instead on airships. At the beginning of 1915 Zeppelin raids started in earnest. On the night of 19–20 January the first air raids against the British mainland occurred when three craft of the Imperial German Navy Airship Division dropped bombs on Kings Lynn and Great Yarmouth, killing five people. In a corresponding 'first' the Royal Flying Corps flew its first night sortie against the airships, but all escaped. By the end of May Zeppelins were attacking London and on the last day of the month seven people were killed and thirty-nine injured. 1915 saw twenty raids, killing 181 people in total and injuring over 400

Hornsea Mere RNAS, East Yorkshire, in 2007. The tea room and workshop were both commandeered by the RNAS and used as workshops throughout the First and Second World War.

more. Clearly something had to be done about home defence. The RNAS made valiant attempts to bring down the marauders; however, due to a lack of serviceable aircraft, coupled with the high altitudes that the Zeppelin's operated at, success was limited. Zeppelins could, by dumping ballast, easily out climb the fighters of the day. This surprisingly rapid manoeuvrability also made ground fire at best inaccurate and often totally ineffective.

Naturally the search was on for suitable locations for airfields to protect Britain and deter the enemy. The following report is interesting as it indicates the ground covered by surveyors at this time. It also serves to demonstrate the diversity of sites considered and shows the reason why many aerodromes are now unlocatable.

19th June 1915

I beg to confirm my verbal report with reference to proposed Air Station at Scarborough, as also the suggested landing stations at Redcar and Hornsea respectively.

I beg to submit that the disused race course situated two miles to the west of Scarborough Town is the most suitable, possibly the only suitable place in that district, and it can be readily adapted for the use and requirements of a permanent Air Base. The district between Scarborough and Whitby offers very few facilities for landing, and the district between Whitby and Redcar practically none. At Redcar itself, however, I can obtain use of the race course, which gives us immediate facilities. The district between Scarborough and Hornsea is suitable for landing almost anywhere. It consists of large fields with low hedges and few

Hornsea Mere RNAS, East Yorkshire, in 2007. The generator house and general workshop constructed in 1916. Other surviving infrastructure include the pay office, toilet blocks, a magazine and slipways.

> trees. At Hornsea itself, I experienced no difficulty in finding a suitable landing station, but have deferred making any arrangement pending your decision with reference to utilising the large expanse of still water for the purpose of a seaplane base. This lake, although it does not run into the sea, approaches the coast to within 1500 yards.
>
> (PRO AIR 1/2558)

The first thing to note is the use of racecourses. Both Redcar and Scarborough went on to have flying stations set up on them as did Beverley, Driffield and a multitude of other locations. This may be important, especially when considering the positioning of airfields along the east and south coasts. Noting the fact that aircraft could land anywhere between Scarborough and Hornsea indicates the slightness of any infrastructure that may be associated with these early landing strips. It should be remembered here that aircraft all-up-weights were often so slight that they required practically no ground preparation at this point, therefore a landing out field might be no more that a requisitioned barn and a few bell tents, leaving no archaeological evidence what so ever.

Hornsea is different. The Mere was indeed utilised for seaplane operations and the first thing the construction unit did was requisition the tearooms of the Hull and Hornsea Railway Co. and convert it into workshops. The railway line had been opened in 1864 primarily to carry tourists to Hornsea but it also carried agricultural products, animals and coal to Hull and onto the Scarborough main line. The Mere, the biggest freshwater expanse in Yorkshire, was a firm favourite with travellers. Surprisingly quite a large amount of the subsequent flying station survives including the tearoom, a singular workshop, the power house, pay office and the officers' toilet block. The remains of the base of the magazine, compass swing circle and slipways are also in evidence.

## The Home Defence Station

A change in policy as well as tactics was desperately needed. The problem was that the War Office had never addressed the initial ad hoc way in which the RNAS inherited, by necessity, the role of Home Defender. Now the RFC had become far more powerful and it naturally demanded it be sole defender of the islands. Finally after much argument and posturing the Cabinet approved a new plan: from 10 February 1916 the RNAS would be responsible for stopping aircraft reaching Britain and any that did would be brought down by the RFC. One of the first RFC Home Defence Squadrons to be formed was No.36, on 18 March 1916 at Cramlington, Northumberland, it was tasked with the defence of the east coast between Newcastle and Whitby.

## Places in the Landscape

A cursory look at No.36 Squadron's footprint reveals the complexity of the archaeological situation regarding Home Defence Stations. Investigating squadron bases is also a useful way, in this period, to demonstrate the positions for the majority of aerodromes throughout 1915–16. Cramlington had actually been operational since November 1915, when three flights of BE2c aircraft had been stationed there. These flights were reformed as 36 Squadron a few months later. The initial the area of responsibility was around Newcastle; however, by May 1916 this had been expanded to include the Tees and Forth areas. In October 1916 the squadron operated over four main sites – the HQ at Jesmond, Newcastle, and flights at Seaton Carew, Ashington and Hylton. With the formation of the Royal Air Force 36 Squadron headquarters was moved to Hylton and the aerodrome renamed Usworth. Of course, the range and duration of aircraft operated at that time dictated that each site had a landing ground for emergencies and refuelling or arming. These sites were, by their very nature, sparse, provided with a basic level of hutting or on occasion using farm buildings or cottages as billets, and further confused by the use and reorganisation of existing sites. The total number of sites used throughout the war by No.36 Squadron was twenty-one, and this figure increases if we consider the search light and anti-aircraft batteries that made up the rest of the Home Defence Area.

Further down the coast the evidence is little different. Recent work by Mike Davies has revealed an even more complicated story; it serves to list all known sites to demonstrate the complexity of the issue. After the Cabinet proposals of early 1916, No.33 Squadron RFC was based at Bramham Moor near Tadcaster. The main task of No.33 and, later that year, No.47 Squadrons was the patrol and protection of the Humber region. Along with the HQ at Bramham Moor, No.33 Squadron had flights at Beverley, Coal Aston and, for a short time, Doncaster and Knavesmire, York. No.47 Squadron had formed on the opening of Beverley and operated one flight from the aerodrome. Again landing grounds were utilised at a number of sites. These were Atwick, Bellasize, Beverley, Brampton, Carlton, Coal Aston, Cullingworth Manywells Height, Dunkeswick, East Retford, Ecclesfield, Elmswell, Gilling, Goxhill, Hedon, Helperby, Middleton, North

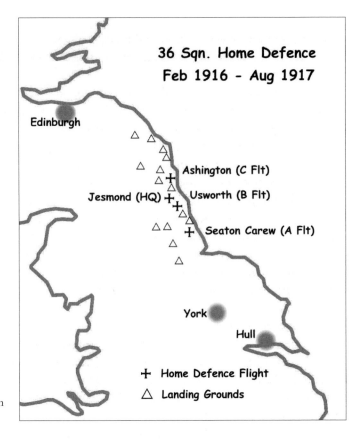

**36 Sqn. Home Defence
Feb 1916 - Aug 1917**

Edinburgh

Ashington (C Flt)

Jesmond (HQ)    Usworth (B Flt)

Seaton Carew (A Flt)

York

Hull

✝ Home Defence Flight
△ Landing Grounds

No.36 Squadron Distribution
between 1916 and 1917.

Coates Fitties, Pocklington Barmby, Pontefract, Redmires, Seacroft, South Cave, Thorne, Winterton and York.

This arrangement did not last, and by the end of 1916 No.47 Squadron had been detached to Salonika, Greece, whilst No.33 Squadron was relocated south to Lincolnshire. Now their HQ was at Gainsborough with flights at Brattleby/Scampton (A Flight), Kirton Lindsey (B Flight) and Elsham Wolds (C Flight). Landing grounds were also reorganised, with the squadron using Bellasize, Beverley, Blyborough, Brampton, Brancroft, Broomhill, Horncastle, Carlton, Cockthorne Farm, Cuxwold, Caistor, Doncaster, Eastburn, East Retford, Gainsborough, Greenland Top, Harpswell, Hedon, Kelstern, New Holland, North Coates Fitties, Owthorne, Redmires, Thorne, Wigsley and Winterton. Searchlight squadrons were stationed at Blyborough, Blyton, Boltgate, Elsham Wolds, Fillingham, Flixborough, Heapham, Goole Fields, Kirton Lindsey Aerodrome, Potter Grange Farm, Saxilby, Scampton, Stow, Twigmore Grange and Wootton.

Meanwhile No.76 Squadron assumed the defence of Yorkshire, particularly the coastal regions. The HQ was at Ripon, yet another aerodrome making use of a racecourse, and three flights were stationed at Copmanthorpe, Helperby and Catterick. Landing grounds were at Appleton Wiske, Barmby, Bellasize, Binsoe, Dunkeswick, Manywell Heights, Menthorpe Gate, Murton, Shipton, South Cave, South Otterington and Thirsk. Landing grounds would appear to be classified night, city defence or patrol and could range anywhere between 28 and 80 acres in the case of the north-east. Presumably a number of criterion dictated this widely varying area – natural obstacles, drainage and even whose estate it was on all made a difference.

One major driver in Home Defence planning was the type of enemy intruder it needed to protect against – the Zeppelin. The majority of raids were launched from occupied Belgium and many made landfall between the Humber and Flamborough Head, a well-known visual reference point. It is not surprising, therefore, that a well-appointed defensive network had developed there by the end of 1916. Nevertheless, this aerodrome landscape was not total coverage and demonstrates the level of defensive strategy considered appropriate against the known threats to the British mainland.

Arbitrary raids took place on town and city ports along the east coast for the next eighteen months. By 1918 attacks had decreased due to the accuracy of anti-aircraft fire and the increased effectiveness of the RFC air defence strategy. Zeppelin raids were never great bringers of destruction; however, they did succeed in killing civilians and subsequently became valuable psychological weapons. They also served to tie up RFC squadrons that should have been operating in France; by the end of 1916 twelve squadrons were committed to Home Defence but this effort was not to be wasted.

On a hazy day, 28 November 1916, in London the first air raid by powered aircraft took place. Again it was not massively destructive but did signal a change in policy by the German High Command. A lone Gotha bomber had made its way to London where it released six bombs. The aircraft was subsequently brought down near Dunkirk by the French, whereby the observer was found to have a large map of London in his possession. Clearly the Zeppelins had been replaced by something far deadlier. March the following year saw attacks increase and by the end of October the south-east coast and London had suffered 484 dead and at least 400 wounded. One of the most devastating raids on London took place on 13 June 1917. Involving at least fifteen aircraft, it flattened Liverpool Street Station and Upper North Street School, killing over 160, including many children. On 7 July sixteen Gothas headed for London again but this time they were met by thirty-six RFC and RNAS aircraft. Disappointingly, only one German was brought down. The public was not impressed and the situation forced a Cabinet meeting to discuss re-equiping the Home Defence squadrons. Eventually more squadrons were committed to the scheme, including one's equipped with the new and highly effective Sopwith Camel. The Camel was so successful that it forced a change in German planning – the Gothas switched to night-time operations, attacking London for six consecutive nights at the end of September 1917.

This move to night attacks brought about a much needed reappraisal of Home Defence locations. Rather than bunching all defences around perceived targets, often causing fatalities on the ground via anti-aircraft fire or shooting down the wrong aircraft, defences would now be arranged more logically. A series of defensive zones incorporating either anti-aircraft guns or aircraft were laid out. Each complemented by searchlights and a line of tethered balloons was constructed to act as a last wall of defence. The balloon defence of London in 1918 consisted of seven 'aprons' formed by a chain of balloons linked by cross cables. The cables carried weighted wire streamers so that any aircraft straying into the area would be cut to pieces. The aprons were designed to force enemy aircraft to use a restricted height band which, in turn, was covered by fighters or anti-aircraft guns.

Henry Farman HF 20s at Farnborough in 1915.

## The Training Landscape

By the start of the Battle of the Somme on 1 July 1916 the Royal Flying Corps could boast thirty-one operational squadrons, with 410 aircraft stationed in France. Unfortunately with this impressive set of figures came an equally depressing set of casualties. Michael Armitage, in his history of the Royal Air Force, suggests that in the July to mid-November period the Royal Flying Corps lost 308 airmen. Demands from General Haig to increase the number of squadrons to fifty-six and by a further twenty squadrons by the end of the year placed massive pressure on the dwindling aircrew reserves. The immediate answer was to open further flying schools in Britain and form twenty reserve squadrons in Canada.

This impressive increase in 'trained' pilots did initially slow the incessant demand; however, there were those on the front line who considered far more experience was needed before rookie pilots were cast into battle. Up to 1916 training had been an ad hoc affair, with pilots receiving only a few hours solo at an Elementary Training School (TS) before completing a night flight. They would then take their Flying Certificate test, awarded by the Royal Aero Club, gaining their 'ticket' before moving on to a higher or advanced TS for specialist instruction. It became apparent that training accidents were claiming nearly as many pilots as the enemy. This alarmed squadron commanders, among them Robert Smith-Barry, one of the early Larkhill pioneers and a member of the first RFC course at CFS Upavon in 1912.

Smith-Barry, Commander of No.60 Squadron based at Savy-Aubigny, convinced Trenchard that pilot training was less than adequate. If the attrition currently being experienced on the Western Front was to be stemmed then training needed a radical re-shaping. He was familiar with the French training system, an 'all through' concept that ensured pilots were fully proficient before posting them to the front line units. Trenchard challenged him to prove his theories, sending him back to Britain to command No.1 (Reserve) Squadron, Gosport, in December 1916.

What Smith-Barry devised revolutionised flying training with some concepts still utilised today. For years the student had taken the back seat during dual flying, watching the instructor's actions and occasionally taking control of the aircraft. Now the student sat in the front seat with a complete suite of controls and instruments, whilst the instructor took the rear seat. Thus the student became accustomed to the position he would be in during his solo flight and as a result accidents were cut. Nevertheless, this was only a minor improvement. Would-be pilots now received extensive classroom lectures covering characteristics of flight and how to control a multitude of airframe types, prior to receiving instruction on them. Once the student had achieved both the solo flight and his 'ticket', he received further dual training. This is where Smith-Barry's new flying instruction course differed radically from the previous arrangement: pilots were shown not how to keep out of danger but what to do if a dangerous situation arose. Previously men had to hope that they did not end up in a spin if the aircraft stalled during combat, and if they did end up recovering from such a dangerous situation it was often more to luck than judgment. The spin − along with various other aerobatic manoeuvres − was actively encouraged and saved many allied pilots' lives during dogfights in France. By July 1917 the School of Special Flying was formed at Gosport with the sole intention of

RNAS Lee-on-Solent, Hampshire, shortly after opening on 30 July 1917. Note the very temporary nature of the station.

RFC Yatesbury, Wiltshire, in 2003. A squadron hangar of the Southern Training Brigade.

RAF Waddington, Lincolnshire, on 5 April 1918. The station opened in 1916 and displays the pre Training Depot Station layout. Servicemen from the United States were instructed here during the First World War.

Interior of Hut, 28 Squadron No 1 Camp, Yatesbury.

Royal Flying Corps Training Brigade Station Yatesbury, Wiltshire 1916. Conditions were sparse for trainee pilots. Note the beds are not much more than planks and can be seen leant against the walls.

teaching a new breed of instructors. These experts were posted throughout the country, improving flying training and saving many lives in the process.

Training stations were also reorganised from late 1916 and a new dedicated organisation in the form of the Training Brigade appeared. The Brigades were initially established on existing aerodromes such as Catterick and Northolt but a number of new airfields were also built to expand the scheme including, in late 1916, Yatesbury. Yatesbury officially opened in November 1916 and was, from the outset, two separate airfields. Two reserve squadrons were stationed at the aerodrome and the layout still survives for one. Two hangars and an aircraft repair shed are still in evidence; however, the repair shed, in the English Heritage 'monument at risk' category, has recently collapsed.

Stations were spread across the country to capitalise on the influx of local volunteers now eager to fly; however this was still quite disorganised and clearly needed some form of standardisation. By January 1917 the Training Brigade scheme had developed into Reserve (Training) Squadrons and rapidly grew from thirty-seven to ninety-seven, including nearly twenty bases in Canada. By November the same year the newly appointed Inspector of Training, Brigadier-General Ludlow-Hewitt, initiated a major expansion. A new specialist training unit appeared on the landscape, one that was to set the foundation of many airfields that survive today – the Training Depot Station.

No. 6 Training Depot Station, Boscombe Down, 1917. The construction of the airfield infrastructure
is well under way – note the roof truss laid around the partially completed hangars. (Courtesy of the
Ministry of Defence)

## Training Depot Stations

Training Depot Stations (TDS) are one of the most important archaeological airfield
components in the landscape. As noted above some earlier sites were developed into
the TDS scheme, although the majority were new builds. These are important as some
stations remain in use today and thus owe their existence to the requirements of the
Royal Flying Corps some ninety years past. Initially seven stations were built at Stamford,
Lake Down, Lopcombe Corner, Hooton Park, Easton-on-the-Hill, Boscombe Down and
Feltwell, but by the end of 1918 the number had swelled to over sixty.

The Training Depot Station system seems to have resulted from a visit by Smith-Barry
to inspect the French training programme. The French had training centres running
an aerodrome, operating numerous satellites and delivering all-through training. The
beauty of the TDS was in its economy; hitherto, pilots had been posted to Elementary
Training Schools and, on graduation, to a Higher Training School, critically at a different
station, followed by a further move to a specialist centre. The TDS provided all-through
training, ensuring a cost-effective training plan that required little further instruction on
completion. No.6 TDS trained daylight bombing pilots, utilising its closeness to Salisbury
Plain, and this explains why the majority of bombing-orientated stations were originally
located on the Plains southern fringe. Later the coverage became national, diffusing any
opportunity to demonstrate a pattern. What is important archaeologically, here is the
station layout, especially since the structural arrangement can still be recognised at a
number of surviving stations.

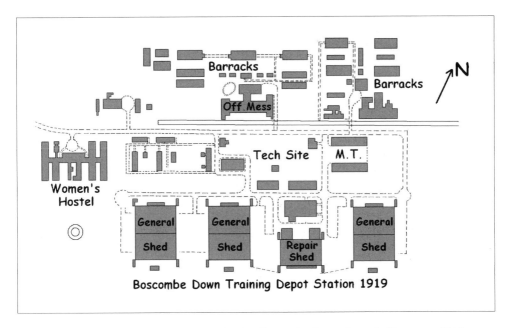

Boscombe Down Training Depot Station 1919

The general layout of No.6 Training Depot Station, Boscombe Down, in 1918. (Courtesy of Mike Stone)

Building 84, Duxford. Built in 1917, double-span hangars were designed to accommodate one squadron of aircraft.

No. 11 Training Depot Station Old Sarum, Wiltshire, in 2007. Originally opened in mid-1918, this single-span hangar was used for aircraft repair and servicing. Note the two associated workshops attached to it.

The purpose-built Training Depot Station had a very distinctive layout, demonstrating its ability to house three squadrons and provide the comprehensive repair facilities required when operating a training squadron. To house the resident squadrons three trussed roofed, coupled general purpose sheds were built, usually aligned north-east to south-west. Between them a single-span repair shed, usually with attached workshop, was built, often slightly forward of the other three. Behind that shed was located the woodwork and doping workshop, often in a double-span, single storey; close by a blacksmith and other technical services were built. At Boscombe Down, Duxford and Old Sarum the domestic site was detached from the technical side by a road; other stations such as Bicester and Andover had the domestic site further away. Regardless of the topographical differences experienced on such sites the majority of TDS were segregated into three separate entities – flying, technical and domestic – a concept that was to survive, albeit modified, until the introduction of the dispersed site in 1941/42.

## Halton

We would be amiss if one of the RFC's and later RAF's greatest institutions, Halton, was not mentioned here. By the middle of 1916 over 1,000 pilots a month were being trained. Men need machines to fly in and it soon became apparent that whilst a shortage of pilots would ground aircraft, a lack of skilled groundcrew would also ensure that no matter how many pilots there were they would not be able to fly. Until that point the RFC had heavily relied on skilled Army mechanics requesting a transfer or recruitment from civilian engineering disciplines. With the introduction of specific mechanic instruction came the opening of one of the Royal Air Force's, if not the world's, most famous groundcrew training centres – RAF Halton.

Halton's aviation roots were pre-First World War; No.3 Squadron of the Royal Flying Corps deployed to Halton Park in 1913 and were involved in army manoeuvres supporting the operations of a brigade of Guards, Battalions of Black Watch and Munster Fusiliers. A temporary airfield was erected on pasture – once it had been cleared of the resident sheep – which later became the parade square area to the Maitland barrack blocks. All this was under the invitation of Alfred de Rothschild, head of the famous society bank. The following year over 20,000 troops arrived at Halton Park after an agreement between Rothschild and Lord Kitchener that the Army could use the land. In 1916, the Royal Flying Corps moved from Farnborough, basing its training for air mechanics at the park. This immediately dictated an increase in accommodation and technical workshop space and what is now known as 'The Old Workshops' was constructed by German POWs at a cost of £100,000. By the Armistice an incredible 6,000 British and Australian male mechanics, 2,000 female mechanics and 2,000 boys were under training by 1,700 staff.

With such a major construction effort being undertaken across Britain, it was inevitable that POWs became embroiled in the work, and this was not restricted to Halton. The hangars at Boscombe Down were the work of German prisoners, as were a good many other airfield structures around the UK. POW camps were often located close to, and on occasion at, RFC stations: Upavon, Netheravon and Yatesbury to name but a few. Strictly speaking, German POWs were allowed by the Haig Convention to work in non-war-based industries, such as farming, as long as they were paid. However, by 1917 they were not only employed on the land, covering the shortage of labour the war was causing, they were also involved in construction works at training airfields.

Not all stations were built by press-ganged POWs. By 1916 a specialist unit had been created for the construction of stations both at home and abroad. The Airfield Construction Corps (ACC), as it was know, based at Pulham, was responsible for much of the airfield infrastructure but surprisingly little remains of their records. Many of the men were classed as Air Mechanics (General) and were subsequently referred to within the RNAS as 'Generals'; however, they were, where possible, mainly recruited from the building trades. It would appear their speciality was the airship station, but work on the TDSs from 1917 and a number of aerodrome builds in France was to account for the majority of their time in the latter part of the war. Luckily when the RAF was formed a request as to the manning of such units was lodged with the Commanding Officer on 17 May 1918:

> In reply to your signal of the 16th. instant, the present establishment of an A.C.C. Company is as follows:-
> Carpenters (40); Constructional Fitters (24); Bricklayers (4); Riggers (10); Sheeters (10); Machinists (4); Plumbers (2); Blacksmiths (2); Painter (1); Unskilled (50).

The question of the complement of an A.C.C. Company is, however, under discussion and the new complement for which approval is expected at an early date. In addition to the above the A.C.C. Companies carry cooks, transport drivers, plant drivers, etc. in accordance with the needs of the Company.

Lieut. Colonel, RAF, Tom Mackie, Commanding Officer, A.C.C.

(PRO AIR 1/72/15/9/140))

The title 'unskilled' is not qualified anywhere in the document and one wonders if these are the POW components of construction teams. If the company was to be deployed to France then the skill base changed slightly with the addition of draughtsmen and surveyors (two), writer (one) and storekeepers (three). The ACC was not concerned purely with aerodromes; 5th Company had been building Naval Mechanical Transport Establishments in France at the time of the switch to the RAF. Clearly there was little distinction between departments in the Navy.

The war period, then, had a number of facets to it. In the one extreme it saw the development of aerial warfare, laying the foundations for what was to reach its developmental zenith just over eighty years later when Coalition air forces effectively neutralised Iraq's total defence capability before ground troops were committed. The First World War also left a mark on the archaeological and architectural record with the appearance of specialist stations for the protection of British coastal waters. This concept continues to the present day, although the leviathans that conducted this during the war had disappeared by 1930 and now only one site, Cardington, can be readily recognised as an airship station. The most easily recognisable aspects of the RFC on the landscape are the Training Depot Stations, a number of which survive in various states of completeness across Britain. However, even where evidence is slight it is still possible, as is the case with Boscombe Down, to recognise the First World War layout in later positioning of structures. The same cannot, unfortunately, be said of the Home Defence stations. These often slight landing strips were rapidly returned to agriculture after the war. Such was the pace of abandonment that it is difficult to place some in the landscape, whilst others are just names in the record with little chance of pinpointing the exact location. By the beginning of 1918 the United Kingdom contained a vast array of air stations. Nevertheless, soon after the Armistice the focus changed from one of national survival to one of the air force's survival.

three

# THE WINDS OF CHANGE 1918–33

In the final year of the First World War air combat became the preserve of a new service, the Royal Air Force. However, concern that the new service would not be able to finish the war under its own direction nearly stifled the venture at birth. This opinion was to prevail throughout the inter-war period and it certainly had an effect on the archaeology of the airfields and associated stations. This section investigates Trenchard's struggle to build a credible air force to police both acquisitions abroad and provide home defence for the British Isles. This cannot be adequately demonstrated in isolation; subsequently the story of the RAF and its airfields in the inter-war years is placed in context with the major political events of the period. It is also a very complex period regarding the distribution of airfields. Many were disposed of immediately after the war, only to become the object of intense and often protracted negotiations a few years later.

*Genesis*
The bomber raids over London throughout 1917 had a profound effect on the British Government. Not only did they change the public's perception of warfare, now civilians were on the front line, dictating military procurement and the need for a credible large home defence network. The network set up to combat the Gotha bombers and increasingly rare Zeppelin raids removed many squadrons from service in France, depleting the front line for a while. However, the introduction of American aircraft onto both the Western Front and throughout Asia Minor meant that shortfalls were not long term.

The crisis was discussed at the Imperial War Cabinet in London, the organisation that Prime Minister David Lloyd George had formed in the spring of 1917. The body was intended to co-ordinate the Military Policing of the Empire for the duration of the war. Subsequently it comprised distinguished individuals from Canada, India, Australia and New Zealand; representing South Africa was Prime Minister Louis Botha and Jan Smuts. Smuts, a distinguished soldier, was tasked with investigating the future of air power, including the home defence situation. By 17 July the first of two reports had been circulated. The first recommended that all aircraft, searchlights, balloons and observation posts needed to be under the same command, building faster reaction times. All this was to be organised under the guise of the 'London Air Defence Area'.

In the second report, presented to the War Cabinet on 17 August 1917, Smuts reviewed the entire British air effort and in so doing laid the foundation stone of the Royal Air Force. This far-sighted work concluded that air power could not be divided between services, requiring instead a dedicated chain of command. Both the Army and Navy would require a flying wing; however, the main bulk of the air responsibility had to be controlled independently of them. By 1917 it had become clear that aircraft were weapons of strategic importance. The first faltering sorties had been nothing more than observation for artillery and ground force concentrations, by the time of Smut's paper this had expanded into a major component of the battlefield. Further, aircraft could attack targets well beyond the reach of artillery, something not wasted on the Germans with their long range bomber fleet. Just as important was the fact that the British aircraft industry could now manufacture craft in such quantities as to fully supply losses whilst building up strategic reserves. Reasons for this included the introduction of women into war industries and the eventual placing of those industries onto a war footing. Smuts concluded:

> In our opinion, there is no reason why the Air Board should continue in its present form and there is every reason why it should be raised to the status of an independent Ministry in control of its own war services.

Opposition to the paper came from all sides, but not all were outwardly hostile to the principle of an independent air force, just its timing. Senior ranks in the Royal Naval Air Service and Royal Flying Corps were concerned that the chaos surrounding a new venture such as this was not a good idea during wartime. Others such as General Haig were outwardly scathing of the report as was, surprisingly, Trenchard. He considered that the reorganisation of the flying wings could lead to a shortage of aircraft and men on the Western Front, and this could lead to defeat. Better to leave the reorganisation until after the war. None of this deterred the British Government from acting and on 16 October 1917 a bill was introduced to Parliament called the Air Force (Constitution) Act; on 29 November it received Royal Assent as the Air Force Act. On 2 January a new Air Council was formed and on 1 April 1918 the Royal Air Force came into being.

### Armistice

After it became clear that the Germans were not going to break the Armistice of 11 November 1918 the British Government naturally looked into drastically reducing its defence spending. At the forefront of this was the air fleet, itself coupled with vast tracts of donated and requisitioned land used for Training Depots, Home Defence, Air Acceptance Parks and the multitude of landing grounds. The massive expenditure of the First World War had turned Britain, in four short years, from a creditor to a debtor nation. The capital debt in 1914 stood at £706 million; six years later that had risen to £7,875 million. The war had left Britain with far more overseas commitments and a poorer strategic position than when it started. Estimates suggest that at the end of the war the Chief of the Imperial

WAAF at Hendon, 1920. Originally the WAAFs were to fill the posts of male mechanics; however, they soon covered most jobs around the station. The organisation was disbanded in 1920.

General Staff had over 3.5 million men still deployed overseas; by 1920 this figure had been reduced to 370,000. The Royal Air Force was at the forefront of cuts. It had inherited the largest air force in the world and had collected some powerful enemies, especially in Whitehall along the way. Now, with a reduction in defence spending it looked like the RAF would be snuffed out.

At the end of the conflict nearly 100 squadrons were based in France alone. Manpower stood at just over 300,000 in late 1918; however, by 1920 this had been reduced to just 29,500. To give some idea of the logistical problem of demobilisation the British Government formed an agency whose sole remit was the disposal of war surplus aircraft. Imaginatively titled the Aircraft Disposal Company Ltd (ADC) it oversaw the removal of nearly £6 million worth of assets in 1919 alone, including over 30,000 engines, 10,000 aircraft, 100,000 magnetos, 350,000 sparkplugs and an incredible 1,000 tons of ball bearings. In an indication to the scale of the demobilisation the ADC was still converting and disposing of aircraft as late 1930.

By the signing of the Armistice aerodromes − covering all definitions of the term − were the length and breadth of Britain. The Training Depot Station scheme had sixty-one locations alone. Some airfields had more than one wing operating from it making interpretation doubly difficult; Yatesbury being one such example. Of over 300 sites in Britain, not including the multitude of landing fields that were quite simple just that, Colin Dobinson has suggested that an incredible 271 were disposed of by March 1920. Many reverted back to the original land owners, often through straight forward contracts or cancellation of rental agreements, a great number were cleared almost immediately. Being grass strips and mostly timber construction means that little, if anything, survives today.

## Training for the Defence of a Nation

Trenchard readily acknowledged that the new RAF was an easy target for cost cutting. In 1919 he proposed a number of measures to ensure a good foundation on which to build any future force. Titled 'Permanent Organisation of the RAF − Note by the Secretary of State on a Scheme Outlined by the Chief of Staff', it soon became known as the Trenchard Memorandum.

Trenchard described the remnants of the Royal Air Force as comparable to the prophet Jonah's gourd:

> … the necessities of war created it in a night, but the economics of peace have to a large extent caused it to wither in a day, and we are now faced with the necessity of replacing it with a plant of deeper root…

Clearly if a major reduction in the Royal Air Force was to be less than catastrophic then it would have to be carefully planned. Any concentration in resources would best serve the RAF if it was planned as a foundation layer, preferably focussing on training a well as a provisioned core force. Central to this would be the retention and expansion of certain training establishments, especially Cranwell, Halton and Andover.

RAF Cranwell, 1929. The Cadet College opened in 1920 but work to improve accommodation conditions was still ongoing at the end of the decade. Buildings being demolished can be seen on the left of the picture. (Courtesy of Malcolm Holland)

### 'The RAF depends on you far more than on me'

The training footprint in the early post-war period centred on three established stations, Cranwell, Halton and Andover, and these were considered by Trenchard to be pivotal to not only the competence of the RAF but essential to retaining its identity and independence.

### Cadet

Cranwell is typical of the complexity encountered when interpreting stations beyond their initial conception. Three distinct phases are apparent in the first five years of its existence and since construction it has housed a myriad of training establishments. Cranwell is a unique site and should be viewed as such; its place in British military aviation history and the fact that it has been the focus of the RNAS, RFC and RAF makes it an aerodrome worthy of investigation.

The Admiralty Aerodrome Selection Committee first identified Cranwell, or more accurately an area west of the village, as a possible location late in 1914. By November 1915 the Ministry had acquired, through purchase and requisition, over 2,500 acres of farmland, primarily on the Earl of Bristol's estate. Construction of a hutted camp began the following month and on 1 April 1916 the Royal Naval Air Service Central Training Establishment Cranwell opened. For the next eighteen months both air and ground crews were trained in powered flying or airship operations; this included a boys' training wing, a forerunner to the famous RAF apprenticeships, or 'Brats'. With the formation of the Royal Air Force, Cranwell continued to train until the end of the war. After the conflict Trenchard chose the station as the location for the RAF Cadet College, primarily because it was 'marooned in the wilderness, cut off from past times they could not organise for themselves, the cadets would find life cheaper, healthier and more wholesome'. The first course commenced in February 1920.

Conditions at the station were less than ideal; the majority of Cranwell comprised temporary wooden huts erected at the height of the war. In 1922 it was suggested that a permanent college be built on the site, improving conditions and giving an air of permanency to the Royal Air Force. The economy, as will be discussed later, dictated otherwise; work did not start until 1929.

## Boy

Halton has already been described in the proceeding chapter with regards to its war period operation. In 1919, after the death of Alfred Rothschild, the wealthy banker and owner of the Halton landholding, the Air Ministry, under pressure from Trenchard, purchased the entire estate for the sum of £112,000. That same year the Apprentice Training Establishment transferred from Cranwell, forming the No.1 School of Technical Training. To house the new school a major building programme was initiated to replace the acres of wartime timber huts covering the site, culminating in the construction of the Groves and Henderson Barrack complexes on East Camp. Whilst these new facilities were under construction the first group of 'boy entrants' were accepted for training at Cranwell in 1920. By 1922 the first of 155 Aircraft Apprentice intakes were accepted to RAF Halton.

## Staff

The Royal Air Force Staff College was formed on 1 April 1922 to provide staff training to selected officers, usually of flight lieutenant or squadron leader rank. The year–long course comprised twenty RAF officers along with up to ten further officers from the Navy, Army or Empire Armies, to enable them to undertake staff officer duties at the Air Ministry or Command/Group HQs. On opening the 'new' facility Trenchard commented:

> Remember that the one thing to which you should at all times apply your thoughts and brains is the expansion of the power of material and personnel without increasing either.

This was a clear pointer to the lean times that lay ahead. Andover could not have underpinned that more. The ideal building to house such a high profile course should have been Halton House, by now owned by the Air Ministry, but the financial constraints were so tight that abandoned wartime hutting was pressed back into service at Andover instead. The reasons for these financial constraints are best understood when the political and social aspects of British life, especially throughout the 1920s, are investigated.

## Politics damned politics

The first important years of the RAF were a microcosm of the entire political landscape during the inter-war period. Governments lasted a matter of months as did, on occasion, the premiership. By 1920 Lloyd George was at the head of a newly formed coalition Government; however, he showed little regard for domestic politics, concerning himself instead with the trappings of a victorious country. Subsequently the coalition soon began to fall pray to inter-party disputes. One issue dominated internal politics in the immediate post-war period – the 'Irish Question'. Since 1919 Lloyd George had actively pursued the IRA in their war of independence. Atrocities were visited on both sides until talks in December 1921 halted the violence. By January the following year just six counties in the north-east of the country were under British rule. The situation on the mainland was little better, as strike after strike beset the workforce threatening the pace of Britain's fragile economic recovery. Miners, railwaymen and even the police entered into the nationwide disputes often broken up by the use of troops. Issues surrounding the miners were pivotal and would fester until the General Strike of 1926.

A mood of pessimism had even swept over the peace treaties. The whole process of reparations was brought into sharp focus when it became clear Germany could suffer economic collapse, subsequently weakening the entire Continent. Voices in the Government now demanded isolation. Andrew Bonar Law, destined to become Prime Minister, pointed out that as Britain's Empire had expanded so it must reduce its involvement in Europe especially through treaty commitments, the root cause of British involvement in the war. By October 1921 this involvement had all but become a reality as a dispute with the recent enemy, Turkey, over territory promised to the Greeks threatened war. The Greco-Turkish War had been raging since 1919 and eventually this had threatened the security of the strategically placed Dardanelles. It was not long before a stand-off developed. The area still contained a major British contingent and Harrington, General on the ground and Allied Commander in Constantinople, was only just managing to keep the situation under control. There were those in the Government who demanded action but common sense prevailed and the Greeks were convinced they should withdraw and cede any territory they had won to the Turks. Suddenly Lloyd George, hailed in 1918 as 'the man who won the war', was viewed as a dangerous autocrat bent on international adventurism. Right wing elements of the coalition Government collapsed and Lloyd George was ousted on 19 October 1922. Perhaps now Britain would return to some form of normality.

By the mid-1920s Lloyd George's 'land fit for heroes' was anything but, especially for many of the working class – the very people who had fought for the nation's survival. Social housing had developed in 1919 and for the next three years over 200,000 were built on subsidies initiated by Liberal Minister Addison. This was, unfortunately, a drop in the ocean as major industrial areas of the United Kingdom continued to house the majority of people in high-density housing that had rapidly turned into slums. This was so bad in some areas of Britain that they were at the point of environmental collapse and as capital investment further waned, especially in coal and steel, the conditions reached breaking point.

## Air Policing

The 'war to end all wars' destabilised the entire European Continent, sweeping away remnant empires such as the Austro-Hungarian and Ottoman, whilst bolstering others

RAF Halton Groves and Henderson barrack complex in 1922. This brand new complex was to be the home of RAF apprenticeships between 1920 and 1993.

such as acquisitions in the Middle East for Britain. This increased the country's overseas commitments way beyond these of pre-1914 levels and in order to control them adequately a cost-effective compromise would be needed. It turned out that the compromise would save the Royal Air Force from extinction.

When Germany orchestrated the withdrawal of Russia from the war by encouraging the revolution, little did anyone know they started a process that would take over seventy years to resolve. As it was British services had become embroiled in the Russian Civil War and were stuck between Turkish and Greek warring factions. The situation in other areas was little better.

Nonetheless, trouble so soon after the 'Great War' opened up new possibilities for the RAF. 1920 witnessed a demonstration that aircraft were far more cost effective than ground forces when Trenchard utilised the RAF against the 'Mad Mullah' in British Somaliland. Four Army expeditions had failed to dislodge him but airpower concluded the twenty-year-old dispute almost overnight.

The following March a conference held in Cairo, discussed the worsening situation in the Middle East and investigated ways of maintaining the British position at low cost to the Treasury. They agreed to pay off the less troublesome frontier tribes in the region, subsequently allowing the withdrawal of British and Indian Army units. By October 1921 Churchill had sold the idea to the Cabinet, indicating the substantial savings the involvement of the Royal Air Force would allow over the use of ground troops. The concept of 'Air Policing' was introduced in Iraq from 1922 and again in Yemen and Aden. The Cairo conference proved a turning point for the RAF; it served to demonstrate that an independent force was indeed an essential aspect of the country's defence strategy. Others in Whitehall did not see it that way.

In the wake of renewed public demands for disarmament the argument for an independent air force slowly petered out, as did the financial ability to pay for it. Prior to the formation of the RAF it will be remembered that the Navy – under the Royal Naval Air Service and Army as the Royal Flying Corps and its predecessor – had their own flying branches. The RAF had only been formed out of necessity and now that necessity had expired it was thought that both services should reabsorb their respective air forces. The first steps towards permanency came in the form of a report by the Committee on National Expenditure chaired in 1921 by Sir Eric Geddes. It concluded that contrary to service demands 'without separate existence' it was unlikely that Britain could 'work out developments which might in the next decade or so entirely revolutionise methods of attack and defence'. Further Geddes went on to demonstrate the 'very large economies' that would be made by the retention of an independent force, effectively mirroring Churchill's comments some months earlier. By March 1922 the House of Commons had reaffirmed its intention to retain an independent air force; however, the Navy did not go quietly and continued the pressure for a separate naval air wing. That same month the Secretary of State for War introduced the Cabinet to the Ten Year Rule, a statement that rapidly became policy, noting that the 'Empire would not be engaged in any great war during the next ten years'. This seriously influenced spending throughout the inter-war years and was not abandoned until March 1932.

Throughout all this Britain continued to pursue a policy of peace and arms limitations talks, although it was seriously undermined by lack of armed forces. As always negotiations go better from a position of strength; unfortunately this was not possible for Britain and the only option was to lead by example. Whilst this gave Britain the moral high ground it did not discourage those who were in the process of rearmament, nor did it dissuade other League of Nations members from taking the law into their own hands.

On 9 January 1923 the French Government announced that Germany was in default on their coal deliveries, part of the severe reparations imposed on the country after the First World War. Two days later French troops occupied the Ruhr Valley, an area of major industrial output, in order to forcibly obtain payments. The occupation effectively destroyed Germany's post-war recovery; inflation rose through the roof, with workers being paid up to three times a day to try to beat the hyperinflation ravaging the country. Political unrest became rife as left and right fought pitch battles in the street, and in November a little-known group in Munich made a grab for local power. Its leaders ended up in prison but they were destined, ultimately, to bring about the deaths of millions in the following decade. Suddenly the fragile stability of Europe was threatened and the venture led to the British Government investigating its National Defence capability under the chairmanship of Lord Salisbury. The French invasion had profound effects on the Government psyche and ultimately led to the airfield landscape we recognise today.

A sub-committee of the investigation, chaired by Arthur Balfour, heard evidence from Trenchard on the effects of bombing during the last war. He explained to the committee that during that struggle just over 240 tons of bombs had been dropped on Britain. The French, on current estimates, could now deliver that tonnage in less than a day. Clearly what was needed was a force that could protect the shores of Britain but, more importantly, deliver knock-out blows to the enemy's airfields, reducing its capacity for offensive bombing. All this occurred just as the successful conclusion of manoeuvres in Iraq was announced. This did not go unnoticed; the whole endeavour had cost a fraction of a land-based campaign and reaffirmed the Government's commitment to an independent air force. The Salisbury Committee therefore recommended expanding the RAF to fifty-two squadrons as part of the Home Defence Force, to be completed by 1928. Unfortunately enthusiasm for the project, not unlike French belligerence, drained away rapidly. With the financial situation rapidly worsening expansion was cut and finally allowed to lapse to almost non-existent levels. Trenchard however, had already planned for new airfields, with the Aerodrome Board actively seeking out new and previously owned sites.

## The First Expansion Scheme

From 1923 Trenchard concentrated on the construction of offensive bomber bases, primarily located in East Anglia and across Oxfordshire/Gloucestershire, with a fighter ring protecting London. To achieve this some sites needed to be re-purchased and practically all would need substantial modernisation if they were to be in any way fit for purpose. The layout of this offensive/defensive network is suggested to be in response to the French invasion of the Ruhr, and to a degree this is the case. However, some sightings are clearly intended to make the most of the existing locations, primarily close to ranges. Boscombe Down and Old Sarum are classic cases in point, their survival and position are investigated later.

## *Building the Estate*

'We are now in agreement that the aerodromes of Upper Heyford and Weston-on-the-Green are in every way suitable to be taken up,' wrote Air Commodore Ludlow-Hewitt in mid-October 1923. These airfields were some of the first identified by the Aerodrome Board and, through the momentum of the Salisbury Committee, had received Treasury approval for purchase that year.

> In the Gloucester-Oxford Area I want one "Grade A" Station, i.e., one to accommodate in peace (and war) 3 Regular Day Bombing Squadrons. The remaining Stations will be of a composite nature, i.e., the combination of one, or at most two, regular squadrons with Special Reserves and/or Auxiliary Squadrons allotted to them. For the grade any station we will select Upper Heyford, unless you consider that Minchinhampton possesses considerably greater advantages for the purpose. In this connection, the time factor is important, as we want to get the Grade A station complete as early as possible.
>
> (Letter dated 19 October 1923 from the Director of Staff Duties (DOSD) (AIR 5/335))

Two things clearly stand out here, firstly the composition of the manning of stations and secondly the involvement of Auxiliary Squadrons. The raising of Auxiliary Forces had been a major component of the original Air Force Act of 1917 but it did not pass into law until 1924; the first visible squadron, No. 502, was formed by May. It is clear that squadrons were considered to be essential to Home Defence by mid-1923 as the previous extract demonstrates. The number of squadrons had risen to nine by 1930 and was to experience a massive increase throughout the Second World War.

By 7 November the Chief of Air Staff, Trenchard, had surveyed the plan and agreed with the President of the Aerodrome Board that 'we should proceed with them'. In spite of this there were some in Parliament who did not relish the re-opening of aerodromes, especially if it was on their doorstep.

> I attended a meeting yesterday at the house of commons at which the Secretary of State interviewed Captain Terrell the local MP for the district which comprises the aerodromes at Upper Heyford, Weston-on-the-Green and Bicester. Lord Jersey was also there is a use the extensive landowner in this district and is primarily affected by our taking up of these aerodromes.
>
> (Reported by Group Captain Mills from the DDO)

> Since the receipt of the notice from the disposals commission that we were definitely abandoning the stations he has spent considerable sums in reinstating his property in carrying out work which he would not contemplated had he thought it possible that the stations will be reopened. He indicated that if we persisted in our policy to take up Heyford and Weston he will be compelled to leave his house and property and we might anticipate heavy claims for compensation.

Lord Jersey clearly considered he had much to lose; including a stud farm adjacent to Weston-on-the-Green which he suggested would cost a minimum of £20,000 to relocate. Further he argued that his house would become untenable if the stations were opened, clearly tea on the lawn would be a thing of the past. What worried the Secretary of State (SofS), Sir Samuel Hoare, was not so much the acquisition of airfields in the area but the increasing bad publicity it could cause.

> Captain Terrell stated that there will be organised opposition to our taking up of aerodromes in the Bicester localities from the whole countryside and it may be anticipated that this, led by Lord Jersey who apart from being a large landowner is Lord Lt of the county, would have considerable weight.

Trenchard was not happy. 'This attitude of big people like Lord Jersey in inspiring the county to object to the Air Force I call most unpatriotic and is bound to do a certain amount of harm,' he wrote at the end of November. But worse than that was the amount of additional expense the location of a new site or sites would incur. Part of Trenchard's vision was that to be cost-effective stations were to be grouped, allowing for the rapid transfer of men and equipment between the proposed bomber stations. For this reason Upper Heyford, Bicester and Weston-on-the-Green had been identified as prime aerodromes, and they needed to be further augmented within the next few years by two more stations. Any dissent could be dealt with via compulsory purchase orders, but bad press would not help and opposition in Parliament was even more difficult to manage, especially in the face of a reduced defence budget.

'Lord Jersey's death of course completely alters the situation,' wrote SofS Hoare to Trenchard on 2 January 1924 in a fortuitous twist of fate, but not before the Lord had forced the CAS to look for alternative sites, including one near Wallingford. As it turned out the Wallingford site was not to be constructed until 1938 – better known as Benson. Weston-on-the-Green also escaped redevelopment, primarily due to initial concerns over claims by Jersey. It, too, did not come under the Air Ministry until the war period.

Upper Heyford was re-acquired and it was here that Trenchard set about building his 'Class A' airfield. The initial concept was a technical site comprising workshops and the latest design in aircraft hangars, the 'A' Type. Married quarters were also introduced with the stipulation that:

> They should be as remote as is practicable from the remainder of the outlay, consistent with avoiding large additional expenditure on acquiring new land and extension of barrack services.
>
> (J.L.B.Vesey, DOSD, 19 October 1923 (AIR 5/335 minute 3))

## Bicester

Bicester, just a few miles to the south-east of Upper Heyford, was identified at the same time as a component of Trenchard's Oxford bomber group. It had opened very late in the First World War as No.44 Training Depot Station with the usual 3 Squadron arrangement. After downgrading to No.44 Training School it finally closed in December 1919; soon the entire site was cleared and the flying field reverted back to agriculture. The field and some additional areas to the east of the site were back under Air Ministry control by

1925. However, the proposed series of structures never materialised due to a noticeable deceleration of airfield funding from the Treasury. Bicester, although not completed within the period, has been identified by English Heritage as one of the best preserved bomber bases from this period and has received listed status for the majority of its structures.

Two more airfield sites, further west near Stroud, were under investigation during 1923–24. Both Minchinhampton and Leighterton were under consideration as bomber group stations, but neither was considered 'nearly so well situated' as Upper Heyford, Bicester or Weston-on-the-Green. What makes them interesting is that they display, by their very location, the concept of stations being tactically grouped. This underpins the doctrine that when legacy airfields are considered in the 1920s they must conform to that basic requirement. It has to be remembered that these two sites were both RAAF stations from late 1917 and were subsequently operated as a pair by the 1st Wing of the Australian Flying Corps until May 1919.

In 1924 the Government reaffirmed its commitment to fifty-two home-based squadrons, still only 10 per cent of the entire budget allotted for defence, a fact pointed out by the House of Lords in the face of Navy opposition. Stanley Baldwin, assuming the Prime Minister's role on the death of Bonar Law, demanded that British air power:

> … must include a home defence and is of sufficient strength adequately to protect us against attacks by the strongest air force within striking distance of this country.

Again politics were destined to get in the RAF's way; that same year the Labour Party, under Ramsay MacDonald, came to power. Their ethos was quite different, preferring negotiation and parity through arms reduction. Nearly a full year was lost as international disarmament was sought through the League of Nations. This policy was overturned again when, just ten months later, Baldwin's Administration had been returned. During this period Trenchard set about capitalising on a renewed popularity of the aircraft by holding spectacular flying displays at RAF Hendon. The fact the Air Ministry did not actually own the site was quickly remedied.

## Hendon

Hendon was one of the pioneer airfields in Britain with the Bristol Aeroplane Co. establishing, with Claude Grahame-White in late 1910, one of the early flying schools. By mid-1911 an oval flying field surrounded by sheds and rudimentary workshops covered the area once known as Colindale. By the middle of the First World War the site had become a major manufacturing airfield with the Grahame-White Aviation Co., Aircraft Manufacturing Co. (Airco), and Handley-Page all using it for test flights.

Almost inevitably the airfield became an RFC Aircraft Acceptance Park and by 1917 the factory site planned a further expansion, this time including housing in a development known as Aeroville. This development, not dissimilar to the Shorts construction at Cardington in 1917, was designed for both workers in the factory and had the potential to billet service personnel. In the event this was limited to just one road as work constructing aircraft ceased at the end of the war. The company limped on for a few years building cars, but it never regained control of the airfield.

Hendon became central to publicising the Royal Air Force after the war; first, in June 1919, the Victory Aerial Derby and then from 1920 the RAF Pageant were held at the aerodrome. However, this was not a harmonious relationship and by 1924 Grahame-White had called in the receivers. The following two years were complicated; protracted negotiations between the Air Ministry and the Treasury were clearly done out of sight of Grahame-White:

> The application to the Court by Messrs. Grahame-White in respect of the Receiver's powers has been adjourned until the 15th. instant. In the meantime Treasury Solicitor is of the opinion that we might open up negotiations (without prejudice) with the Receiver for possession of the land and buildings required for immediate occupation and we suggest subject to your approval that the application should in the first instance include all the land and buildings.
> (Captain W.W. Palmer of the Directorate of Lands 3. b. (DL3.b.) 6 October 1924 (Air 2/258))

> We agree. If we can have the land 5 buildings specified above we shall be able to proceed with the formation of the Squadrons. This matter is becoming most urgent – we had hoped to form these units in August.
> (R. Mills, handwritten note, 8 October 1924 (Air 2/258))

By December 1924 the RAF were planning what was to be stationed at Hendon, apparently already considering the acquisition of the site a success:

> With reference to minute 16, the Sub Committee of the RAF Building Committee visited Hendon on the 25th November and its proposals for the necessary work to enable the existing accommodation to be temporarily occupied by two squadrons of A.A.F. are being formulated.
> (H.S. Oakley for the Director of Works & Buildings, 9 December 1924 (Air 2/258))

The proceedings moved on when the Receiver finally accepted the Government's intention to compulsorily purchase the site. The Government paid a paltry 5 per cent of the original market value, however:

> The Crown would forthwith be given possession of that property as though the purchase had already been completed.

Clearly the Government knew that if it waited long enough then the cost of the site would be a fraction of its trade value.

Protracted negotiations were not restricted to Hendon, although not all were as outwardly questionable. Boscombe Down, closed by 1920, fell once again under the spotlight. The Air Ministry, during the development of the Wessex Bombing Area, considered the site and set about re-acquiring it in 1924. Studying Boscombe Down also presents the opportunity to investigate the fate of other bases in the area during the immediate post-war years.

## 'Buildings so entirely out of harmony'

A prime example of the changing fortunes of airfields can be demonstrated by those stations located immediately to the south of Salisbury Plain. Five Training Depot Stations (TDS) were constructed in quick succession and whilst the story of each is interlinked not all have the same outcome. Their interpretation is also important in relation to the survival of two of their number, Boscombe Down & Old Sarum.

No.2 TDS at Stonehenge was opened in November 1917 with the first aircraft taking up station there the following month. By December 1918 it had been renamed the No.1 School of Navigation & Bomb Dropping and was continuing to expand. By the time training ceased in July 1919 Stonehenge had eight linked GS Sheds and one Aircraft Repair Shed as well as four semi-permanent Handley Page sheds and numerous workshops and accommodation.

The Aerodrome Board Quarterly Survey of Stations of the RAF (British Isles) contains the following information on Stonehenge:

Function

The School is a finishing school for Pilots and Observers in both Day and Night Bombing. The Pilots must have previously have graduated 'B' at a Training Station. The School is divided into two Squadrons, one for training Day-bombers, and the other for the training of Night-bombers on Handley-Pages.

Aerodrome

Maximum dimensions in yards 1,450 x 850; Area 230 acres of which 30 acres are occupied by the station buildings. Height above sea level 330ft. Soil loam on chalk. Surface fairly good though somewhat rough and very rolling. The general surrounds open Salisbury Plain Country. Fairly flat in the neighbourhood.

(Air 1/453/25/312/26)

What the record forgot to mention was that the aerodrome lay less than a mile south-west of one of Britain's most famous monuments – Stonehenge. A number of people were not prepared to accept the aerodrome as such a permanent feature:

Whatever may have been the reasons which determined such a site, a choice entailing the complete disfigurement of the surroundings of the most famous of British Monuments, it must be conceded that nothing short of absolute necessity can justify the retention there of a set of buildings so entirely out of harmony with the venerable traditions of the place.

This was written by Mr. C.R. Peers acting on behalf of the Society of Antiquaries in a letter to the War Office on 20 December 1919. He went on to point out that:

… whatever preservation or no, the monument remains utterly disfigured, by a vandalism which has been reserved for our time to perpetuate.

No.14 TDS Lake Down, Wiltshire, in 2007. Lake Down Airfield was removed by 1920. This water tower and workshop stand as a monument to the site.

After the letter had circulated other Government offices for nearly a year it fell to an Air Ministry official to reply. It is here that the reason for Stonehenge Airfield's existence and retention is noted:

> The value of Stonehenge Aerodrome however lies in its close proximity to Lark Hill and other Artillery Camps and ranges close by, since the experience of the late war proved not only the necessity for the co-operation of aircraft with artillery but also the need for the very closest touch between officers of the two services if such co-operation is to give the best results.

The Ministry sympathised with the Society of Antiquaries' plight and promised to consider the case carefully throughout 'the ensuing summer's training'. However, for the time being the aerodrome was staying put.

Not all sites in the area were retained. Lake Down was constructed throughout mid-1917 but had a very short history compared to Stonehenge, some 2 miles south west of the aerodrome. It had originally been designated No.2 TDS but this was moved in December to its neighbour and a day bomber unit flew in. By June 1918 Lake Down was re-designated a TDS, this time No.14 of 33 Wing which, incidentally, had its HQ at nearby Druids Lodge.

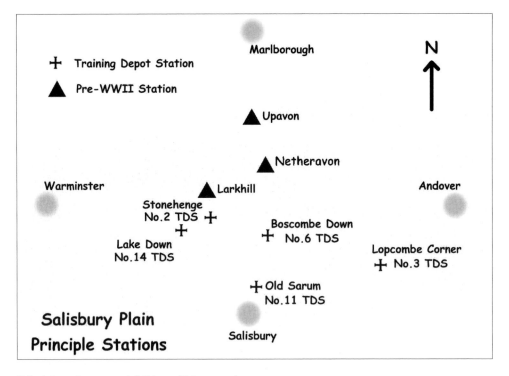

Principle stations around Salisbury Plain around 1919–20.

Lake Down was more the 'traditional' layout of a TDS, comprising the three pairs of linked GS sheds and the stand alone aircraft repair shed surrounded by workshops, stores and training facilities. By mid-1918 the station contained three units whose primary concern was the training of day bombing. Again it was located very close to Salisbury Plain and made continued use of the area until the beginning of 1919 when Lake Down was re-designated No.14 Training School. This was, however, short-lived; by 1920 the site was abandoned. The various buildings were disposed of through auction by the Disposal & Liquidation Committee, whilst the land reverted back to sheep grazing. So by 1920 little remained and now only a workshop and the water tower stand testament to the site.

The same can be said of Lopcombe Corner, some 5 miles to the south-east of Boscombe Down. It is worth introducing some squadrons and dates here, if only to demonstrate the complexity of tracking RFC and later RAF forces. No.3 TDS was formed on 5 September 1917 with three flights, A Flight from Harlaxton, B Flight from Yatesbury and C Flight from Dover (Swingate Down). By July 1918 the station had accepted 157 Squadron, formally A Flight from Chattis Hill. The airfield accepted two fighter squadrons from France within a week of each other in February 1919, Nos 74 and 85, their kills totalling 140 and 99 respectively. No.91 Squadron arrived from Kenley at the beginning of March and by the end of May No.52 Squadron had flown in from Netheravon. All had been disbanded by the end of October 1919 and Lopcombe Corner itself had been closed by 22 January 1920.

Boscombe Down can also be viewed as a 'typical' Training Depot Station. Opened in October 1917 and initially known as Red House Farm after the site near by, it had the

No.3 TDS Lopcombe Corner, Hampshire in 2007. Lopcombe Corner demonstrates the short life of some sites. Opened on 5 September 1917, flying ceased at the end of October 1919 and the site had been extensively removed by January 1920. Five structures remain.

usual suite of buildings associated with this type of airfield. However, by the time of the Armistice the aerodrome was far from complete. Designated No.6 Training Depot Station, Boscombe Down was again concerned with the training of aircrew in day bombing. The slowness of the construction work was such that officers were billeted at the George Hotel in Amesbury whilst the men, and women were under canvas until the end of 1918. By then the women's accommodation, incidentally 154-strong in September 1918, were the only buildings anywhere near completion.

At the time of the Armistice Boscombe Down had only just got into its stride, but training at the base was to be short-lived. On 15 May 1919 the TDS was disbanded and the site was used for aircraft storage until April 1920 when the aerodrome finally closed. The airfield then appears to be split between two concerns. The land reverted back to its original owner and the majority of the buildings went to Messrs Wort and Way who, amongst other things, used some of the hangars to store building equipment and engines. Private ownership did not last long.

> We have under consideration the re-acquisition of the aerodrome at Boscombe Down. It has not yet been actually decided to take up the ground and it is quite possible that we may not require it. At present we are collecting all the necessary information.
>
> (E. Ludlow-Hewitt, Air Commodore, president of the Aerodrome Board, 25 April 1924
>
> (AIR 2/254))

RAF Boscombe Down, 1931. A substantial amount of wartime clearance had been undertaken on reoccupation. The TDS Hangar layout can be clearly seen as well as the addition of one A Type. (Courtesy of the Ministry of Defence)

Four days later, at a meeting with the Chief of Air Staff, the decision was made 'as to taking Boscombe Down'. One of the most famous airfields in Britain had been given new life, this time as an offensive site directed, in the first instance, at the French.

In a letter to the Chief of Air Staff dated 2 December 1924 the proposed occupants of the aerodrome were noted:

> You agreed at a meeting on 29 July last that we should adopt BOSCOMBE DOWN as a peace station for 2 regular T.E.B. [Twin Engine Bomber] Squadrons and a war station for 2 regular and 1 A.A.F.T.E.B. Squadrons. The existing sheds, after some reconditioning will serve to take the regular squadrons.
>
> (J.L.Kerry, DOSD, 2 December 1924 (AIR 2/254))

This was a little premature as the current owners Messrs Wort & Way had not yet agreed a price for the redundant site. Since they purchased the site from the Air Ministry back in 1920 they had put the buildings to good use and clearly were in no rush to part with them:

> The last letter on these negotiations from Messrs Wort and Way intimates that they will be prepared to attempt to meet us when we are in a position to discuss the matter with a view to purchasing and are able to make a <u>firm offer</u>.

RAF Boscombe Down, 1932. As part of the Wessex Bombing Area, Boscombe Down was provided with a bomb storage area. This is one of the few remaining in the country. (Courtesy of the Ministry of Defence)

> It is very difficult to say how far Messrs. Wort and Way are prepared to reduce their present demand for £25,000, especially as they are using the hangars for housing their many engines etc., for which they will have to find other accommodation at the same time I am quite certain that if a firm offer could be made this sum could be reduced very materially; this has been our experience at other Stations where similar cases have occurred.
>
> (Lt Col. Archibald Thompson, Department Land 3. b., 15 January 1925 (AIR 2/254))

As was the case at Hendon earlier the previous year Department Land 3b (DL3b) were well versed in the 'waiting game'. As it was they had managed to reduce the financial aspect of the deal from a possible £42,000 to the £25,000 now on the table. However, there were those in the Treasury who felt sure the offer could be further reduced:

> As regards the price to be paid for the buildings, the Council had, perforce, to ask for sanction to pay up to £25,000, as this was the final offer made by the owners during the preliminary negotiations. There is little doubt, however that if a firm offer of, say, £10,000 is made as a basic negotiation, the result will be the acceptance of an amount considerably less than £25,000.
>
> (R.E. Holloway, HM Treasury, 22 January 1925 (AIR 2/254))

RAF Boscombe Down, 1931. A clear view of the domestic site built between 1928–30 after the re-acquisition of the airfield by the Ministry. (Courtesy of the Ministry of Defence)

The Treasury finally got its way on 10 March 1925 when contracts were exchanged with Wort and Way to take possession of the proposed land, including all the airfield buildings, for a substantially reduced £15,000. The key to Boscombe Down being re-purchased turns out to be its surviving buildings. The President of the Air Board made this perfectly clear when he pointed out that refurbishment of the major structures would save the public purse in excess of £50,000.

Officially it would be another twenty years before Boscombe Down became an experimental station; nevertheless, landing tests had been undertaken in 1918 to look into grass strip performance:

> The difference, for example, in the general flying qualities and behaviour of light training machines such as those used at BOSCOMBE DOWN during the war, as compared with the big heavy night bombers for which the ground will be required in the future could be emphasised. Tests with heavy night bombing aeroplanes were actually carried out on the old landing ground and it was shown conclusively that the slopes are too steep to permit of a heavily loaded twin-engined bomber taking off up the slope, except possibly in a strong wind.
>
> (E. Ludlow-Hewitt, Air Commodore, president of the Aerodrome Board, 9 January 1925
> (AIR 2/254))

The fifth site in the group, Old Sarum, has similar beginnings but a different story again. Originally named Ford Farm after the site it replaced, the airfield did not fully open until mid-1918, making it a full RAF base as No.11 TDS. By then it had a full suite of technical buildings; the majority of personnel, however, were billeted in tents. The station was re-designated No.11 Training School in July 1919 and later became part of the Army School of Co-operation, running courses for both RAF and Army observers and pilots. Naturally the station's position close to Salisbury Plain played a major part in Old Sarum being retained by the Ministry.

When all five sites are considered it becomes clear that the most appropriate site for retention has to be Stonehenge. The aerodrome was closest to the ranges at Larkhill and had very few obstacles, bar the henge monument. The aerodrome also boasted far better facilities than the other four, so it was with this knowledge that the Air Ministry elected to keep Stonehenge on and form the No.1 School of Night and Day Bombing there. Lake Down and Lopcombe Corner were quickly removed from the landscape, whilst Boscombe Down was sold on. Only Old Sarum remained active, continuing to train day bombing pilots until late 1919. This, too, was clearly on run down as throughout May 1919 surplus building material from the site's construction and hutting was offered for sale by local estate agents Woolley & Wallis.

A number of factors altered the post-war airfield landscape in South Wiltshire, not least pressure from the Society of Antiquarians. By late 1920 the Air Ministry had decided to move the New School of Army Co-operation to Old Sarum and dispose of Stonehenge. The distribution of structures started in June 1920 when the Ministry of Munitions began holding sales. Included was the 'Night Camp', erected so that trainee pilots could sleep during the day. Crucially the notice posted in the *Salisbury Times* on 18 June and again on 25 June noted that 'The buildings are not for sale, for removal'; Stonehenge was destined to disappear like the neighbouring airfield at Lake Down. By 1922 the rest of the site was up for sale, including the Day Camp, four aircraft sheds and the YMCA hut. At no time was the site offered as functional and all structures were, by terms of the sales, to be removed within three months. However, disaster struck, at least for the Society of Antiquarians. It transpired that whilst the buildings had been sold for demolition, allowing the purchaser to realise the scrap value, there was no legislation stopping those buildings being sold on in situ, and that is exactly what happened. Mr Crook, the landowner, from whom the Ministry had originally rented the land, subsequently bought some of the buildings from the original purchaser. As he was the legal landowner the Government had no way of forcing him to remove buildings, and even if they tried to enforce the three-month rule it would not prevent Mr Crook rebuilding. The last of the structures were formally removed in 1930 and with them went the airfield the Ministry had been desperate to retain. The only evidence of the site today is a pile of bricks in a recently laid copse to the south west of the Henge. Old Sarum survives as a working airfield, albeit now in private hands, due to the pressure exerted to move Stonehenge, whilst Boscombe Down remains operational due, in part to Messrs Wort and Way who utilised many of the hangars both agriculturally and for scrap storage.

## The General Strike

Since the end of the war the Government had aimed to return Britain's economy to the 'Gold Standard'. This was reintroduced by the then Chancellor, Winston Churchill, in 1925, immediately making British exports prohibitively expensive. Coal exports, especially, had reduced since the French had started selling reparations coal on the world market. Now inferior seams and expensive market prices forced the industry deeper into crisis. The Government underwrote miners' wages for a nine-month period until April 1926, however, negotiations at the TUC came to nothing and the unions brought the country to a standstill for ten days. Not all public services were hit. Both the TUC and Government were worried about the downward spiral into anarchy that a total cessation in public services would bring, no doubt encouraged by certain militant elements. Subsequently only key working groups were requested to support the miners; food and health orientated services were to remain functional. Just as suddenly as it had started the TUC called the strike off; only the miners, with nothing to lose, stayed out. The strike achieved little beyond damaging the union power base, the Government legislated against further mass picketing and Civil Service involvement, and the miners who did return to work had to face years of lower wages.

Problems with finance were also hitting the rearmament programme hard. Site acquisitions had slowed and those airfields already back in Ministry hands were undergoing constant modification. RAF Bicester never achieved the intended complement of buildings due to the downturn. It also had a detrimental effect on defensive thinking, especially against enemy attacks. Late in 1925 the OC of RAF Kenley, Surrey, voiced concerns that his airfield was inadequately protected against air attack and discussed this with his superiors at No.6 Group HQ. They, in turn, wrote to HQ Inland Area at Uxbridge:

> It is very strongly recommended that adequate arrangements should be made at every Aerodrome for defence against low bombing. Unless these arrangements are made in peace time there is every chance that their installation will be too late to be effective in case of war.
> (Air Commodore Commanding No.6 Group, 18 January 1926 (AIR 5/515))

John Salmond, Air Officer Commanding of the Air Defence of Great Britain (ADGB), replied on 2 February 1926:

> The risk of a low day flying attack on most aerodromes would appear to be negligible except perhaps Tangmere and Hawkinge. Even low night attacks are most improbable until higher ones have been tried and failed.

This is important because it demonstrates tactically why the bomber bases especially were placed in the areas they were. Clearly Salmond considered the aerodromes were too far inland to attempt an attack. However, the true nature of the refusal to fund additional protection, was revealed the following month when:

> … existing conditions will not permit of special provision, entailing expenditure, being made in connection with the Defence of Aerodromes against low flying attack.
> (Group Captain Mills, DOSD, 27 February 1926 (AIR 5/515))

The Air Defence of Great Britain (ADGB) was a new formation encompassing all units of the Royal Air Force's Home Defence Force. This was subdivided into Wessex Bombing

RAF Cranwell, College Hall. Originally intended to be completed by 1925, the building was not finished until 1933. (Courtesy of Malcolm Holland)

Area, controlling all regular bombing squadrons, Fighting Area, covering all regular fighter squadrons, and an Air Defence Group (later No.1 Air Defence Group), which consists of the cadre and auxiliary squadrons.

Whilst the country was reeling from such social upheaval Trenchard had endeavoured to keep the RAF in the public eye. On 26 September 1927 Flight Lieutenant A.M. Webster won the Schneider Trophy for the first time. Meanwhile, abroad, the RAF were being utilised in 'Air Police' operations in Aden and during the Afghan rebellion aircraft were used in the transport support role. As the RAF had won the Schneider Trophy it fell to the British to host the following event, scheduled for 1929. The RAF, flying a Supermarine S6 designed by R.J. Mitchell, were victorious. Unfortunately this was to be the final race sponsored by the Government. A memo released by the Cabinet put the cost of the two seasons as £196,000 and £220,000 respectfully and summarily pulled the plug on more financial aid and on the use of RAF pilots. Industry went on to back the event held in 1931; however, once the costs had been taken over the Government, not unsurprisingly, relented and allowed the RAF to supply the flight crews.

One major casualty of the financial climate was the building of Cranwell's College Hall, eventually started in 1929. The initial building design was undertaken by the Ministry of Works, but when published the Secretary of State for Air, Sir Samuel Hoare, rejected the plans out of hand; he commissioned the architect James West who, reflecting the influence of Sir Christopher Wren's work at the Chelsea Hospital, designed the building that stands today. The college building was completed in September 1933 and officially opened a year later. The price tag was a little over £321,000.

RAF Abingdon, Oxfordshire, in 1932. Abingdon was one of the last pre-expansion stations to be constructed. The A-Type hangars, indicative of the 1920s construction programme can be clearly seen.

Not all were happy with the continuing – if slow – expansion of the airfield network. In early 1929 Mrs Katherine Atkinson wrote to the Air Council to tell of her dismay in having Tangmere Aerodrome still on her rental property's doorstep:

> During the War, however, the Tangmere aerodrome was erected in some fields exactly opposite the house – my tenant was told the Aerodrome would be dismantled after the War. As a matter of fact it <u>was</u> closed and offered for sale. However, the sale did not take place and the Aerodrome was re-opened and enlarged.
>
> (AIR 2/343)

With six months left on the current agreement Mrs Atkinson, clearly expecting her tenant to move out, appointed agents to try and sell the house on. The ten-bedroom property in its own grounds attracted lots of viewers – but no takers:

> Nobody would undertake it at any cost owing to the nuisance from the aerodrome, machines flying over the house all day and the noise being continuous.
>
> (AIR 2/343)

Unfortunately no compensation or purchase of the property was to be forthcoming from the Government, as Sir Samuel Hoare explained in a reply on 21 March 1929:

> Tangmere is only one of many new aerodromes which the air defence of Great Britain makes it necessary to establish throughout the country, and I cannot admit that the owners of houses near these aerodromes, who may maintain their attractiveness has suffered, are entitled to compensation. The amenities of residential property are, of course, constantly being effected through a variety of causes – by the increase of motor traffic due to the opening up of a new arterial road, for example, or by the erection on adjacent land of factories or lower-class

dwelling-houses – and the owners have to accept the position without being able to claim
that their losses should be made good.

(Secretary of State for Air (AIR 2/343))

In 1929 Ramsey MacDonald was returned to office with a renewed optimism for the
new decade. Unfortunately this did not see the year out; that October the American
stock market crashed, taking any chance of trade recovery with it. Unemployment went
through the roof and within two years peaked at over 3 million, and those were just
the ones who were registered, millions more had no Government support whatsoever.
Naturally the working class looked to the Labour Party for some form of respite
– none was forthcoming. Conditions rapidly deteriorated as Britain's outdated modes of
conducting business left it open to aggressive competition. Years of over-manning, low or
non-existent investment and poor efficiency effectively crippled any chance of a speedy
recovery. Some form of drastic reform was clearly necessary and by August 1931 it was
obvious the MacDonald Government would not last much longer. A run on the pound
and subsequent accusations that the Government's mismanagement had caused industrial
ruin was the last straw and on 24 August 1931 a National Government took over,
surprisingly still with MacDonald at the helm. After a number of groundbreaking reforms,
including renewed social housing and agricultural initiatives, the National Government
was returned for a second term still with MacDonald although another political name
was now waiting in the wings – Neville Chamberlain. As the Prime Minister was to
demonstrate to the House of Commons, thoughts were now turning to rearmament:

I think it is well, also, for the man in the street to realise that there is no power on earth that
can protect him from being bombed what ever people may tell him, the bomber will always
get through the only defence is offence, which means you have to kill more women and
children more quickly than the enemy if you want to save yourselves.

(Stanley Baldwin, 10 November 1932)

## Organisation Throughout the 1920s

Naturally the organisation of the RAF is as complex as the many different factors shown
to dictate airfield positioning. It seems more appropriate to lay out the basic framework
of the 1920s and early 1930s at the end of this section as some facets survived up to the
Second World War whilst others went through periods of transition and amalgamation just
a few years after the First World War. It is important to have a level of understanding here
as the decisions driving the organisation were also responsible for the bases constructed
throughout this period.

Just a few weeks after the formation of the Royal Air Force its forces were reorganised
into five geographically designated areas. Each area had a number of groups that could
cover anything from fighters to training.

No.1 Area became South-Eastern Area
No.2 Area became South-Western Area
No.3 Area became Midland Area

RAF Duxford, Operations Block in 2007. This structure was built in 1927 and is now protected by listing.

*Above:* RAF Duxford, Station Headquarters Building in 2007. This structure was built in 1933 to an earlier pattern.

*Left:* The distribution of fighting area aerodromes around London in 1928.

No.4 Area became North-Eastern Area
No.5 Area became North-Western Area

This was further complemented in August with the formation of No.11 Irish Group, not surprisingly covering all bases in Ireland, at this time still incorporated the entire country. In September 1919 a significant move was made towards working with the Royal Navy when Coastal Area was formed from South-Western Area's No.10 Group to control all units working with the fleet in home waters. Crucially the officer commanding Coastal Area was jointly responsible for the Admiralty and Air Ministry. By the end of the year Britain had been streamlined into just three areas, Southern, Northern and Coastal Area. The Irish Group, Cranwell and Halton reported directly to the Chief of Air Staff.

In 1920, the RAF's second birthday, these groupings were further altered when Northern and Southern areas were amalgamated into Inland Area. This new area covered a wide variety of stations and activities, everything from training to bombing, stores to fighters. The Fleet Air Arm of the Royal Air Force was formed on 1 April 1924 and included all RAF units based on aircraft carriers, catapult launch or float planes, with personnel from either service. The following January the organisational layout was altered once again; this time a single formation covering all home aspects was devised, named the Air Defences of Great Britain (later renamed Air Defence of Great Britain, or ADGB). This was further subdivided into the Wessex Bombing Area, controlling all regular bombing squadrons, Fighting Area, controlling all regular fighter squadrons, and an Air Defence Group, comprising the cadre and auxiliary squadrons. By the time Hitler came to power the organisational aspects of the RAF, simplified here it has to be said, had undergone many transformations, virtually all still reliant on station positioning rather than function. The coming rapid expansion was to see further change and the advent of some far more recognisable 'commands'.

Between 1924 and 1930 the number of airfields had slowly risen and at this point it is worth taking stock of those stations in that latter year. By 1926 the ADGB contained the Fighting Area, a defensive ring around the capital comprising nine aerodromes, the Wessex Bombing Area with six stations and the Coastal Area with eight sites. A further twelve aerodromes comprised the Inland Area and ten were operated for reservist squadrons.

Those airfields under the Fighting Area were Northolt, Kenley, Biggin Hill, North Weald, Tangmere, Martlesham Heath, Hawkinge, Hornchurch and Duxford. Whilst the majority of the stations were open for aircraft by 1928 work continued on a few, in particular Duxford and Biggin Hill, until 1932. The Wessex Bombing Area comprised Upper Heyford, Bicester, Bircham Newton, Manston and Worthy Down, with Boscombe Down still being modified and Harwell and Abingdon under proposal.

The Inland Area consisted of a mixture of sites, including the Central Flying School at Wittering, Rollestone Balloon Training Camp on Salisbury Plain, Old Sarum and the School of Army Co-operation, No.1 FTS Netheravon, No.2 FTS at Digby, No.3 FTS Spitalgate (Grantham), No.5 FTS Sealand and the Officers School of Aeronautical Engineering at Henlow, Aircraft & Armament Experimental Establishment (A&AEE) at Martlesham Heath and Orfordness, West Drayton, Uxbridge, Eastchurch, Catterick, Royal

RAF Henlow in 1932. Throughout the 1920s Henlow was home to fighter squadrons, repair depots and even the Parachute Training Wing.

Aircraft Establishment Farnborough, North Coates Fitties, Sutton Bridge and Catfoss. To this can be added a number of storage depots and offices not furnished as a flying centre and therefore not featuring as part of this study.

   This first expansion programme had been more than just an attempt to modernise; it had been a fight for the very survival of the service. As it was financial constraints had seriously curtailed Trenchard and Salmond's aspirations but at least some structure had been possible, if only with thanks to the French. What was to follow was the biggest capital works of the century as it became clear that the French were not the threat they were earlier considered to be. As Hitler came to power in Germany, Britain was a country on the rebound; politically things were more stable and welfare reforms were improving the lot of the average family. The political turmoil spreading throughout Europe would soon erupt into war but for the time being Britain hung its hopes on a successful disarmament conference at the League of Nations.

four

# REALISATION NOT RATIONALISATION: EXPANSION POLICY 1933–39

If the post-war period had been years of cost cutting and internal disputes, often due to external influences, the years after the Wall Street Crash were anything but. On 4 March 1935 the British Government published its intentions to rearm. After more than a decade of poor investment and rundown, the Royal Air Force was to be modernised, primarily in the face of growing European unrest and German militarism. The directive did far more than reshape military strategy; it was to have a radical impact on the British landscape. A massive expansion programme swung into action constructing the majority of airfields still in existence today. With it came some of the country's most distinctive military architecture and some of the most famous place names in aviation history.

*Expansion and the Alphabet Schemes*
By late 1934 it had become clear that Britain's almost obsessive policy of 'Peace' had failed. Successive Governments had actively pursued disarmament through a mandate with the League of Nations but now acknowledged:

> The Disarmament Conference had virtually come to a standstill. Further negotiations, it was clear, would be hampered by the fact that Germany was not only rearming openly on a large-scale, despite the provisions of part V of the Treaty of Versailles, but had also given notice of withdrawal from the League of Nations and the Disarmament Conference. Japan also had given notice of a withdrawal from the League. All the larger powers except the United Kingdom were adding to their armed forces.
>
> (Statement relating to defence, March 1935 (PRO 30/69/620E))

British newspapers were quick to report the turnround:

> Explaining the government's policy shift Stanley Baldwin said: 'Our attempt to lead the world towards disarmament by unilateral example has failed.' German rearmament now threatened to put peace at peril. Despite claims by Germany's leaders that they wanted

peace, Britain could not ignore the way Germany's forces are constantly being mobilised, he added.

(The Guardian, 4 March 1935)

Clearly a modernisation programme was needed if Britain was to protect both the United Kingdom and supply routes to and from the Empire. Central to this was to be reconditioning and rearmament schemes; the first for air had actually been approved in late 1934 by the Cabinet. Inventively known as Scheme A, it required the RAF to have aircraft number parity with the Luftwaffe by 1939. Estimates suggested forty-one bomber and twenty-eight fighter squadrons; 1,544 aircraft in all. A number of aircraft were to be based in Singapore in response to Japan's increasingly militaristic belligerence in the Far East. Anti-aircraft defences, at that time still the provision of the Army, would also require a major increase. This was to be no small undertaking as the Government readily admitted:

> In the air we virtually disarmed ourselves in 1919, and, subsequently, from time to time postponed attainment of the minimum air strength regarded as necessary to our security in the face of air developments on the Continent.

(Statement relating to defence, March 1935 (PRO 30/69/620E))

Along with the increase in production of machines for the RAF came a building programme to augment and improve the current airfield situation. As indicated previously the fifty or so sites ascribed to the RAF by 1934 were less than ideal. Few were in a fit state to provide homes for new squadrons equipped with modern aircraft, and even fewer had the range of technical buildings that were now deemed essential. Scheme A, continuing current RAF doctrine, demanded the development of a bomber force, albeit a medium range one. This was as much an attempt to dissuade Germany from its rearmament path as to promote an arms race. Unfortunately, like many good intentions, it did not quite work out that way.

Throughout 1935 a series of new stations were commissioned at Marham, Feltwell, Cranfield, Stradishall, Waddington and Church Fenton. That year work also started at Harwell, originally intended in 1926 to be part of the Wessex Bombing Area. Further to these developments a number specialist bases were planned. At Thorney Island a torpedo school was developed alongside other marine-orientated structures. A site at Odiham was developed as an Army Co-operation Station and Manby built as an armaments specialist centre, whilst Ternhill, was designated a Flying Training School. Armament training facilities were built at Woodsford and Henlow received a massive increase in hutted accommodation. Investigating the new build stations from 1935 it becomes apparent that the planners' primary concern was protection of the east coast. From Church Fenton, at its northern most point, a chain of seven 'Standard Function' stations runs south in an arc to Harwell. The arc encompasses Yorkshire, Lincolnshire, Norfolk, Sussex and Oxfordshire. Ternhill, Shropshire, was placed well away from the east coast making its role as an FTS less vulnerable, but Thorney Island needed to be at the coast. One final aspect is the role played by Manby. Naturally ranges were needed for bombing orientated training and, along with two other coastal bombing ranges at Languard and Theddlethorpe, a specific site for Manby, just a few minutes flying time, was constructed at Skipsea on the site of an

Scheme A stations.

RAF Harwell, Oxfordshire, in 2004. Initially proposed in the Wessex Bombing Area development, the station was finally built in 1937. The C-Type hangars are still visible within the later development.

earlier range. Far from being haphazard this series of developments was clearly designed to give the best cover with the shortest possible time frame.

## The Station of 'Standard Function'

Expansion scheme planning did much to standardise all aspects of airfield design and layout. Prior to 1935 reconstruction work had often been to locally approved designs, considering immediate needs rather than the long-term view. Indeed the entire outlook of the RAF had followed this restricted path throughout the 1920s and early '30s. Now a new standardised type of station was required, promoting economy in design and little deviation from set piece construction – the Standard Function Station was born.

As one would expect the initial process whereby a location was chosen was protracted. In the preceding two decades the majority of stations were located on previously used land. However, with the Expansion Schemes the Government once more entered into land acquisition. The Airfield Board, often utilising nothing more than the Ordnance Survey map, selected potential parcels of land and then forwarded the choice to the Directorate of Works (DoW). The DoW then dispatched engineers and surveyors into the field to conduct a preliminary site suitability survey. This had a wide remit with particular attention being paid to the geological nature of the area. Soil type, contour and drainage were noted along with obstructions, local amenities and potential location for airfield technical and domestic structures. The team also enquired as to the capacity of quarries and local brick merchants, along with agricultural and power companies output. The survey for Finningley serves to demonstrate that much more than ground works were at stake in some areas.

When the site of the proposed airfield was first investigated it became clear it lay within the South Yorkshire coalfield. Naturally this caused some concern and two independent reports were commissioned by the Director of Works and Buildings to investigate the effect on mining in that area:

> The Air Council explain that it is proposed to acquire 559 acres of land at a cost exclusive of mineral rights estimated at £16,000. The Council have decided not to purchase the mineral rights in view of the heavy cost involved being advised that there is little prospect of the coal seam underlying the site being worked for a number of years, and that, if it were so worked, the resulting subsidence would not seriously affect any buildings on the surface.
>
> (J. Phillips, Treasury to the Air Ministry, 26 August 1935 (AIR 2/4293))

During the First World War sites had, on the whole, been rented on contract from the owner and normally reverted back soon afterwards. Now the Ministry was intent on purchase and was prepared to acquire the land at a price set by the Treasury and 'for the exercise, if necessary, of compulsory powers for the acquisition of the land'. As time went on this option was 'exercised' as not all landowners were keen to relinquish land.

The majority of expansion period airfields were furnished with grass strips or landing grounds; only nine paved surfaces were in existence at the outbreak of war. Naturally the first requirement of any station site was suitability of location, ideally a square or rectangular piece of land, requiring little modification. Within that was a flat area at least 1,100 yards in diameter, known as the 'bombing circle'. The bombing circle was a throwback from the First World War when iron weights or darts were thrown at a circular white target. On expansion period stations the circle indicated a safe practice area. Usually four landing strips were marked out across the circle, one of 1,300 yards x 400 yards and two of 1,000 yards x 200 yards. The main strip was doubled as it was laid to the prevailing wind, a critical consideration in the construction of any airfield.

Drainage was a major factor in designing any grass strip. Water had to be removed from the area as quickly as possible and a number of techniques were developed to do just that. The longer water was allowed to stay on or under the strip the more unstable the subsoil was likely to become. The load-bearing capacity would subsequently be reduced, forcing any aircraft in flight to divert to other airfields. Special grass that had a high absorption rate was sown and the ground slope was designed into the airfield promoting water run-off. Under surface drainage – allowing the water to be channelled away and a reduction of the water table level, often by aggressive pumping close to the airfield – ensured the area was kept dry. To achieve this the landing area received substantial modification. The entire area was subsoiled and materials such as ballast, clays and sands were mixed with the subsoil; the bombing circle was then fertilised with manure, lime, harrowed and finally rolled to produce the ideal turf growing environment. However, it was the architecture of the station of 'Standard Function' that was to become such a recognisable part of the British landscape.

As we have seen in previous periods a degree of standardisation has always been desirable when connected with airfield construction; most recognisable to date had been the airship and Training Depot Stations of the First World War. Now, as part of the expansion schemes, this requirement was further explored. This led to the design of a whole suite

RAF Finningley, Yorkshire, in 2006. Officers Mess. One feature of the expansion period was the standard of architecture designed with the help of the Royal Fine Arts Commission.

of structures intended to perform the latest technical function and yet not appear too out of place with the local surrounding. Architects soon came up with an unassuming yet aesthetically pleasing Georgian theme, utilising locally made materials where possible. The Royal Fine Arts Commission reviewed all designs as they were made available and, in conjunction with the Society for the Preservation of Rural England, had a major hand in the architecture we see today. Interestingly the majority contain elements of typical Art-Deco modernist architectural styles, mirroring on occasion designs that would not look out of place on the local Odeon cinema. As the pace of construction grew throughout the period some sites received concrete versions of the same architectural design, but on the whole building was executed using hand-made bricks or occasionally local stone. The layout of the technical and domestic sites owed much to the shape of the airfield. In nearly all new build airfields of the expansion period a standard plan was implemented only to be deviated from if the local conditions, especially geological, dictated it so. Subsequently it is possible to readily recognise expansion airfields from the ground plan alone.

Baldwin's abandonment of the path to peace in 1935 would turn out to be an extreme piece of good fortune, as the following eighteen months were to demonstrate. The first casualty of the abandonment was Scheme A. By May the Government had approved a revision – Scheme C. Scheme C also instigated work on existing stations at Catterick, Cranwell, Halton, Hornchurch, Leuchars, North Weald, Sealand, Tangmere, Turnhouse, Upper Heyford and Wittering, each receiving improvements costing around £35,000. It

The expansionist agendas of Mussolini and Hitler throughout the 1930s indicated to the world the problems on the horizon.

needs to be pointed out here that the missing letters in the series are those proposals that never received Government backing. Now the requirement was for a front line force with parity to that estimated to be held by Germany by 1937. The requirement for bombers, some now light, remained but would it and the subsequent building programme be enough to dissuade the dictatorships developing in Europe from an arms race?

## Countdown to Catastrophe

In September 1931 the Japanese Imperial Army invaded Manchuria. It was intended to be the conclusion of a modernisation through an expansion scheme promoted by the Japanese army. The depression of 1929 had hit the Japanese economy hard and the population increasingly listened to army-derived political voices rather than the weak civilian government. By 1931 it was clear any expansionism into Asia would need a mainland springboard. Manchuria was the natural choice. A full naval and aerial bombardment of Shanghai and the execution of thousands of Chinese farmers brought swift condemnation from the League of Nations; Japan withdrew from the League in March 1933. Its expansionist aspirations in the Far East were now obvious and British interest were now clearly under threat.

On 3 October 1935 troops from the Italian Army crossed the Eritrean border into Abyssinia. This move, supported by a smaller force from the south, was a clear act of aggression and, worse, it was unannounced. By 7 October the League of Nations was imposing sanctions – rubber, camels and donkeys were no longer allowed to be exported to Italy; interestingly oil and other materials essential to the Italian war machine were not mentioned. By May the following year (1936) Abyssinian opposition eventually collapsed in the face of repeated use of mustard gas from artillery and aerial bombardment.

## Scheme F

Scheme F, ratified by the Cabinet in February 1936, was heavily influenced by the Italian-German rearmament programmes, so much so that it now acknowledged Germany was likely to become the aggressor in the near future. That said, the main driver for Scheme F was the possibility of having to bomb Italian targets if directed by the League of Nations. Italy's main industrial centres were located in the north of the country but were just too far away for the RAF to bomb. Scheme F, influenced by the new Deputy Director for Air Plans, none other that Arthur Harris, switched the emphasis from light to medium bomber aircraft. Procurement specification orders 29/36 and 30/36 were subsequently issued; the first steps towards the Handley Page Hampden and Vickers Wellington.

Organisational changes also occurred throughout 1936, introducing some classic departments. First to go was the Inland Area. This became Training Command No.1 Group in May and by the beginning of July both Cranwell and Halton came under its command. Then, on 13 July the Air Defence of Great Britain was abolished and Bomber Command, Fighter Command and Coastal Command took over.

This change of emphasis naturally had an effect on the airfield building programme, as did the increase of squadron complements from twelve to eighteen aircraft. To cope with this airfield designers standardised the capacity of each station, enlargement of communal buildings were subsequently required:

> The Council add that they are satisfied that the revised estimates are fair and reasonable and that, apart from the fact that officers' and sergeants' messes have been provided in all cases as for heavy bomber stations and institutes as for the larger establishment of medium bomber stations in order to meet the need for stations being interchangeable.
>
> (R.N. Nind Hopkins, Air Ministry to Treasury, 10 November 1936 (AIR 20/8539))

By July 1936, Britain had managed to convince many of the League of Nations members that the sanctions should be lifted, ineffective as they were, recognising Mussolini's annexation of the country. This level of appeasement, costing Samuel Hoare his job, was a blatant attempt to keep the Italians' favour, possibly as a counter to Germany's clear expansionist hopes, expansionism that had been demonstrated a few months earlier in the Rhineland.

On 7 March 1936, in direct defiance of the Treaty of Versailles and Locarno Treaty, Germany marched troops into the demilitarised Rhineland. Versailles was specific about what constituted a violation:

> ARTICLE 42
>
> Germany is forbidden to maintain or construct any fortifications either on the left bank of the Rhine or on the right bank to the west of a line drawn 50 kilometres to the East of the Rhine.

ARTICLE 43

In the area defined above the maintenance and the assembly of armed forces, either permanently or temporarily, and military manoeuvres of any kind, as well as the upkeep of all permanent works for mobilisation, are in the same way forbidden.

ARTICLE 44

In case Germany violates in any manner whatever the provisions of articles 42 & 43 she shall be regarded as committing a hostile act against the Powers signatory of the present Treaty and as calculated to disturb the peace of the world.

Churchill, naturally, demanded a military response; however, he was in the minority and the governments of Britain, France and Belgium, beyond complaining to the League of Nations, did nothing. Alan Bullock in his hugely influential *Hitler: A Study of Tyranny* later quoted the Führer as saying of the venture:

> The forty-eight hours after the march into the Rhineland were the most nerve-racking in my life. If the French had then marched into the Rhineland we would have had to withdraw with our tails between our legs, for the military resources at our disposal would have been wholly inadequate for even a moderate resistance.

He need not have worried as the remilitarisation met a mixed but decidedly ineffective reaction in Britain. Bar Churchill, who was on the back bench at the time, the sentiments were decidedly pro-German. Baldwin claimed that public opinion would not agree to military force and Britain still lacked the resources to enforce any treaty commitments. Anthony Eden, Secretary of State for Foreign Affairs also set about discouraging military action by the French and was against the imposition of any financial or economic sanctions on Germany. The Government considered that if the German administration collapsed under external pressure it would again take Europe with it, just as it had through the mid-1920s.

## Spanish Civil War

In June 1936 a failed coup by Nationalist forces in Spain led to a bloody three-year civil war. What alarmed politicians in Britain was the immediate pledge of equipment from Italy and Germany for General Franco, leader of the Nationalists, whilst Stalin, naturally, supported the democratically elected republican government. It appeared that the situation could very quickly lead to war and subsequently the British and American governments remained neutral. This did not stop many ordinary people from around the world joining the fight for democracy by joining the Republican International Brigade. This included American pilots who, under the guise of the *Patrolla Americana*, eventually operated a squadron of twenty. Nevertheless, it was Germany that was to benefit from involvement in the war. Hitler considered aid to a fascist cause such as Franco's a pre-requisite. Subsequently *Unternehmen Feuerzauber* (Operation Fire Magic) was sanctioned. It his book *The Spanish Civil War*, Hugh Thomas suggested that Germany's involvement was an attempt to manipulate raw materials and this appears now to be the case. However, the involvement of the Luftwaffe, formed into the Condor Legion for the expedition, and the experience it would gain were not lost to the Reich:

The Fuehrer thought the matter over. I urged him to give support under all circumstances, firstly, in order to prevent the further spread of communism in that theatre and, secondly, to test my young Luftwaffe at this opportunity in this or that technical respect.

   With the permission of the Fuehrer, I sent a large part of my transport fleet and a number of experimental fighter units, bombers, and antiaircraft guns; and in that way I had an opportunity to ascertain, under combat conditions, whether the material was equal to the task. In order that the personnel, too, might gather a certain amount of experience, I saw to it that there was a continuous flow, that is, that new people were constantly being sent and others recalled.

(Herman Goering with Counsel Dr Otto Stahmer, *Morning Session*, on Thursday
14 March 1946, Nurnberg)

By the time the Condor Legion withdrew its forces in 1939 it had combat tested the Heinkel HE111, Junkers Ju 87 Stuka and the highly effective Messerschmitt Bf109 fighter; not to mention giving nearly 20,000 of its personnel valuable experience on both the ground and in the air.

   As Hitler was marching into the Rhineland a further – if less well-defined – distribution of RAF airfields was laid in. This time nine stations of 'standard function' were built running from Dishforth in the north down through Yorkshire and on into Cambridgeshire. As with any project as the size increased naturally so, too, did the costs.

## Dishforth

Planning for the acquisition of land to site an airfield at Dishforth in North Yorkshire had started by early 1935 and on subsequent advice from the DoW proposals were forwarded to the Treasury. Dishforth was to be home for 'two Heavy Bomber Squadrons included in the approved expansion scheme for the Royal Air Force'. It was also proposed to purchase land at Leconfield for the same purpose:

> The areas which it is proposed to acquire are at Dishforth, 402 acres and at Leconfield, 496 acres, the cost of the acquisition, inclusive of severance and compensation to tenants, been estimated at £20,000 and £23,500 respectively, chargeable to Vote 4 subhead F. It may be found possible to dispose of an area of some 45 acres at Leconfield, but further consideration is deferred pending approval to the layout of the permanent station buildings.
>
> (Commissioner to the Treasury, C.M. Brigstocke, 26 October 1936 (AIR 20/8539))

The target date for occupying the site was laid at the end of 1936/37; both airfields were initially to be occupied on a temporary basis at a cost of £25,000 per station. Work to prepare the aerodrome landing ground was estimated to cost between £6,000 and £9,000 for each site. Further to this preparatory work the Air Council also proposed five C-type hangars should be built at both sites, 'the cost of these hangars will be in the neighbourhood of £165,000 in each case'. As the stations would not be home to permanent squadrons until 1938/39 the hangars once built 'will be utilised for the storage of the reserve aircraft at the aircraft to the squadron station there a temporary basis'.

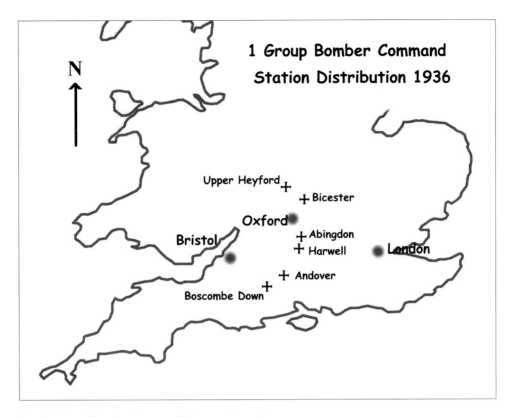

Distribution of Bomber Command Group 1 in 1936.

1936 saw the development of new stations expanding well beyond those plans laid in the 1920s. The pace and scale, demonstrated in the following extracts from a letter to the Treasury from the Air Council, was such that modification was needed in the construction effort. The initial concept had been to build temporary camps for almost immediate occupation followed by permanent construction once established. By 1936 the construction of permanent structures was becoming wide spread and as a matter of course the level of resources being demanded by the programme rapidly increased, dictating that some stations would remain 'temporary' right through the 1930s and '40s.

The council proposed to commence in 1936 the permanent construction of Shawbury, a flying training School required in connection with the expansion scheme approved in 1934, and the following six stations required in connection with the scheme of expansion approved in May, 1935.

Dishforth, Finningley, Driffield, Stations in Yorkshire each required for the accommodation of two heavy bomber squadrons. Scampton, Lincolnshire – for two medium bomber squadrons. Upwood, Huntingdon – for three light bomber squadrons. Debden, Essex – for three fighter squadrons.

At three further sites already acquired as squadron stations, vis; Hemswell, Leconfield, and Wyton, it is proposed that work in 1936 should be confined to the completion of the erection of hangars, and the preparation of the aerodromes, and such work as construction of roads, drains, etc and the provision of water, light and power services which are essential, not only for the permanent station, irrespective of the type of construction, but also for the temporary camps to be erected in 1936 for occupation on or before the 31st of March, 1937.

Separate applications will be made to their Lordships the sanctions to provide hangars and prepare aerodromes for two further flight training schools when authorities sought for the purchase of the requisite sites, while sanction has already been sought for the construction of hutted accommodation of a semi-permanent character at three new armament training camps, viz; Penrhos (Hells Mouth), West Freugh (Luce Bay) and Woodsford (Chesil Beach).

(J.S. Ross, Air Council to the Treasury, 24 February 1936 (AIR 20/8539))

## Manpower Problems

This explosion of construction was not restricted to the building of airfields. Other Government projects were demanding more and more manpower as well as raw materials. Social housing was one area that the National Government had prided itself on developing, but by 1936 there were fears that this could quite easily be brought to a standstill due to the loss of skilled labour. This loss was all the more apparent due to the shortage of apprentices to the building trade. The problem was that the depression caused by the Wall Street Crash had squeezed builders and the first sign of any rationalisation involved letting any trainees go. This, coupled with the increased wages being offered on some Government projects by contractors, was stripping the domestic market. Further problems were acutely experienced by the Air Ministry due to the location of airfield sites, by their very nature remote and rural, and any spare labour was immediately absorbed.

Those airfields started in 1935 were nearly all completed by 1937 but those in the 1936 batch were immediately effected by the shortage of labour. Naturally this started to increase costs as slippage bit into the allotted contract times:

The estimates which are based on the latest available information as to the prices of building works materially exceed previous estimates for similar stations, the increased cost being due to the following factors.

(a) A general rise in prices, particularly in the cost of steelwork.

(b) The adoption of concrete construction for technical buildings, this course being necessary in view of the shortage of bricklayers.

(c) The adoption of protective measures against incendiary bombs in the case of certain buildings such as the operations block, sick quarters, wireless station and petrol installation.

(d) Increased requirements, e.g., the provision for bomb storage has been increased to 144 tons at each bomber station.

(A.H. Self, Air Council to the Treasury, 16 September 1936 (AIR 20/8539))

RAF Finningley, Yorkshire, in 2006. Station Armoury, with the shortage of bricklayers caused by the expansion programme designers switched to concrete construction.

Concrete construction, utilising similar designs to those in brick, eventually made up around half of the entire technical buildings on airfields in the expansion period. This, too, brought its problems. It transpired that the transition to concrete did not increase the speed at which airfield construction progressed. Simply put the problem of the lack of skilled bricklayers was replaced by a lack of carpenters who could perform the shuttering operation. Subsequently the estimates for building Dishforth had increased within the first year from £430,000 to £525,000 whilst Finningley, comprising concrete where possible, still rose by £100,000.

Scheme F also saw renewed interest in the deployment of balloons to ward off enemy bombers. The concept had been first introduced as a defence against the Gotha bomber attacks of 1917–18 over London. Known as a balloon apron, seven were deployed in defence of the capital. In November 1936 the Air Council made its intentions to form a Balloon Barrage around the capital known. Planning now dictated that a ring of balloons were set up around London forming a defensive circuit of 45 miles. The concept being that bombers would be forced to fly higher, avoiding the cables, meaning they would be in the sights of anti-aircraft guns for longer. Unfortunately this proved ineffective as any aircraft making its way to London simply 'hopped' over the balloon obstacles and then assumed its bombing run. This limited balloon defence was placed under the control of Fighter Command.

1936 then became a pivotal year. Not only did the building programme accelerate, so did the aircraft types considered essential for the offensive defence of the country. Scheme F saw the realignment of the organisational structure of the RAF against a worsening political background. Two problems remained – how to get industry to increase production and what to do with the aircraft once built. The answer came in the form of the Aircraft Storage Unit and the shadow factory.

## Aircraft Storage Depots

The development of the Aircraft Storage Unit (ASU) saw a detachment from standard airfield design. Many, primarily due to their location, survive to this day. The stations were designed to receive aircraft straight from manufacture, often still in component form, assemble, function and flight test them before dispatching them to the squadrons. Twenty-four were eventually constructed and the ASU, more than any other unit, typifies the planning and design that went into expansion period thinking.

One area of major concern for military planners was the problem of how to make good wastage. Reports to the Air Staff covering this issue in 1933 estimated a fighter force of fifty squadrons losing 1,000 aircraft per month. Further meetings chaired by Sir Robert Brooke-Popham at the Royal United Services Institute in 1934 discussed any future conflict using statistics from the First World War; it added to the already grim reading. The average life of an aircraft in war was estimated to be no more than two months. Indeed the fledgling Royal Air Force had suffered a 45 per cent monthly loss rate during its brief seven months in battle. If the RAF was to be prepared for the future it needed to be able to make good any losses whilst increasing production and maintenance wherever possible. A number of facets were obvious. Production rates would need to increase to make good any shortfall, aircraft would need to be repaired and planning would need to be accurate and far sighted. At present none of this was in place.

If repair stations were able to return 50 per cent of damaged aircraft back to the front line it would leave industry to make up the 500-strong shortfall – every month. Naturally there would be a time lag between placing orders and aircraft being produced so a reserve stock equivalent to around six weeks would be needed. This reserve stock had been held at the airfields on which they were to be used; however, numbers now required a major rethink. By 1936 what was to become Maintenance Command proposed a network of twenty-four Aircraft Storage Units each to hold 400 aircraft in various states of readiness. During the war this massive number was reduced to 200 per site but still ensuring nearly 5,000 were in reserve by late 1940.

ASUs fall into two broad categories, those located on Flying Training School airfields such as Hullavington and self-contained units with their own landing areas including Kemble which, incidentally, cost £625,000. ASU hangarage was the most diverse of any station often featuring C, D, E, L and outlying Robins hangars. A number of Lamella sheds also appeared on site; these were, bizarrely, based on a German design. There was method to this diversity. ASUs were to all intense and purpose production lines, generating aircraft to replace losses or equip new squadrons. In the case of overseas deployment, especially to Asia, this also involved the dismantling and packing of aircraft for shipping. By the outbreak of war the ASU had become an integral part of the aircraft production process.

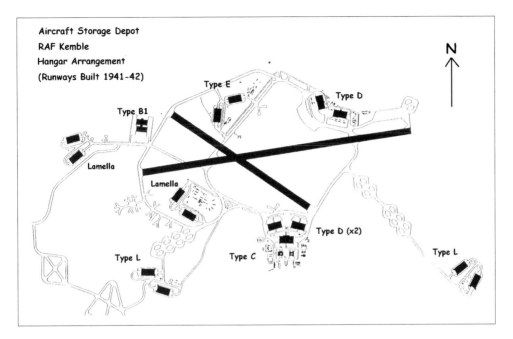

RAF Kemble Aircraft Storage Unit. (After Paul Francis)

As the speed of rearmament increased so did the size of production contracts to the aircraft manufacturers. These were, in the main, satisfied by producing aircraft in unit parts and then finally building and testing on the ASUs.

## Landscape

A cursory glance at the distribution of the Aircraft Storage Units (ASUs) demonstrates a geographically distinct grouping. No stations appear to the east of the Pennine line and the furthest south they occur is North Wiltshire. The reason for this is clear. Airfields with reserve aircraft stocks would be a prime target in any future conflict and attack would come most likely across the east or south coast from Continental Europe. Basing major aircraft reserve stocks in the north and south-west, therefore, moved such critical wartime assets as far as possible out of harm's way. A deeper consideration is evident when one considers aircraft manufacture and the role of the shadow factory scheme.

To build an adequate reserve the Government embarked on a scheme of expansion in the aircraft industry, interestingly also in 1936. Seven sites were initially identified, expanding to nine per year after initial work started. These new factories complemented expansion work at existing aircraft producing firms, again underwritten by the British Government. From its conception to the outbreak of hostilities the scheme was supervised by the Air Ministry. Of those original seven, two – Austins and Rootes – were designated airframe construction sites whilst the other five at Daimler, Humber, Standard, Rover and Bristol were all concerned with engine production. In 1937 a further two factories were started for the building of propellers at de Havilland and Hobsons, manufacturing carburettors specifically. Shadow factories, whilst a prudent idea that was to pay dividends in the coming war, at their

RAF Wroughton, Wiltshire, in 2005. The D-Type hangar was reinforced concrete and was for the safe parking of aircraft once assembled at the ASU.

RAF Wroughton, Wiltshire, in 2005. Aircraft Storage Units often had a reduced number of service staff on them, necessitating smaller facilities. Here the SHQ is single storey.

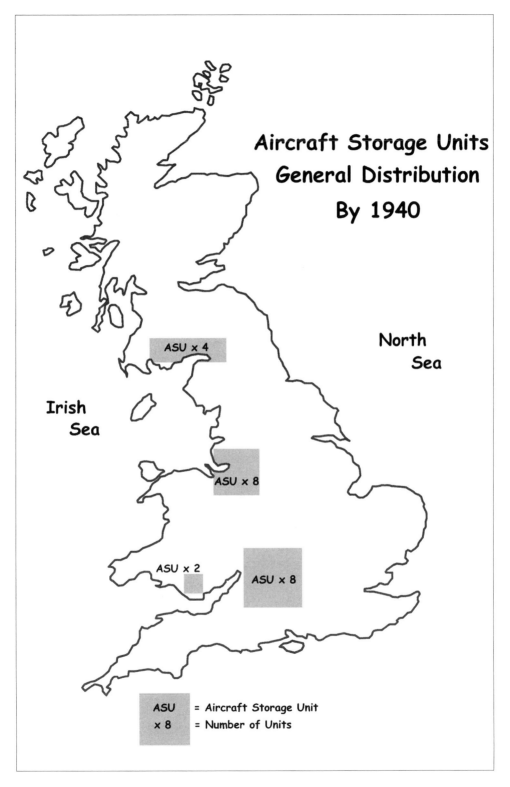

Distribution of ASU demonstrating western locations.

conception brought rise to many problems. Companies such as de Havilland were already producing aircraft and components and were well versed in the approaches needed for peak efficiency. Unfortunately the same could not be said for companies such as Rover, and the Air Ministry struggled to make the firms aware of aircraft production in the initial years of use.

The locations of the shadow factories do help us interpret the positioning of Aircraft Storage Units. Clearly access to ports at this time did not feature too heavily, the involvement of the USA being a minor concern. However, the primary function of the ASU was to create a buffer of around six weeks between squadron wastage and the production of replacements. Naturally it made sense to locate the ASUs close to the factories producing the replacement, not too close to make them a liability but close enough to move the components by road and rail efficiently. This is most obvious when the distribution of the ASUs are considered.

The ASUs fall into four distinct areas on the British mainland. There are major concentrations in the West Country, centring on Cirencester and the industrial north-west, centring on Stoke-on-Trent. Manufacturers in the north-west include Rolls-Royce, Fairey, Avro, English Electric, de Havilland and Lucas, as well as premises owned Ministry of Aircraft Production (the shadow factories). Whilst those in the west are close to Bristol Aeroplane Co., Gloster Aircraft Co., Rolls-Royce, Smiths & Phillips and Powis Aircraft Ltd (later Miles), both these groups are clearly allied to the major aircraft companies and between both contain 70 per cent of the ASU scheme storage capacity. A further group containing four airfields is distributed loosely around the Solway Firth and two more are located at the Maintenance Unit, RAF St Athan and just two miles away at Llandow. Two further sites are located in Northern Ireland and are allied to the new, Government-sponsored factory started, again, in 1936 for Shorts and Harland & Wolff.

The Aircraft Storage Unit was one of the first aerodrome types to take full advantage of local cover. By their very nature they were designed to be concealed. Containing far more aircraft than a normal station the ASU would become a tempting target in any future conflict. Other station types were concerned with local flying obstructions and whilst the same can be said of those ASUs on FTS sites the actual infrastructure, especially the hangars, readily welcomed them. Pure ASUs such as Wroughton and Kemble noticeably deviated from other airfield designs, not least in their dispersed nature. Local topographical conditions are also exploited. Wroughton covers an area of around 5 sq.km and has differences in landfall of up to 15m in places. These were exploited by the planners who dispersed the various hangars across six sites around the extensive perimeter. Each group of hangars was a minimum of 750m from the next group, making targeting from the air difficult. During the war the ASUs expanded enormously; Wroughton doubled in size as more surrounding land was requisitioned by the Government for aircraft parking and a similar situation prevailed at other stations. Quite a number of ASUs prevail, many surviving as RAF stations until the big disposals due to the 'Peace Dividend' era of the early 1990s, their distinctive hangar layout still clearly visible.

## Aircraft Repair and Maintenance
Aircraft by their very nature breakdown or, more correctly, become unserviceable (US); they also require periodical maintenance if they are to maintain maximum serviceability.

RAF Aston Down Aircraft Storage Unit, Gloucestershire, in 2007. 'E'-Type Hangars were designed to take aircraft still in packing cases delivered from the manufacturer.

This can, to a certain level, be carried out at the aircraft's home base; however, on the scales predicted in wartime this would in all probability take up precious space at front line airfields. To relieve this pressure the Air Ministry planned a number of dedicated airframe and engine repair stations, massive in scale and where possible civilian manned.

St Athan, South Wales, and Sealand, Chester, were both planned during 1936 and were under construction by 1937. They were yet another radical detachment from the 'Standard Function' Station. Primary to these new sites was the level of efficiency that could be achieved with the careful positioning of the structures. Accordingly, at both stations substantial barrack blocks, modelled on the high density Maitland mess area at the RAF Apprentice School at Halton, were built. These three-storey constructions were built as close as possible to the workshops, which were in turn built close to the main hangar complex. Both stations were far beyond the considered enemy bomber range and subsequently this high-density messing could be tolerated. These stations were to prove ideal sites for ASUs and it was at RAF St Athan that one of the largest complexes of the war eventually developed. St. Athan was also upgraded to a technical training establishment during the latter part of 1936 and the station, along with the former airship station at Cardington, received timber hutting capable of accommodating 4,000 trainees. The hutting was to be a temporary measure whilst the RAF built its pre-war strength. Those at St Athan were not removed until the late 1990s.

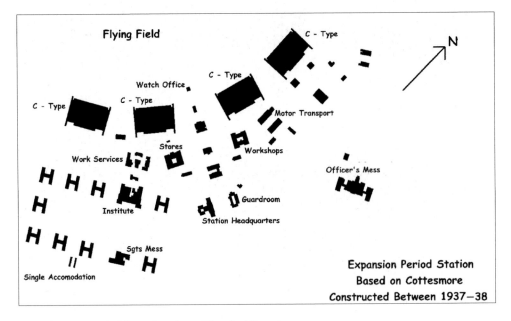

RAF Cottesmore. A Scheme J station of Standard Function.

## Scheme J

By 1937 a new arc of stations had been planned for eastern England, from Linton on Ouse, north of York, down to Benson, south of Oxford. The bulk of the standard function stations lay inside the Norfolk/Suffolk bulge, allowing a degree of flexibility dependant on offensive or defensive requirements. A further ten stations received upgrades to existing facilities including Boscombe Down. Here a singular C Type was constructed on the site of the motor transport depot, a bulk fuel installation and substantial expansion of No. 1 explosive area took place, increasing the station's bombing capacity. It was also in 1937 that the new Squadron Balloon Depots were started. These had been designed during Scheme F but only received financial authorisation a year later. Four were initially built at Kidbrooke, Hook, Stanmore and Chigwell as part of the London defence network. Scheme J is important insomuch as the requirement now tabled by the Air Ministry was on Heavy Bombers, 896 to be exact. More important still they had to be able to reach targets in Germany.

Not every construction was to standard function design; Fulton Block at Cosford, designed in 1937, was to signal a change in training environment, especially for groundcrew.

## Fulton Block

Fulton Block was initially planned as a permanent construction for 4,000 personnel, incorporating instructional workshops, lecture halls and domestic arrangements such as messing and billeting. The building was destined to become unique as, by 1938, it was clear such structures were neither practical nor economically viable. Not only was it unique, it was also a quarter of the proposed size. The block was so named in memory of Captain Fulton who is widely recognised as one of the forefathers of the Royal Air Force. In fact Fulton was one of the Larkhill pioneers, flying at his own expense until the foundation of the Air

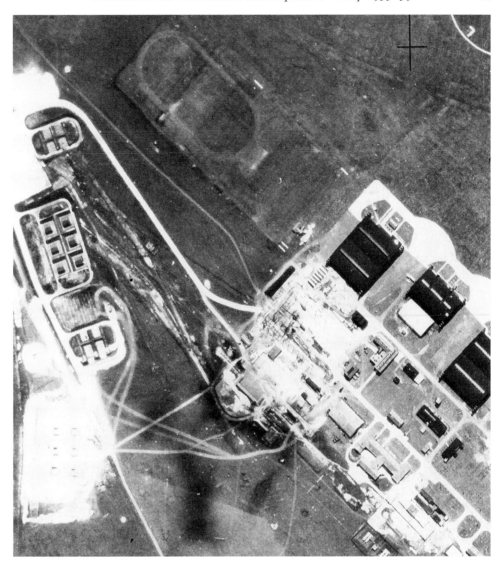

*Above:* RAF Boscombe Down.
Expansion of existing stations in 1937
included Boscombe Down. Here a
new C-Type hangar, station workshop
complex and extension to the bomb
dump is in progress. (Courtesy of the
Ministry of Defence)

*Right:* RAF Cosford, Shropshire, Fulton
Block built in 1938–39. The design was
intended to appear on all training sites;
however, the economies of the national
purse dictated otherwise.

RAF West Raynham, Norfolk, in 2006. Following on from the TDS layout all C-Type hangars were set out in a sweeping arch with the air traffic building central to them. (Courtesy of Mike Digby)

Gloster Gauntlet K4083 (centre) was delivered to No.19 Squadron at Duxford on 25 January 1935. By 20 April 1937 it was scrapped after a heavy landing. The squadron was later equipped with Spitfires. (Courtesy of Malcolm Holland)

Battalion, in which he commanded No.2 Company until his untimely death in 1915. Fulton Block cost just short of £250,000; however, the higher density of recruits coupled with the cost dictated that the majority of recruits were housed in timber accommodation.

In late December 1937 there was an important shift in policy. Until then all schemes had aimed to maintain parity with German Bomber Force numbers, with the ultimate aim of delivering a knock-out blow to the enemy. This thinking had been prevalent since the first expansion period in the early 1920s but now the emphasis changed. Thomas Inskip, Minister for the Co-ordination of Defence from 1936, suggested that the United Kingdom need not spend anything like the projected costs on long-range bombers, far better to invest in light- or medium-range aircraft and increase the fighter cover for Britain. The shift was now towards the prevention of an enemy delivering a knock-out blow to Britain more than the RAF delivering one to them, the end of Offensive Defence. Yet another scheme, this time 'L', was tabled in April 1938 to support this, against a backdrop of the worsening situation in Europe.

1938 proved a turning point in the expansion of the Royal Air Force. Until that date there was always the possibility that Germany would be contained by its European neighbours, but by March Hitler demonstrated that he was intending to expand Germany's frontiers.

## *Anschluss*

Since his rise to power Hitler had made no secret of his intentions for Austria, the place of his birth, under the guise of uniting all German-speaking peoples. An attempt to bring Austria into line politically happened in July 1934 when a coup by the far right party ended in chaos and the assassination of the much-respected chancellor, Engelbert Dollfuss. Hitler renewed his unification demands in early 1938 when he pointed out to the new chancellor, Kurt von Schuschnigg, that unless the Austrian Nazi Party was legalised he would be forced to invade and install the party in government. Schuschnigg eventually resigned over the matter and was replaced by Dr Arthur Seyss-Inquart, a leading Austrian Nazi. The day after he took office, 11 March 1938, Seyss-Inquart 'requested' the German army be sent in to restore law and order. The next day he declared *Anschluss* and Austria disappeared into the Greater German Reich.

## *'Peace in our Time'*

Next on the list was Czechoslovakia. Again Hitler cited the unification of all Germanic peoples as his reason for wanting to annex the Sudetenland, the frontier region on Germany's border. Goebbels stepped up the pressure by portraying the ethnic Germans as a persecuted minority, when in reality they enjoyed better conditions than some in other areas of Czechoslovakia. In May Hitler decided to move in; Britain, France and Russia all warned that an invasion would bring about an immediate military response. Throughout the summer the Nazis engineered a number of incidents, including a claim that 300 Sudeten Germans had died in police directed brutality. By the tenth Party Conference at Nuremberg in 1938 Hitler was openly demanding 'self determination'; the Sudeten Germans rioted on the signal and many were killed or arrested.

Diplomacy now came to the fore as Neville Chamberlain orchestrated a series of summits to discuss a peaceful way forward. The first meeting was held at Hitler's mountain retreat at Berchtesgaden on 15 September. Subsequently Chamberlain, with the backing of the French government, told the Czech president that if he was to go to war over the Sudetenland he could not count on their support. By the second meeting, on the 22nd, Chamberlain told Hitler he would not stand in his way, as long as a timescale was adhered to. However, Hitler, now convinced no one would appose him, demanded immediate possession of the Sudetenland and mobilised his troops. The Czechs did likewise and war seemed inevitable. A way out came at the eleventh hour when Italy called a conference to be held at Munich in an attempt to break the deadlock. On 29 September 1938 Czechoslovakia, who was not represented at the conference, was dismembered losing lands to Germany, Poland and Hungary, whilst being split into the Czech and Slovak nations. Hitler promised that this was his last territorial demand in Europe and Chamberlain declared to a large crowd on landing at Heston Airport:

> We, the German Führer and Chancellor and the British Prime Minister, have had a further meeting today and are agreed in recognising that the question of Anglo-German relations is of the first importance for the two countries, and for Europe. We regard the agreement signed last night and the Anglo-German naval agreement, as symbolic of the desire of our two peoples never to go to war with one another again.

In the subsequent Parliamentary debate on 3 October on the signing of the Munich Agreement Chamberlain commented that the crisis had been dangerous – 'Now that we have got past it, I feel that it may be possible to make further progress along the road to sanity'. That 'sanity' was not to last as on 21 October Hitler ordered the German Army to ready itself for the takeover of the remaining areas of Czechoslovakia. If the British people thought peace was assured they soon realised it could well be short-lived; the affable 'Mr Hitler' instigated one of the worst excesses to date on the Jewish population of the Gross Deutches Reich. Kristallnacht, as it became known, saw a week-long series of attacks on Jewish businesses, homes and people that shook the British public to its core. Families had been fleeing persecution for a number of years but this demonstrated that a corner had been turned. If the Nazis were capable of carrying out such brutality then they were clearly capable of lying to get what they wanted territorially.

During all the negotiations the expansion of the RAF continued apace. As short-lived as scheme L was it still had a major effect on the landscape. It was clear by now that any diplomatic efforts were not considered to be a permanent arrangement; accordingly L concerned itself with the expansion of accommodation for training and the subsequent increase of personnel that would be based at aerodromes after that. Training establishments were increased at Yatesbury, Compton Bassett and Hednesford to the tune of 4,000 trainees each, whilst the colleges at Henlow and Cosford were further enlarged, utilising timber hutting. An incredible twenty-five sites already in existence or still under construction also received increased accommodation to absorb the extra personnel. Ten Aircraft Storage Units were started along with an ASU attachment to the new airfield under construction at Kinloss. One of the biggest bases in the British Isles was also started at Burtonwood, again with an ASU attached. Hospitals appeared at Ely and Wroughton, and more sites were investigated to further expand the network. Standard Function stations also appeared at Colerne, in conjunction with an ASU, Coltishall and Horsham. Complementing the airfields were a number of extra balloon barrage stations covering major industrial areas' population centres and ports. These seventeen stations, from 1 November 1938, came under Balloon Command with HQ at Stanmore, one of the original four London stations.

The prospect of war soon loomed large when Mussolini, whilst addressing the Fascist Grand Council in November 1938, outlined his programme for the next few years. Now Italy demanded territories from France including areas in North Africa, Tunisia and Corsica. Naturally the French were outraged and refused point blank to consider ceding to a fascist government, especially since the fascist successes in Spain now meant the country was being pressed on three frontiers. Chamberlain again stepped into the middle but by now it was clear that the fascist states of Europe were not going to stick to their agreements over territory. That same month the Air Ministry proposed scheme M to the Cabinet, a scheme which radically increased development in all areas. Aircraft development was to see the Halifax and Sterling enter production in earnest whilst fighter production, especially for Hurricane, Spitfire and Defiant, was increased. The final indication, if one were needed, came on 15 March 1939 when Dr Emil Hácha, the new Czech president, was 'invited' to a night meeting with Hitler and other German officials. Hitler demanded he sign the instrument of abdication of Czecho-Slovakian sovereignty or he would bomb the country into submission. That night Hácha was subject to physical

RAF West Raynham, Norfolk, in 2006. Standard H block airmen's accommodation. The flat roof was to make sure incendiaries did not penetrate the roof space, making them difficult to deal with. (Courtesy of Mike Digby)

abuse to the point where he had to be brought round by injection. Hitler got what he wanted and troops moved into Bohemia and Moravia unopposed.

This was too much for many in the British Government and on 31 March 1939 Chamberlain announced to the House of Commons that any threat to the independence of Poland, clearly next for annexation, would be met with force:

> As the House is aware, certain consultations are now proceeding with other Governments. In order to make perfectly clear the position of His Majesty's Government in the meantime before those consultations are concluded, I now have to inform the House that during that period, in the event of any action which clearly threatened Polish independence, and which the Polish Government accordingly considered it vital to resist with their national forces, His Majesty's Government would feel themselves bound at once to lend the Polish Government all support in their power. They have given the Polish Government an assurance to this effect.

Naturally all eyes were on what Germany would do next, so it came as something of a surprise when Italy declared its intention to occupy Albania. Mussolini, interestingly, had hoped Hitler would stick to his word over the Munich Agreement. When he did not Mussolini considered he had been personally humiliated. By 7 April the Italian expeditionary forces were landing on the Albanian coast virtually unopposed. The

Station Headquarters
Aberporth, West Wales.
Aberporth opened as an
Anti-Aircraft Gunnery
School, supported by a
small airfield for target
towing a few miles
inland.

government fell within days; the whole episode prompted Britain to extend its guarantees to Greece and Rumania. When Hitler demanded access across the Danzig corridor, the scene was set for disaster.

Construction was now hastily started at seventeen more Standard Function stations including Binbrook, Leeming, Swinderby, Oakington and West Malling. However, as war approached a new building concept came to the fore – austerity measures. This was ruthlessly applied to all stations still under construction from mid-1939. It also meant that all those stations that had temporary constructions on them suddenly found they were permanent, Lyneham being one such airfield. Further increases to the training establishments were approved as well as building two further hospitals, this time in timber.

## Coastal Command

Coastal Command was very much the poor relation to Bomber and Fighter Command. For years the role of the RAF in naval affairs had caused much consternation and faced repeated opposition from the 'Senior Service', to the point where the Command had played a subservient role to the surface fleet. The Command had been formed in 1936 with three groups with HQs at Plymouth, Chatham and Rosyth. Each was jointly manned by air and naval staff. By 1937, as part of Thomas Inskip's reorganisation, all carrier-borne aircraft were transferred to the Fleet Air Arm whilst all land-based aircraft remained in RAF service. Throughout the expansion period schemes Coastal Command received little in the way of funding, with the Government quite happy to follow Navy assurances that it could handle any issues in that environment. The only noticeable exception was S.25 Short Sunderland, a development of the 'C' class flying boat, whose maiden flight was 16 October 1937.

Other than that the force was in no way ready for war. Apart from the Sunderland its equipment was at best adequate. In 1936 the Command had been equipped with Ansons after a design competition between Avro and de Havilland. The aircraft subsequently formed No.48 Squadron, stationed at RAF Manston, in March 1936. In 1938 the British Purchasing Commission, occasionally known the 'Anglo-French Purchasing Board' and based in New York, arranged the production and purchase of the Lockheed Hudson, the company's biggest order to date. The commission also arranged the purchase of armaments from other North American manufacturers, circumventing the Neutrality Act by paying for the equipment in gold. By February 1939, Hudsons began to arrive in Britain, initially equipping No.224 Squadron at Leuchars.

As you would expect many of Coastal Command's airfields are situated around the coast. However, as Coastal Area in 1930, only a handful of bases were utilised including Calshot, Lee-on-Solent, Gosport and Portland, with training carried out at Leuchars, Donibristle and Mount Batten. During the alphabet expansion schemes it is possible to pick out some work for Coastal Command, or at least naval co-operation. In 1935 work was sanctioned at Thorney Island for torpedo training, whilst Leuchars received funding 'to replace unsatisfactory accommodation'. In 1937 further increases to establishment sizes were seen at both Bircham Newton and Mount Batten and in 1938 Silloth and Aldergrove were both expanded to receive ASUs. Further accommodation was provided at Leuchars and a small airfield was constructed at Carew Cheriton. St Eval saw the building of a General Reconnaissance airfield for work in the western approaches. Even with this work Coastal Command was extremely inadequate at the outbreak of war.

So, can we see a pattern in this rapid expansion? Interestingly, what stands out here is the constant obsession with the Bomber. Trenchard, Baldwin and others, driven by personal experience and lessons learned whilst observing other countries, all pointed towards the requirement of a long range, heavy bomber force. Underlying this was the continued insistence of an independent naval force, culminating in the re-formation of the Fleet Air Arm. Inskip, from 1936, argued otherwise, as did the newly appointed Commander-in-Chief of Fighter Command, Air Chief Marshal Sir Hugh Dowding. Interestingly Peter Grey has recently suggested that Dowding's 'promotion' be considered sidelining due to the primacy of the Bomber Force. These two voices would be instrumental in the Battle of Britain four years hence, their insistence on a fighter force being pivotal to the outcome. Moreover, the dual path of bomber and fighter now meant the Royal Air Force would go some way to being a multi-tactical force by the outbreak of war. Luckily only Britain would build such a force. This was to become its saviour and Germany's eventual undoing.

five

# THE SECOND WORLD
# WAR 1939–42

The Second World War prompted the Royal Air Force to construct nearly 450 new airfields. Thousands of labourers and engineers, along with hundreds of designers and construction companies, were involved in one of the biggest building programmes Britain has seen. Operational requirements and rapid advancement in aircraft technology constantly dictated the design of the new aerodromes, consequently changing the majority from grass to paved runway construction. Material shortages forced building design down a different architectural avenue than had been prevalent in the late 1930s. During 1942, the peak construction year of the war, an average of one airfield every three days was being handed over to the Government by construction consortiums. That same year sixty-three existing airfields received major upgrades, notably in the addition of lengthened or new paved runway and taxiway networks. The reasons behind this vast expansion will be familiar to the reader; events as they unfolded dictated the development of the airfield network. Subsequently it is intended to investigate the different developments in airfield construction using those events as a backdrop to help understanding. Further a watershed in airfield construction was reached at the end of 1942 and this is a convenient place to split the period into two distinct sections. This chapter looks at the years punctuated by defeat, evacuation and isolationism.

*The Fall of Poland*
On 3 September 1939 Neville Chamberlain addressed the nation:

> I am speaking to you from the Cabinet Room at 10, Downing Street. This morning the British Ambassador in Berlin handed the German Government a final Note stating that unless we heard from them by 11 o'clock that they were prepared at once to withdraw their troops from Poland a state of war would exist between us. I have to tell you now that no such undertaking has been received, and that consequently this country is at war with Germany.

It had been an intense three days, discussions between France and Britain covering everything short of actually going to the direct aid of the Polish government. One thing had become apparent: Hitler was in possession of a well-trained, tactically effective army, supported by an equally effective air force. When used together as Blitzkrieg they easily pushed aside the Polish forces, so much so that the invasion of 1 September had already reached Warsaw seven days later. The Germans proceeded to lay waste to vast areas of the city from the ground and from the air in an attempt to force the resisters to surrender. The successes of the Nazis took Stalin by surprise. Not wanting the Germany Army on the Russian border, he launched an attack on 17 September. The Battle for Poland was over by the end of the month; however, Stalin now set about annexing the three Baltic states and making demands for territory from its northern neighbour, Finland, and on 30 November 1939 Stalin mobilised over a million men against them. 160,000 Finns kept the Soviets at bay for four months before the weight of numbers forced a surrender.

Britain, conscious that it had given no more than moral support to Poland, attempted to support Finland with both men and supplies. However, this was to be thwarted as land routes across Norway and Sweden, both neutral, had been blocked to military traffic and the only usable Finnish port had fallen to the Soviets early on in the conflict. In Central Europe the Germans took the opportunity to regroup and prepare for an attack on Denmark and Norway; in Britain the period became known in the press as the 'Phoney War' and even rather comically as 'Sitzkrieg'. However, not all Government departments had been 'sitting it out'.

## 'Requisitioning'

Before the outbreak of hostilities the process whereby the Government acquired land for airfields was, as has been demonstrated in the preceding two chapters, slow, cumbersome and very often expensive. This process had dramatically changed in the weeks before September 1939. The Emergency Powers (Defence) Act 1939 provided, from 24 August, the necessary powers of immediate possession of land or structures deemed essential for the defence of the country. In a flash, thousands of acres were 'requisitioned' for the construction of airfields and other war-related activities. The Lands Branch struggled from the outset. Whilst a number of potential sites had been investigated throughout the expansion period, a large number had been deemed unsuitable for aerodromes. Now, those files were reopened as the Aerodrome Board increased its requirements ten fold and taking land through requisition orders was just the tip of the iceberg. Aircraft production now stepped up a gear. All the shadow factory assets were turned over to aircraft production, but it was not enough and staff from the Lands Branch were tasked with the requisition of factory space, the valuation of it and any compensation claims arising.

## Site Reconnaissance

The selection of potential stations was the responsibility of the Airfield Board; any site under consideration needed further field investigation. Throughout the war this task fell to the Reconnaissance Engineer. Often given just a few days notice and armed with little more than a notebook and level, the engineer was responsible for identifying the geological conditions, soil and sub-soil matrix, any major obstructions, including those underground such as mining works and the local water courses, and for estimating the water capacity for accelerated run off, along with the identification of local quarry for ballast and brick manufacturers, paying particular attention to output. Food, a critical consideration by 1940, was also the concern of the engineer and contact was made with local agricultural committees. An incredible 750 sites were investigated by a team of under ten men during the war, not including the sites rejected.

The engineer's report was submitted to the Air Ministry Directorate of Works who decided whether a full survey was required. This fell to the Land Surveyor, often a civilian just out of college, who again received little notice as to the proposal. The task of finding the landowners also fell to the surveyor and once notice had been served under the emergency power act, things moved very rapidly. Airfields covered, on the whole, 600 acres and took around ten days to adequately survey. Such was the pace of development that ground work often started immediately, having to be modified due to local conditions as the work progressed.

The war demanded immediate economies on all fronts, coining the phrase 'austerity construction'. This is most clearly demonstrated in the building techniques utilised on the airfields by 1940; however, in one area expense was destined to go through the roof. By May 1939 it was clear that some airfields, especially those designated heavy bomber stations, would need to have paved runways if they were to remain operational all year round. Furthermore the grass strip was just not up to the punishment of multiple landings by heavy aircraft; in winter this caused noticeable drag on take-off. However, by the outbreak of war only nine stations could boast all-weather runways; the remainder, including those proposed or under construction, were still expected to have grass strips.

This development had a dramatic impact on the British landscape. The inclusion of a runway surface, usable in practically all weather conditions, was to prove essential in both the defence of Britain and the Offensive Bomber Campaign. Nonetheless, due primarily to the Treasury's reluctance to authorise even more expense, only a few were planned. This had not been for the want of trying as demands for all-weather runways had come from the top:

> The initial cost of the runways will of course be high but, apart from their operational necessity, they will pay for themselves hand over fist in 10 years. This eternal tinkering with the drainage of aerodromes will not be necessary.
>
> (H. Dowding, 1938 (AIR 2/2067))

Subsequently by the end of 1939 twelve stations were selected for hard runways measuring 800 x 50 yards which were linked to the technical site by a 50ft wide taxiway. By 1940 that length had been increased to 1,000 yards. Alterations to the specification continued as bomber bases were provided with three paved runways from the end of 1940. Each new build had one principle surface of 1,600 yards and two of 1,100 yards; however, the ideal dimensions should be 2,000 yards and secondary 1,400 yards, if required. By the end of 1942 a major programme of expansion directed that all bomber stations were to conform to the listed 'ideal dimensions wherever practical'.

Occasionally Ministry directives changed the layout or construction technique leading to discord between the labourers and management. One such incident is worth repeating here:

RAF Cottam, Yorkshire, in 2007. Built originally as a bomber base, it suffered such bad weather that the field was turned over to bomb storage soon after completion. This standby generator house and a handful of other derelict structures are all that survive.

The men had just been asked to produce record outputs of concrete, and as soon as a portion of the runway was finished instructions were received that it was to be taken up, because the line was to be altered. In order not to dishearten the men, his firm took the extreme step of refusing to carry out the instructions, and by going through the various channels – resident engineer, superintending engineer, and so on – they managed to delay doing anything until some new requirements enabled the runway to remain in the position in which it had been built.

(S. W. Cox, Institution of Civil Engineers, 1948)

Concrete was not the only medium employed in constructing runways, hard standings and taxiways. Naturally each process had its own problems and advantages over the other. Figures published in 1948 give some indication as to the variety of methods and materials utilised by the construction companies at 444 airfields:

Concrete paving, no additional surfacing other than sealing coats of tar or bitumen.
Concrete paving, with the whole or parts surfaced with either single or two-coat asphalt, bituminous macadam, or tarmacadam
Stone pitching with asphalt, Bituminous, or tarmacadam surfacing. Extensions in concrete surfaced with asphalt.
Stone pitching with asphalt, Bituminous, or tarmacadam surfacing. Extensions in concrete unsurfaced.

Stone pitching with asphalt or tarmacadam surfacing.

Sand mix

(P. Hudson, *The Development and Construction of Airfields and Runways
for the Royal Air Force, 1939–1945*)

The figures are staggering and worth quoting here. By 1942, the peak year for airfield construction, 60,000 men were employed on the groundwork and construction of runways alone. C.M. Kohan, in his 1952 publication *Works and Buildings*, likened the amount of paving laid throughout the war to an area equivalent to the total size of Birmingham (39,000 acres) or a 30ft-wide road nearly 10,000 miles long. This equated to 18,000 tons of cement, 90,000 cubic yards of aggregate and 50 miles of drainage piping per average bomber airfield. Each one, by 1942, costed a minimum of £500,000 and that was before any structures were built. The constant demand on labour resources began to cause some major headaches for the Government.

## Norway

Whilst Finland was in the final throws of battle an act by the Royal Navy sealed the fate of neutral Norway. On 16 February 1940 crew of the destroyer HMS *Cossack* boarded the German supply ship *Altmark* in Norwegian waters and liberated her cargo of around 300 British prisoners, the victims of the *Graf Spee*. A clear signal was sent to the Norwegian government that it was neither in control of its waters nor had it the power to stop either Britain or Germany carrying out whatever operations they saw fit. The control of Norway was important to both sides, primarily due to the passage of Swedish iron ore through the country to Narvik, the main port.

The first British troops landed in Norway on 15 April but were unable to stem the flow of the German army. The Navy, however, faired better, sinking ten German ships to the Royal Navy's two. The Germans had made a dash for airfields early in the conflict and subsequently obtained air superiority as a matter of priority. The air attacks became so debilitating that the majority of British troops had been evacuated by the end of April. The remaining did not leave the Narvik area until a few days before the Norwegians surrendered on 8 June. The fall of Norway left Britain with a problem, it was geographically well positioned, and could allow the Germans to launch bomber attacks into Scotland and the north of England, especially from the air.

## Offensive Air Operations

It was now that Bomber Command should have swung into action. Throughout the 1930s the bomber force had been the bedrock of Air Force policy; however, now that the opportunity arose serious shortfalls were discovered. Bomber Command had been seriously denuded at the outbreak of hostilities with a number of squadrons being detached to France. Other aircraft were just too obsolete to carry out any operations involving the enemy. Training was at an all time low; a combination of part-time personnel coupled with either unfamiliar new or redundant, unserviceable old equipment, along with the rapid expansion of the Command had left the force in a dangerous position. Subsequently the long planned strategic air offensive never materialised, but the level of competence was only part of the reason. On 1 September 1939 President Roosevelt had appealed to all protagonists not to repeat the bombing of civilian targets in light of the horrors of the Spanish Civil War. Both sides agreed – Hitler, as populated areas were not a component of Blitzkrieg, happily so – however, by agreeing to it Chamberlain relegated Bomber Command to the rank of anti-shipping and leaflet delivery. Marshal of the RAF Arthur Harris later described the situation:

> In the earliest stages of the war we were not allowed to bomb anything on land, and our only possible targets were therefore warships, which we could attack only by day. Our losses from enemy fighters and flack were prohibitive and we therefore desisted before we had done ourselves or the enemy much harm. Meanwhile the Whitleys and Wellingtons were put to the questionable employee of dropping pamphlets all over Europe, a game in which we never had the slightest faith. My personal view is that the only thing achieved was largely to supply the Continent's requirements of toilet paper for the five long years of war.
>
> (Sir Arthur Harris, 1947, Bomber Offensive)

The very first bomber raid against German units outside Wilhelmshaven on the first day of the war was abandoned due to bad weather. The following day fourteen Wellingtons and fifteen Blenheims flew again against naval targets; seven aircraft failed to return for little damage on target. Throughout December 1939 attacks against naval targets continued, with the losses mounting. On 18 December twenty-two Wellingtons arrived over Wilhelmshaven to be greeted by effective fighter defences and thick flak; twelve aircraft were lost over the target while three more crashed on landing. It was rapidly becoming clear that daylight bombing without fighter escorts was near suicide. Strangely the leaflet bombing had been carried out at night and tactically was probably of more use than the daylight raids. Aircrew on those sorties were now accustomed to operating over enemy territory at night and this soon became the norm for Bomber Command.

The turning point came during the Norwegian campaign. Air attacks against German-held airfields and naval targets in Norway started on 9 April, again with little success. However, on 12 April a force of eighty-three aircraft, the biggest so far mustered, attacked targets along the coast. Success was limited and the losses were such that Bomber Command now realised it could no longer support such an erosion of men and equipment. If offensive air operations were to be undertaken without fighter escorts it would have to be at night. The wider implications of Norway were clear. The Royal Air Force was simply not prepared for air operations during daylight hours whilst on detachment. In all the expansion years the tactics had centred on 'offensive defence'; the harsh reality was that the RAF was certainly not 'offensively' capable and with the losses it was facing in France it might well not be 'defensively' capable either.

## Advanced Air Striking Force

Further examples, if ones were needed, were on the horizon. The British Expeditionary Force (BEF) had an air contingent comprising Lysanders, Blenheims and Hurricanes, to be expressly deployed with the British troops only. A further ten squadrons, including Battles, were deployable across the Allied Front. This could be further complemented by bombers from Groups 2, 3, 4 and 5, still stationed in the United Kingdom. On 10 May at 5:30a.m. the German army unleashed the Blitzkrieg on the Low Countries. Airfields

Handley Page Hampden, 1940. The Hampden, like the airfields it operated from, was a clear product of expansion period thinking. Here P1333 of No.49 Squadron is being bombed up for a raid, probably at Scampton.

across the region were key targets for the Luftwaffe and fifty were attacked on the first day alone. A large number of Fairey Battles and Hurricanes were lost on the ground, primarily due to the lack of radar cover; however, arranging aircraft in convenient lines did little to alleviate the problem. Within three days of operations the bomber force of the RAF alone was reduced from 135 to seventy-two. Importantly the Germans lifted the embargo on the bombardment of civilian centres when on 14 May the Luftwaffe bombed large areas of Rotterdam in an attempt to force the Dutch surrender. The German forces now made a dash for the coast in a pincer movement intended to entrap the remaining French forces and BEF units, reaching there on 20 May. Units of the beleaguered BEF and the remnants of forty French divisions headed for Dunkirk as a large assortment of ships was hastily organised for an evacuation. Operation Dynamo has gone down in the annals of British history and it was a great achievement. However, along with Battle of France, it served to demonstrate that Britain was not ready to fight the superior German war machine. Some hard lessons were learned by the RAF – who had lost over 50 per cent of the fighter force in the endeavour – including how important it was to disperse aircraft around the airfield.

Churchill, who had taken over as Prime Minister on the same day the Germans attacked, pointed out to the House of Commons on 18 June, 'What General Weygand called the Battle of France is over. I expect that the Battle of Britain is about to begin.' The Air Ministry hoped it would not be immediate!

## The Battle of Britain

An invasion after the fall of France was considered imminent, but it took precious months before Hitler thought his war machine ready to cross the Channel. By then the RAF had worked at making good its losses, although whether this had been enough was at the back of the minds of everyone in the Air Ministry. The Battle of Britain is also important to our story of the airfields and subsequently requires substantial expansion at this point.

The Royal Air Force possessed one thing on mainland Britain that it had lacked in France – The Chain Home network. With this rudimentary radar system Fighter Command was able to detect enemy aircraft up to 100 miles away and scramble aircraft accordingly. The advantages this gave the RAF at a time when they were subordinate in numbers to the enemy was to be the trump card. Aircraft did not need to fly standing patrols ensuring precious aviation fuel and subsequently operating hours were not used up unnecessarily. Further the strain on aircrew was substantially reduced. To complement this a network of the Observer Corps covered the majority of the British Isles controlled by Fighter Command. Anti-aircraft Command had around 1,000 heavy AA guns and over 600 light ones, and Balloon Command had around 1,400 barrage balloons ready for deployment across the major target areas.

The effort of constructing airfields, storage depots, shadow factories and the associated infrastructure was now to be put to the ultimate test. Throughout June and early July the Luftwaffe busied themselves with the disruption of shipping around the south and east coast with only sporadic attacks inland. As the formations became larger with more fighter escorts, it became apparent that the entire concept of offensive bombing and defensive fighter cover, something the RAF had spent years training for, had left the service at a distinct disadvantage.

The Blitz, 1940. Moving tactical bombing away from the airfields and on to British cities proved to be the ultimate folly.

## Organisation Level

By the time of the Battle of Britain Fighter Command had reorganised the defence of Britain into four Groups, Nos 10–13. Each group contained a number of sectors and within these lay the fighter stations. What makes the layout important to our investigation is seeing how many of these stations already existed and how many were expansion period bases. Scheme M was in the final throws of completion in 1940 but just how accurate had the planners been in building bases for the RAF from 1935? To answer this it is first necessary to look at the stations involved in the battle. Naturally most airfields were, at the time, involved in some way or other; this section concentrates on the fifty-one controlled by Fighter Command HQ from Bentley Priory.

No. 10 Group contained an HQ at Box and two Sector Airfields at Filton and Middle Wallop. Below these were the fighter stations at Boscombe Down, Colerne, Exeter, Pembrey, Roborough, St Eval and Warmwell. No. 10 Group concentrated its efforts from Southampton west into the Atlantic approaches.

No. 11 Group HQ was at Uxbridge, and Fighter Command HQ, at Bentley Priory, also fell within this Group. Protecting the approaches to London, No. 11 Group had seven Sector Airfields at Biggin Hill, North Weald, Kenley, Hornchurch, Tangmere, Debden and Northolt. Fighter stations were Croydon, Detling, Eastchurch, Ford, Gosport, Gravesend,

Hawkinge, Hendon, Lee on Solent, Lympne, Manston, Martlesham Heath, Rochford, Stapleford, Thorney Island, Westhampnett and West Malling.

No.12 Group HQ controlled the east coast with its HQ at Watnall, and five sector airfields at Digby, Duxford, Kirton-in-Lindsey, Wittering and Church Fenton. Fighter stations were at Coltishall, Ternhill and Leconfield.

No.13 Group HQ was located at Newcastle with sectors at Acklington, Dyce, Turnhouse, Wick and Usworth. Fighter stations were Catterick, Drem, Grangemouth, Kirkwall and Sumburgh. No.13 Group concentrated on potential threats from occupied Norway and northern Europe.

What is immediately apparent is the increased number of stations under No.11 Group, and what is very interesting is the fact that six out of the seven Sector HQs, Debden being the exception, originally formed part of the 1926 Fighting Area, a defensive ring around the capital, comprising nine aerodromes. Of the other three, two were designated fighter stations under No.11 Group whilst Duxford had moved into No.12 Group, again as a sector HQ. The Fighting Area came about when it looked increasingly like a war with France was possible, which, when considered in this later context, could be interpreted as incredible good fortune.

The Luftwaffe, with their medium-range bomber force, needed to have forward air bases to hit Britain, and now they had them facing the entire south and east coasts. Raids into British air space throughout the year were to originate from Norway, the Low Countries and France. However, for effective fighter escorts they needed to use the aerodromes in northern France as the duration of the Bf109 was only a few minutes over London. Subsequently Nos 10 and 11 Groups were to experience the majority of German intrusions.

It is interesting at this point to examine the phenomena of aerial warfare. Set piece battles on the ground can have a starting point, D-Day being one such major event. The war started for Britain on 3 September 1939 and finished in Europe on 7 May 1945. But when did the Battle of Britain actually begin and end? The RAF has it that the first recognisable event occurred on 10 July 1940 whilst the Germans have it as 8 August, the day of some big losses for them. The end date as far as the RAF was concerned was 31 October whilst the Luftwaffe have it as 11 May 1941. And the point? Well, it is worth remembering that 'tip and run' against shipping and land targets had been going on since 1939 and it is important to demonstrate that not all is as it seems when dates and records are involved. That the battle was fought is not in dispute and if we take a glance at the losses on both sides it is suggested that the RAF lost 915 aircraft to the Luftwaffe's 1,733 (taking the period of the RAF). The Battle of Britain Fighter Association puts the total aircrew casualties at 1,007 with 507 killed. The period is marked by three German objectives, the denial of ports and safe shipping routes, air supremacy and total warfare. It is air supremacy and the links it naturally forges with the airfields that is of interest here.

*Crater*

On the first (RAF) day four aerodromes, West Raynham, Marham, Honington and Martlesham, were attacked. West Raynham suffered the worst when a hangar caught alight and gutted three Avro Ansons and a Gladiator. Attacks were to continue fairly

Churchill in a familiar pose.

sporadically, interspersed with general industrial targets for the next month. Three days later St Eval suffered minor damage. On the 15th the Luftwaffe attacked airfields in South Wales including Llandow, St Athan and Carew Cheriton. Mount Batten, then Coastal Command and the FAA at Yeovilton also received attention. 19 July saw Nutfield, Norwich Aerodrome, Milton, Abbotsinch and Manston bombed with limited success. Small-scale raids continued until 12 August when things stepped up a pace. Lympne Aerodrome was attacked on two occasions with considerable damage being done to hangars. Hawkinge suffered considerable damage when seven hangars, the services and telephone network, quarters and other buildings were seriously affected by fire and blast. Manston had two hangars damaged and a number of craters closed the airfield for a short time. Bircham Newton, Brookland, Thorney Island, Martlesham, Coltishall and Wattisham plus the Radar stations at Pevensey and Poling all had slight damage. Two days later, on 14 August, Detling suffered major damage. Several buildings were hit, some further damaged by fire, the Germans were using a rudimentary napalm bomb on some raids, with the loss of eight Blenheims, ten killed and more than fifty injured. The headquarters offices at Andover were also attacked, whilst at Eastchurch the landing area was substantially damaged. The opening paragraph by the section officer from Manston on 15 August says it all:

The section officer regrets to report the following and to say the delay in reporting has been necessitated by the fact that all communications were badly damaged and it was necessary for the section officer personally to visit each station to arrange for all the essential services to be maintained.

(Air Publication 3236, 'Works' 1959, Appendix 11)

Manston, due to its location was destined to take the brunt of the onslaught. The section officer's report described how:

Manston was bombed on 12 August and again on 14th. The aerodrome was badly cut up by bomb holes, but was in flying condition in the evening. The work on bomb holes should be completed tonight. The bulldozer from Ashford was used for filling in the holes roughly whilst the R.E.s carried out the work of leveling and rolling. The Ashford lorries transporting and helping in the general clear up. Hangars 155, 154, 1, 127, 106 and 109 have been badly damaged – practically unserviceable. The S. of T.T. Workshops 108, 110 and 142 are almost wiped out.

Two things stand out here, the first being the use of 'wiped out' as a description of the stations' assets; the second, the use of 'Ashford' equipment to repair the damage. During his visits to other stations the officer notes, at Lympne – 'this station is practically wiped out'; Hawkinge – 'all hangars and workshops were practically wiped out'; Eastchurch – 'here again the station is practically wiped out'; and Detling – 'practically the whole of the station is completely wiped out'. Thankfully, cooking was continuing in the sergeants' mess although 'under restricted conditions'.

## The Works Repair Depots

In 1938 the Air Ministry had become concerned that damage by air attack could, if it was not dealt with as soon as possible, close an airfield indefinitely. To counter this the director of works created the Works Repair Depots. Initially each Command was to have its own pool of labour; however, it quickly became apparent that this was unworkable. By 1939 the United Kingdom had been divided into twenty Works Areas, each with a number of depots. The depot was so placed to be as central as possible to the airfields within its area and could carry out emergency repairs on any type of airfield. The initial complement of men, usually drawn from the Ministry of Transport, was forty plus a foreman. As damage to the airfields, especially in the south-east became almost unrecoverable (by 25 August Manston was so badly damaged that the RAF considered evacuation of site) the complement was increased. Work Area 10 saw an increase at Harlow and Eastcote to eighty, whilst Area 13, with depots at Addington and Ashford, was increased to 120. At the outbreak of war a further fifteen staff were located on each station, usually taking over one of the Married Quarters as a base. Nevertheless, these were civilian staff and with the best will in the world could not be expected to repair airfields whilst an attack was still underway. As part of the evacuation of France a large number of Royal Engineers had become available, many of whom had started the quickly abandoned airfield expansion project in the north of the country. The units were distributed across sixty-six airfields in mid-1940 and a further forty-four by the end of the year. However, this was not to be a permanent arrangement especially since a specialist airfield construction team had already existed.

## 'Self Build'

Until 1940 airfield construction was almost exclusively the preserve of civilian contractors, service personnel were utilised on occasion, supplementing the workforce. This was especially the case where supply depots, hospitals and accommodation camps were required. Subsequently troops from the Pioneer Corps and Royal Engineers were drafted onto various projects, especially those with a Bolero (introduced later) implication. However, one small band had been around since the start of the war.

The Royal Air Force, meanwhile, had been reorganising its own airfield construction unit, originally known as No.1 Works Area (France). As the name implies, this small unit was formed in 1939 with the remit to advise French construction companies on the building of airfields for the British Expeditionary Force (BEF). This, naturally, came to a halt when France collapsed and No.1 Works Area personnel made it back to southern Britain over 16–18 June 1940. After evacuation the majority of its fifty-strong contingent was utilised by the Air Ministry in the selection of emergency landing grounds throughout the United Kingdom. On 22 July 1940 the unit was reformed as No.1 Works Area (Field) and set its HQ up in a requisitioned house at Downleaze on the outskirts of Bristol. Divisions were formed at Weston-super-Mare, Somerset, and Lostwithiel, Cornwall. The units primarily worked on airfields in this area.

Throughout the Battle of Britain the repairs necessitated by enemy action were undertaken by the Works Depot Organisation, but soon had to be complemented with detachments of Royal Engineers. Clearly this was not ideal and the Air Ministry quickly reorganised the remnants of No.1 WA (Field) into four Work Squadrons, the forerunner to the RAF Airfield Construction Service (ACS). The ethos here was to act as a local repair agency to a fixed number of stations in the south and south-east of the country. Like all other airfield-centered agencies the Work Squadrons suffered from the lack of qualified labour from 1942, leading to the construction of RAF Mill Green, one of the RAF's more unusual stations. Mill Green, named No.2 School of Airfield Construction, was a disused gravel quarry just outside Welwyn Garden City and twenty acres of it became the testing ground for trainee plant operators throughout the war. But what makes the soon to become ACS important to our story is the work they were destined to do in 1943–44, both across southern Britain and into liberated Europe.

## London

A number of factors have been offered as to why London suddenly became the main focus of German attention. It is likely that the first raid on Berlin on the night of 25/26 August was the catalyst for the return attack on 7 September, but whatever the reason it almost certainly lost Germany any remote chance it had of winning the Battle of Britain. As the Luftwaffe continued to pound London and on occasion other populated areas, Fighter Command was able to rest some of its crews and re-equip. The shadow factory network now came into its own with twice as many aircraft being produced than in 1939. Whilst it has been suggested the Battle of Britain ended on 31 October, the raids on British cities and airfields continued including, on the night of 14/15 November on Coventry. These raids were very successful primarily due to the RAF's inability to get fighters on target. Decoy sites were subsequently developed as clearly bombs dropped on a field are far better than in the middle of a city. However, it was technological improvements that were to prove most effective. Now Night Fighter Squadrons were equipped with Beaufighters and carried the very effective Mk IV interception radar. This coupled with more Ground Control Intercept (GCI) stations coming on line, had by May 1941 accounted for nearly 100 enemy aircraft.

Over the first five months of 1941 the German objective changed. Now the emphasis was on starving Britain of food, raw materials and arms from the Americas. Birmingham, London and Coventry were again targeted; however, the majority of raids now focused on Bristol, Swansea, Hull, Cardiff and Southampton. By the time of the last major raid – on 10/11 May – on London, which incidentally devastated the House of Commons, Germany was already pulling aircraft out of northern Europe in preparation for the invasion of Russia.

## The Standard Operational Airfield

Throughout 1940–41 the development of the Standard Operational Airfield had moved on at speed. This design, by 1942, came to epitomise airfield layouts in Britain. Runway construction called for three paved strips, the main one with the prevailing wind, the other two laid 60 degrees to that. Ground either side of the runways was prepared as were the earlier grass strips and a 30ft margin either side of the paved taxiway. The taxiway was usually 50ft wide and had no building within 150ft of the centreline. Some of its design aspects were already making use of the experiences in France and elsewhere.

## Dispersal

One extremely datable aspect of the paved-surface aerodromes is the dispersal. These developed throughout the war and allow the archaeologist to plot the development of a given airfield chronologically, if indeed they were built at that site. Tactically, parking aircraft in lines has never been a good idea; however it would appear that air forces

RAF Skipton-on-Swale, Yorkshire, under construction in 1942. The Bomber bases located in North Yorkshire were at the furthest extremities of Bomber Commands effect strike arc. This station was home to the Royal Canadian Air Force.

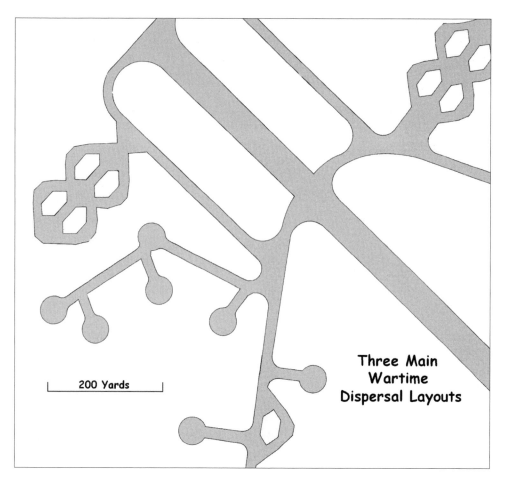

200 Yards

Three Main
Wartime
Dispersal Layouts

Airfield dispersals through the Second World War.

continue to do just that in peace time. A cursory look at any military airfield will demonstrate this. Yet in wartime the traditional flight line is virtual suicide. This had been comprehensively demonstrated on the first day of the Battle of France when a large number of Fairey Battles were lost on one airfield alone. Clearly then, there was a requirement for some form of dispersed parking. Initially temporary tracking was utilised but it soon became apparent that permanent links to the runways would be needed. These early dispersals also needed to be able to cope with light servicing and arming up, especially on bomber bases.

The initial type of dispersal was a circle of 125ft with a long access track leading from it to the taxiway. The problem was that when one aircraft left its dispersal it then clogged up the access track. As squadron numbers increased on airfields so too did the congestion; aircraft in winter often took 'short cuts' and naturally they often 'bogged' in the wet conditions, especially on bomber bases. The answer was to move the dispersal off a singular access track servicing all pans and distribute them around the perimeter track. There was a problem with the circular pan as well. As an aircraft taxied on to the pan it needed to do a very tight 360-degree turn to face back towards the exit. Aircraft undercarriages and tyres are not designed for this and subsequently a number were rendered US by the practice. By late 1941 the dispersal pan had been redesigned and was now a 'spectacle' or loop distributed around the peri-track. The spectacle was a simple revolution and was widely implemented from 1942. It had many advantages including the use of less material for more parking. It allowed aircraft to taxi on at one end and then follow a shallow curve back onto the peri-track, saving fatigue on equipment and, most importantly, it allowed for rapid deployment of an entire squadron, on occasion one every forty-five seconds.

One further development needs to be introduced here. Storage units were given 'finger' parks from 1944 and, as the threat of air attack diminished after D-Day, the regulations regarding the parking of aircraft were relaxed. The finger park, sometimes arranged in star formation, allowed the aircraft to be parked on concrete but it needed to be towed on or off. Therefore, something as mundane as an aircraft dispersal pan can give a good landscape clue as to the development of the airfield, placing it within the context of early, mid- or late war period. This is especially useful when encountering airfields that are little more than crop marks, as many wartime sites now tend to be.

## Buildings

Airfield structures experienced a dramatic change between 1939 and the end of the war. Architectural styles of the war period stations bore little if no resemblance to the preceding expansion period grandiose, driven instead by the need to conserve energy and resources. Indeed the war years were described by Anderson & Biggs in 1948 as 'a period when the romance of building was lacking'. A number of designs became prevalent, often bearing the name of the company or individual that designed them, the Bellman hangar and the British Concrete Federation hut being two good examples. Many books have been published covering this topic, including work by Mike Osborne and others through the Defence of Britain Project; subsequently, in-depth coverage is not required here. However, the layout of airfield structures was important as it helps interpret the archaeology of the stations.

A vast number of buildings had been designed during the expansion period, but by 1939 it had become clear they were neither large enough to accommodate the extra service personnel, quick to build or, most importantly, economical. Furthermore, the layout of structures on airfields changed dramatically with the outbreak of war. The Battles of France and Britain graphically demonstrated the vulnerability of the compact airfield layout, especially to bombers, and subsequently airfields received a radical redesign. From 1940 airfields began to contain 'dispersed' sites, which were further subdivided into technical and domestic areas. Naturally this was to cause many, particularly the Department of Works and the designers, some major headaches.

Initially dispersed accommodation sites capable of housing 150 personnel were built, all being a minimum of 800 yards from the main technical area and at least the same distance from each other. This soon proved unworkable as major delays were experienced in all but the most minor aspects of station operation. Not to mention the extra fuel used transporting men and equipment between one area and another. Subsequently the distances were reduced to 200 yards and levels of accommodation raised to between

RAF Holme-on-Spalding Moor, Yorkshire, in 2007. The parachute store, a typical example of temporary construction to be found on a technical site of a Class A bomber base.

250 and 400 per site, depending on their vulnerability. It was not unusual for airfields from 1941–42 to contain up to twenty dispersed sites within an area of around 1 square mile. Podington, originally a construction for the Royal Air Force during 1941–42 and later taken over as one of the first bases for the USAAF serves to demonstrate the layout of these dispersed sites. The airfield was designated Site 1 and contained the majority of technical buildings, the bomb store, motor transport, fire, control and bulk fuel stores. This needed 160 structures comprising temporary brick, temporary concrete, Nissen, Jane, Laing, Seco and Romney hutting. Two T2 aircraft sheds were provided for some undercover servicing but on the whole work was carried out by 1944 in the open on one of forty-two 'pan handle' or four sets of 'spectacle frame' dispersals.

The domestic aspects of the airfield were catered for by a further thirteen sites dispersed to the north of the airfield. Of these two were taken up with sewage disposal works, one dedicated to the sick quarters, one originally to the WAAF, five for airman, NCO and officers' accommodation, and two communal sites. This comprised a further 266 structures the majority of which were similar types to those on the Tech Site. A further area, just to the north of site 9, was set aside for further expansion tenting if required. This layout changed little over the next few years. It is possible to say the technique of distributing domestic structures some distance away from the airfield made an impact on the landscape by mid-1941, primarily due to the experiences of the first two years of the war.

The new layout naturally brought the construction firms and designers problems. Each dispersed accommodation site required water, electric, sanitation and access roads, so to

RAF Membury, Berkshire, in 2007. Temporary brick stores building. Membury was a further Bolero acquisition. Initially intended as an RAF training station, on completion in 1942 it was handed to the USAAF.

economise services to some areas were kept to a minimum. Bathhouses were linked in with the mess halls as a way of cutting down on water and sewage, leading, especially in winter, to some unpleasant living conditions. Coupled to this was the almost constant revision of building design and requirements, often causing major delays in the early programmes. One such revision was accommodation for the Women's Auxiliary Air Force.

## WAAF

The Women's Auxiliary Air Force (WAAF) was created on 28 June 1939, nearly twenty years after the disbandment of the Women's Royal Air Force. By the outbreak of war the service comprised 1,740 women; it was destined to reach a peak in 1943 of 181,835 women in uniform, by then filling a number of specialist roles, especially in Fighter Command. Accommodation for the WAAF is a good demonstration of the changing social attitudes towards women in uniform. Many 'barriers' were broken down by the war years, in much the same way they had in the First World War. Initially in 1940, when designing the dispersed airfields, everything was duplicated for the WAAF service. Naturally they were provided with a dedicated living site; however, this was extended to messes, institutes and dining rooms costing many thousands more to build. By 1942 it was realised that resources would be better directed with the construction of just one mess, institute and dining room serving both sexes. Some things did not change; WAAF attracted two thirds of the pay of their male counterparts, even when doing the same job.

## *Austerity*

Throughout the expansion period of the late 1930s the concept of temporary accommodation was utilised as an aid to get new stations up and running as soon as possible. These timber huts were no more than a stop gap; however, by Scheme F timber hutting was being extensively used to bolster training establishment accommodation. Furthermore, a number of 'temporary' hospitals, such as one at St Athan, were built extensively utilising timber construction.

Timber hutting, or at least the materials to construct them, had by 1938 become both expensive and scarce. The building type that replaced them became synonymous with wartime shortages – the Half-Brick or more commonly known Temporary Brick Structure. This was not the only type of hut structure to be found – a myriad of others, designed by both Ministry of Supply and private contractors, were developed in an attempt to reduce labour, construction time and resources. These include X, Y, and Z Hutting by Gerrard & Sons, lightweight timber huts utilised up until 1941; Laing Hutting, made a lightweight timber frame structure using felt-clad plasterboard walls; Handcraft Huts from 1942 designed by the Universal Asbestos Co. Ltd; British Concrete Federation huts and a number of Air Ministry designs covering the use of timber, concrete, plywood and corrugated iron.

Along with the temporary building schemes came the reduction of personnel environment. Quarters for airmen before the war were 45sq.ft per person; reducing this down to 38sq.ft per person countered the increases in station strengths. The sergeants'

RAF Wroughton ASU, Robins Hangar in 2005. With the rapid increase in aircraft production many more acres of land were requisitioned. Often a Robins hangar was provided for servicing equipment nearby; Wroughton has eight such structures.

mess and quarters, initially 70sq.ft, were reduced to 58sq.ft. However, the sergeants' mess underwent a radical transformation, as from the late 1930s the introduction of the sergeant aircrew post radically increased the number on each station. Expansion period estimates suggested only 50 per cent of sergeants would require full messing, the rest would presumably be married and live on the quarters patch. With the increase in sergeant aircrew came an increased demand for on-station messing, and subsequently over fifteen designs of messes were built.

## Coastal Command

Coastal Command, as we saw in the preceding chapter, had a very poor start and for the first few years of the war this was set to continue. Duties in the first few months were restricted to reconnaissance patrols over the Channel and North Sea and convoy protection in coastal waters. Whilst the German government had been ready for war, luckily the same could not be said for the fleet. Of the fifty plus U-boats at the outbreak of war, over two thirds were short range, making it fairly safe in the early stages to cross the Atlantic. They did, however, sink substantial amounts of Allied shipping including, on the first day of the war, the liner *Athenia*, operated by the Donaldson Line, causing the loss of 118 lives. The most notable loss in this early period was the *Royal Oak* by U47 in Scapa Flow in October. By the end of 1939 the combined efforts of the Royal Navy and Coastal Command had accounted for nine submarines. However, by mid-1940 this total had risen to twenty-seven whilst only twenty new U-boats had been commissioned. The German fleet also made a poor account of itself during the battle for Norway, a lucky escape for the Allied troops who were evacuated.

Coastal Command at this time was suffering poor equipment procurement with two new airframes proving to be completely useless. The Blackburn Botha and Saro Lerwick, intended to replace the Anson by May 1940, were both cancelled. This instigated severe problems for the RAF. A major gap in Coastal Commands frontline capability opened up as the Botha was designated a strike aircraft. The only airframe now available to fill that gap was the Sunderland. Unfortunately, Shorts had stopped production of the aircraft in favour of the orders for Sterlings placed by Schemes L and M. The production line had to be hastily resurrected whilst further aircraft were built by Blackburn under licence. The biggest blow came with the fall of France. This now meant that U-boats could be based from Spain up to the top of Norway; the increased threat to allied shipping was obvious. If the German Navy could conduct a campaign similar to that of the First World War it was possible that Britain could be severely affected, if not knocked out all together. This period saw the laying of magnetic mines around British coastal waters, effective on their initial use but soon counteracted by the degaussing of ships and the operation of aircraft carrying a large magnetic hoop, causing detonation whilst over the mine.

With the increased threat of invasion in mid-1940 the RAF and Navy had little resources to patrol and protect the western approaches to the United Kingdom. The situation became so bad that by the end of 1940 an average of two ships per day were being sunk and not all by U-boats. The Luftwaffe also began to operate their long range Focke-Wulf 200s from both French and Norwegian airfields, thus patrolling deep into the Atlantic. Once on station they were able to directly attack convoys or guide U-boats onto them. The tactics were not lost on Coastal Command; technologically it was beginning to catch up and such patrols were soon mirrored by the RAF. Naturally, the further west aircraft could be based the longer their patrol range – primary areas were Northern Ireland and the western peninsular.

## Reorganisation

By 1942 the number of airfields operated by Coastal Command had more than doubled from the 1939 total. The approaches to Britain were now the responsibility of No.15 Group, North-West; No.16 Group, South-East; No.18 Group, North-East and No.19 Group, South-West. A further group, No.17, was responsible for the training of all personnel and included sites at Catfoss, Chivenor, Gosport and Squires Gate. The most noticeable expansion is clearly in response to the problems being faced in the north-west Atlantic. The area now under No.15 Group (reorganised in February 1941) had by 1942 expanded from just Aldergrove in Northern Ireland, Hooton Park, Liverpool (also the Anson repair depot) along with Oban, Helensburgh and Abbotsinch guarding the Irish Sea. Northern Ireland became home to Ballykelly, Limavady, Lough Erne and Nutts Corner as well as retaining Aldergrove. An airfield was also constructed at Stornoway on the site of an existing civilian strip and a golf course. The first coastal related aircraft, a detachment of Ansons from No. 612 Royal Auxiliary Air Force had arrived there in late 1940 where they joined No.827 Squadron Fleet Air Arm who were operating the Fairey Albacore at that time. These two aircraft types flew missions into the Atlantic whilst the station was being completed and on 1 April 1941 RAF Stornoway was opened becoming part of No.15 Group Coastal Command. Ballykelly also opened in 1941, as did Nutts Corner and Lough Erne. The stations allowed for much deeper flights into the Atlantic area. So from 1940 it was increasingly clear to the Air Ministry that the northern Atlantic approaches were critical to Britain's survival. What is interesting is that as No.15 Group expanded the threat from the U-boats was diminishing. The German resources were starting to be spread quite thinly by 1941, distribution of Wolf Packs to other areas, namely the Mediterranean covering the North African campaign and Baring Straits, and in preparation for Operation Barbarossa – the invasion of Russia. Throughout 1941, Nos 16 and 18 Groups' aircraft began to be equipped with Bristol Beauforts to complement the Hudsons already on charge, and began developing their anti-shipping tactics in the North Sea and Channel areas. Heavy aircraft losses forced through the redesigned Torpedo Beaufort by late 1942, forming a Strike Wing based at North Coates Fitties, the reopened First World War site it reoccupied in 1940.

With the entry of the United States into the war in December 1941 U-boat activity substantially increased. The total of Allied shipping lost began to rise compared to very few successes against the U-boats. Advances in radio tracking, aircraft-mounted radar, the introduction of the Consolidated Liberator and better weaponry all should have helped. However, effective countermeasures to radar made most devices ineffective. By 1942 the years of under-funding and playing second fiddle to the Fleet Air Arm and Bomber Command meant that Coastal Command was in serious crisis.

## Training

Naturally as the demand for aircrew increased so did the number of aircrew training sites located around the country. As was demonstrated in the previous chapter the tendency was to locate establishments away from the east and south coast and wherever possible this continued throughout the war; however, the majority of crews had a rather convoluted training programme that was often spread around the world.

By the outbreak of war fourteen service flying training schools existed in Britain, including Hullavington, Ternhill and Shawbury, all coupled with Aircraft Storage Units. To support this, a number of Relief Landing Grounds were proposed, totalling twenty-four by 1940 with the same number under construction. Relief Grounds were, by necessity, sparse undertakings often being no more than flying fields in the true sense of the word; however, some eventually made it to parent station status receiving major infrastructural upgrades.

Prospective aircrew attended one of several Aircrew Reception Centres around the country, Lord's Cricket Ground being one such site. From there three months were spent at one of seventeen Initial Training Wings (ITW) often based in large hotels by the coast. Nos 10 and 11 ITWs were located at Scarborough in the Grand Hotel and Prince of Wales both overlooking the South Bay. Then followed a period of basic flying training at one of the many Elementary Flying Training Schools (EFTS) around Britain. EFTSs were a privately-run venture and had been under contract since they were first formed back in 1934. Bristol, which you will recall was one of the first companies to provide training for the military back in 1912, now operated Yatesbury. It had rebuilt part of the site under an agreement utilising a fund set up by the treasury allowing a certain amount of flexibility in design. However, wartime construction endured the same austere restrictions as the military counterparts. A number of Air Observer Schools were set up including Staverton, Jurby & West Freugh, all existing airfields, whilst a beam approach school was established at Watchfield to the north of Swindon. In the first two years of the war another six EFTSs were constructed, bringing the total by the end of 1941 to twenty-nine.

## No.29 EFTS, Clyffe Pypard

On 8 August 1941 a new Elementary Flying Training School was opened at Clyffe Pypard in North Wiltshire. It is worth describing the layout of the airfield here as the majority of EFTS follow a similar pattern. The first entry in the aerodromes operations record book describes the new station:

> Messrs. Marshalls of Cambridge were given the contract as the operating company. The camp was built under the supervision of W & B Air Ministry and was new when occupied by the unit. Accommodation was provided in the camp for 40 officers, 30 sergeants 440 airmen, and 208 civilians. The dimensions of the aerodrome were: North to South 1100 yards; N. East to S. West 830 yards; East to West 1100 yards; S. East to N. West 1100 yards. A perimeter track 10 foot wide laying concrete on top of turf of the aerodrome, was commenced starting from the North-West boundary and running round the South boundary with turning points every 600 yards.
>
> (Operations record book, 8 September 1941 (PRO AIR 29/622))

RAF Yatesbury, Wiltshire, in 2003. The officers' mess and associated structures were built as part of the Air Training Scheme initiated by the Government from 1935. Yatesbury opened in 1936.

No.29 Elementary Flying Training School at RAF Clyffe Pypard in 2006, Wiltshire. Built in 1941 and operated by Marshals of Cambridge, the station was a classic example of temporary construction.

The following day thirty-one defence personnel and eighteen airmen were taken on to ration strength; they had originally been stationed at No.14 SFTS. On 13 August seventy-one pilots were posted to the unit after completing their initial training at No.7 ITW Newquay and No.1 course commenced flying two days later. By now the majority of the camp had been completed in either timber hutting for the accommodation blocks or temporary brick for technical and flight related functions. Four Bellman hangers and fifteen blisters were eventually provided for maintenance and aircraft parking. The perimeter track was not completed until 31 October and this had caused some major problems as areas of the aerodrome had become waterlogged due to worsening weather. The blister hangers were provided on this and other EFTS sites to protect the light flimsy aircraft, predominantly Miles Magisters and Tiger Moths, utilised in this initial part of the training programme. This is one of the identifying factors of the EFTS aerodromes; however, more often than not they have now been removed leaving only slight evidence today.

Naturally these sites tended to operate in groups as much more experience could be gained from flying and navigating around several sites rather than just the one. Subsequently Clyffe Pypard had a number of other airfields within easy reach. These included stand-alone sites such as Yatesbury, where a number of training tasks were being undertaken by 1942. Clyffe Pypard also had existing airfields transferred to its command. One was RAF Alton Barnes located 10 miles south in the Vale of Pewsey. Initially the airfield had been under the control of the Central Flying School at Upavon but on completion of Clyffe Pypard this had been transferred to No.29 EFTS control under No.50 Group. Interestingly not all pilots who commenced their training at these stations completed them at the same place.

> 38 cadets of number two war course were granted embarkation leave, pending overseas posting for further elementary flight training. 60 cadets were attached from No. 1 ARCA (aircrew reception centre) for number one grading course, in accordance with flying training command policy instituting courses of three weeks duration, in order to find the cadets likely to achieve a sufficiently high standard to minimise the danger of there being suspended from further elementary flight training overseas. Such cadets as selected for these overseas postings to have a maximum of 15 hours dual flying, no solo, before being posted, the remainder being absorbed into the ordinary EFTS escorts.
>
> (ORB, 2 November 1941 (PRO AIR 29/622))

The situation by 1942 was such that the number of aircrew requiring training could, quite simply, constitute a major hazard in the skies over Britain. Subsequently the Air Ministry instigated a massive training program with the help of dominion governments. Known in Britain as the Empire Air Training Scheme, the Government proposed the idea in September 1939 that fifty elementary flying schools be established in Australia, Canada and New Zealand. The graduates of these schools would then receive advanced training in Canada before proceeding to Britain for service with the RAF. Agreement was reached on 17 December 1939 after a lengthy conference at Ottawa, Canada, between the interested administrations. Subsequently the number of EFTS was only a fraction of that actually

RAF Clyffe Pypard, Wiltshire. The site was built by the Air Ministry but operated on their behalf by Marshalls of Cambridge.

required, however aircrew often received postings back to training aerodromes such as Hullavington for familiarisation training in map reading, blackout and weather conditions. Specialist training was administered at Operational Conversation Units. Bomber Command also used Heavy Conversion Units, often located on an existing squadron airfield. To complement this they also operated the Lancaster Finishing School with units at Lindholme, Faldingworth, Hemswell, Feltwell, Syerston and Ossington. With all this training one would imagine that such units would be visible within the archaeological record, yet surprisingly the opposite prevails. Training units built during the expansion period do contain some visible differences especially on the domestic sites, however any aircrew training required by specific squadrons was catered for by the standard and class A airfield construction layout. Surprisingly the most recognisable remnant of the entire training airfield network that was constructed throughout the Second World War is the Elementary Flying Training School. Many sites continued on into the 1960s retaining many of their original structural features. Clyffe Pypard trained pilots for the FAA until mid-1947 when the flying field was returned to agriculture, leaving the 198 buildings constructed for training to be used as transit accommodation for RAF Lyneham 3 miles to the north.

*Bolero*

The massing of American servicemen in Britain in advance of the liberation of Europe is well documented, as is the deployment of various units of the United States Army Air

Force and the subsequent operations they took part in. Their arrival increased the pressure on the construction teams across the United Kingdom and clearly increased the number of airfields built in the latter part of the war. However from a purely landscape perspective they have little or nothing to differentiate them from their British counterparts. Naturally excavation should yield artefactual information but that is not the remit of this work.

It is useful to discuss the problems encountered by the work services as they attempted to accommodate the influx. On 7 December 1941 the Japanese attacked Pearl Harbor bringing the economic might of America directly into the conflict. Four days later, during an 88-minute speech in Berlin, Hitler declared war on the USA:

> Faithful to the provisions of the Tripartite Pact of 27 September 1940, German and Italy have consequently now finally been forced to join together on the side of Japan in the struggle for the defence and preservation of the freedom and independence of our nations and empires against the United States of America and Britain.

Many commentators point to this as being one of Hitler's biggest mistakes, bringing as it did over a million American servicemen into the European theatre during the next few years. United States Secretary for War Henry Stimson described Britain's unique position in a memo to Franklin D. Roosevelt on 19 June 1942:

> The allied naval power controlled the seas by only a narrow margin. There was a dangerous and increasing shortage of commercial shipping. With one exception the Axis Powers controlled every feasible landing spot in Europe. By fortunate coincidence one of the shortest routes to Europe from America led through the only safe base not yet controlled by our enemies, the British Isles. Out of these factors originated the Bolero plan.
>
> The British Isles constituted the one spot
> (a) where we could safely and easily land our ground forces without the aid of carrier- based air cover.
> (b) through which we could without the aid of ships fly both bomber and fighting planes from America to Europe.
> (c) where we could safely and without interruption develop an adequate base for invading armies of great strength. Any other base in western Europe or Northwest Africa could be obtained only by a risky attack and the long delay of development and fortification.
> (d) where we could safely develop air superiority over our chief enemy in northern France and force him either to fight us on equal terms or leave a. bridgehead to France undefended.

The first detachments of the United States Army Air Force were due to make landfall by the end of March 1942, to accommodate them eight existing RAF stations were reassigned. Grafton Underwood, Podington, Chelveston, Polebrook, Thurleigh, Little Storton, Kimbolton and Molesworth all required work to be finished prior to arrival.

## Contractual Chaos

Bolero projects were the responsibility of the War Office and came at a time when the Work Services Department was undergoing a major reorganisation. This included the way

RAF Membury, Wiltshire, in 2004. Membury was quickly handed over to the USAAF as part of the Bolero build-up.

in which projects were prioritised, according to labour, material and tactical requirements. Initial discussions between Washington and London were conducted under strict secrecy and it was not until 23 June that junior ministers learnt of the size of the undertaking. Departments were also starting to get wind of the proposals; the Ministry of Works Director General did not like the sound of the idea and sought confirmation.

> I am alarmed by a report that you are contemplating accommodation for one million American troops in this country in the next six months, partly in billets or requisitioned houses and partly in camps. Even if only a small part is to go in to camps, of however rough a description, the demand for labour and materials would be enormous, and I know no means of meeting it from civilian labour.
>
> (Wyndham Portal, 24 April 1942 (from Kohan 1952, 262))

The Bolero programme was slow off the mark as the labour force was simply not present in the numbers required. Even after other projects were combed for suitable workers the problem of relocation arose. Many of those now available were not prepared to move to construction sites far away from home and more often than not in the middle of nowhere. To further exacerbate this, men were now being called up at the rate of 20,000–25,000 per month causing considerable drain on the building workforce. It also has to be remembered that the civilian workforce was not tied to any one specific contract and subsequently many moved industries often in search of better conditions and pay.

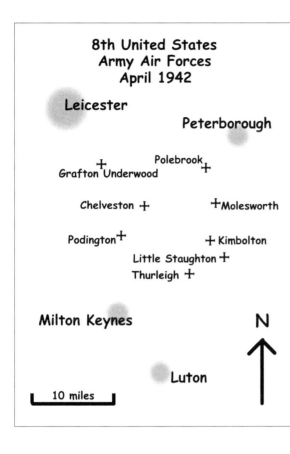

**8th United States
Army Air Forces
April 1942**

Leicester

Peterborough

Polebrook +
Grafton + Underwood

Chelveston +                    + Molesworth

Podington +                    + Kimbolton
        Little Staughton +
        Thurleigh +

**Milton Keynes**            **N**
                             ↑

Luton

10 miles

*Left:* The original eight stations handed to the USAAF detachment.

*Below:* RAF Horham, Suffolk, hospital complex in 2007. RAF Horham was originally planned as a Bomber Command station; however, as part of Bolero it was handed to the 8th Air Force. The hospital is another example of temporary, dispersed construction.

RAF Davidstow Moor, Cornwall, in 2007. By 1942 the policy of dispersal had ensured a move away from the closely packed sites of the pre-war period. Temporary brick structures such as the Air Ministry Laboratory Bombing Teacher (left) and the Double Turret Trainer are both examples of austerity construction and design.

The situation took a further nosedive when in late November 1942 the Government announced an increased call-up of a further 15,000 per month. Suddenly the Bolero programme looked increasingly in danger as there was no way any major contract could be fulfilled with the current loss of manpower. The then Minister of Production, Oliver Lyttelton, recommended a complete cessation of new works from December 1942; the War Cabinet accepted and all airfield related sites not required for Bolero were summarily cancelled or put on hold.

By December the Bolero programme was just over 80 per cent complete. In relation to airfields a total of 69,500 men had been employed across construction sites destined to be the first USAAF bases. Putting this into perspective the Air Ministry started £71,433,000 of contract work on 1 December 1942 utilising 118,000 men but with a requirement actually put at 190,000. Two British airfield projects were, however, continued – St Mawgan (originally called RAF Trebelzue), where considerable extension was underway, and a new build at Predannack, both in Cornwall. The Secretary of State for Air considered these two airfields essential as they gave aircraft a tactical advantage when operating in the Atlantic, helped protect the western approaches of the English Channel and were ideal centres for operations in North Africa. Incidentally the actual requirement for Cornwall was eleven airfields, but due to the topographical nature of the county only six were envisaged by 1942, including the two previously mentioned. Notably, all eleven, Cleave, Culdrose, Davidstow Moor, Lands End, Parranporth, Portreath, St Eval, St Merryn and Treligga along with the two previously mentioned, were achieved by 1945.

## Underway at Last

On 30 May 1942 the German city of Cologne was the target of the heaviest air raid of the war so far. Commander-in-Chief of Bomber Command Arthur Harris, in the post from February, had planned 'Millennium' over the preceding month and was convinced a decisive blow would shake the enemy's reserve. More importantly than that the RAF had learned from the Germans' mistakes in the skies over Britain, primarily the switch by the Luftwaffe to night-time bombing. This is where Blitzkrieg came back to bite its owner as Harris noted some years later:

> Had they known anything about the exercise of their power – and they certainly knew very little – they would have known that night bombing requires not only a vast amount of specialised training, for which they had left themselves in no time at all, but also very special aircraft and equipment, which they had made no attempt to produce. They had, in fact, no strategic bombers at all, since their whole force of well over a thousand bombers was designed for Army co-operation work and was only used for at attacks on cities when not required to support the German Army.
>
> (Sir Arthur Harris, 1947, Bomber Offensive)

On the night of 28/29 of March the city of Lübeck became the first major German city to receive area bombing. The city was chosen for a number of reasons. Night bombing navigation was still in its infancy and Lübeck was easily recognisable on the Baltic coast. More importantly the 234 aircraft had been dispatched in two waves half an hour apart, the idea being that the fire started by the first wave could be used as a navigational aid for the second. Over half the city was destroyed by fire for the loss of thirteen aircraft. Area bombing was approved, and the following month Rostock was attacked, again on the Baltic, this time over four nights.

Now Harris, with Churchill's blessing, planned for the first 1,000-bomber raid in history. On 30 May, 1,047 aircraft took off from bases all over England, having being literally scraped up from everywhere, including training units, partially formed commands and, in some cases, aircraft straight from the factory were thrown together. The majority of the force, almost 900, reached the ancient city and within two hours had dropped 1,455 tons of ordnance. High explosive bombs blasted roofs open and incendiaries, two thirds of the total bomb load, rained in setting the buildings ablaze. Over 600 acres of the ancient city centre were completely destroyed, 480 civilians were killed and around 45,000 were 'de-housed'. Cologne had widespread implications for both sides. For the RAF it signalled the start of area bombing carried out during night-time raids, and for the Luftwaffe came a shift towards home defence. Aircraft used in close ground support were reduced to 20 per cent of pre-Cologne levels and the production of single engine fighters accordingly increased. The Bomber Offensive, so pilloried in later accounts, did indeed open up the second front demanded of the Allies. On 17 August 1942 the USAAF flew its first strategic daylight bombing mission in Europe, destroying rail marshalling yards at Rouen. The twelve B-17E Fortresses were escorted by an incredible nine Spitfire squadrons and unsurprisingly none were lost.

This is a convenient point to investigate the location of the bomber bases. The first thing to note is that bases were increasing rapidly in number throughout this period. As has been demonstrated in the text so far, from humble, if not critical origins, the force had steadily grown throughout the late 1930s, primarily due to bomber doctrine. The focus of airfields up until this expansion had been the possibility of war with France, subsequently the majority were in the west of England. No.1 Group Bomber Command, formed on 1 May 1936, was based across six airfields in January 1939 – Abingdon, Andover, Bicester, Boscombe Down, Harwell and Upper Heyford. All these have been covered in the preceding chapters but their distribution demonstrates the westerly distribution in the year that hostilities were building.

Naturally, locating the bomber force as close to the target area is a must and by 1942 that is exactly what had happened. The majority of No.1 Group's airfields were now located in a geographically distinct area in South Yorkshire and Lincolnshire. The HQ was formed in July 1941 at Bawtry Hall, Doncaster. The new home bases were a mixture of pre-war expansion period and austerity units. In Yorkshire: Holme-on-Spalding Moor (1941); Lindholme (1940); Snaith (1941); and Breighton (1941). Whilst in Lincolnshire: Hemswell (1937); Binbrook (1940); and Elsham Wolds (1941). Holme-on-Spalding Moor and Elsham were both late opening due to the decision to build paved runways at the airfields immediately, others would be improved at a later date. If this is expanded to view all Bomber Command Groups in 1939 and 1942 respectively the total number of airfields concerned and the spread of expansion aerodromes becomes apparent. By January 1939 Bomber Command was responsible for twenty-nine stations with a great number still under construction; however, in July 1942 this had expanded to fighty-eight stations, many with three home squadrons, and more were to come in later years. Naturally the majority were down the east coast, the shortest possible flying time to the Continent. As groups were formed they invariably took over the airfields becoming available. Unfortunately for No.8 Group, formed on 1 September 1941, the future would not be so rosy. In May 1942 the decision was taken to stop the training of the group and the first of its designated bases, Chelveston, Polebrook, Thurleigh and Molesworth were handed over to American Forces.

*Fleet Air Arm*

One final group requires expansion to complete the pre-1942 airfield story, the expansion of the Fleet Air Arm (FAA). The FAA has its origins in the formation of the RAF back in 1918. As the Royal Naval Air Service was absorbed into the RAF the Navy were left with a carrier force and aircraft stationed on them. These were also to become the responsibility of the RAF by 1920 and so a situation unfolded whereby the Navy operated the ships but the RAF flew the aircraft. This had been rectified by mid-1924 when all flying units became part of the Fleet Air Arm of the Royal Air Force. Clearly this was not popular and Trenchard tried to quieten dissent by agreeing that 70 per cent of its pilots would continue to be naval officers. Thomas Inskip in his 1937 review decided that the

RAAF Short Sunderland 1940 Pembroke Dock. The Sunderland was to become the mainstay of
Coastal Command operations for the duration of the war.

Fleet Air Arm would be more cost effectively run by the Navy and consequently it was announced that the Admiralty was to assume command. The RAF finally relinquished the FAA in May 1939.

Naturally the FAA required airfields and the first to be transferred were Donibristle, Ford, Worthy Down, Lee-on-Solent and Eastleigh. Confusingly, under the banner Royal Naval Air Station, airfields built for the Admiralty now began to appear, and in the main they were radically different from those constructed for the RAF. The primary difference was the number of hangars on site. The general concept, it has to be remembered, was to train personnel for service with the carrier fleets and the acceptance and preparation of aircraft for service in the salt water environment. Just one month after the outbreak of war the first purpose built airfield at Hatston on the Orkneys opened, although it was mid-1941 before the site was fully completed with paved runways and slipways for flying boats. Other airfields soon followed including Arbroath, Crail, St Merryn and Yeovilton, all in 1940.

## After 1942

In mid-December 1942 the Admiralty issued its requirements for the expansion of the Fleet Air Arm. This came at a time when all other considerations were to scale back airfield construction operations. The War Cabinet, on the advice of the Minister of Production, Oliver Lyttelton, had pulled the plug on all new airfield projects from December 1942. This was clearly a clever use of insider information as on 18 December the Admiralty informed the Cabinet of its requirements for 1943. The main reason for the cessation of building had been the lack of manpower available for Air Ministry projects, manning the all important Bolero programme instead. Naturally the Ministry of Works were concerned about the increased labour demand now being made and asked the Admiralty for clarification of the benefits of purpose built airfields. Surely if the labour pool was to be used it would be better served extending RAF accommodation for use by the FAA, argued some in Whitehall. Crucially the FAA airfields were estimated to require 2,000 men per project as opposed to 1,000 by Air Ministry projects. It transpired that the figures relating to production in the Air Ministry had been taken from the construction of Bomber bases in the east of England. Naturally many of the resources needed to construct the paved aspects of the airfields were sourced quite locally to the site. The entire process by mid-1942 had become quite a mechanised programme with many operators being fully versed in the use of it and this year of experience was how the figure the RAF provided benefitted. Those airfields proposed for the FAA were often in areas of poor access, with limited resources and were tarmacadam top surfaces on a hardcore base. Further the topography of the site often required substantial modification to allow for the runways to be set. Eventually a reduced version of the plan was put into action in March 1943.

So 1942 became a watershed and thus is a convenient time to close this section. Britain had managed to weather the losses felt during the Battle of France, primarily due to the Aircraft Storage Units and shadow factory network. The insistence of Thomas Inskip and Hugh Dowding that the bomber principle was fundamentally flawed and a strong fighter defence was needed had provided Britain with a minimum defensive network, capable of repelling attack. Meanwhile the expansion period bomber bases

RAF Boscombe Down, 1941. From 1941 airfields were constructed with paved runways; however, earlier fields received theirs on an ad hoc basis. Teams started work in 1943 at Boscombe Down. (Courtesy of the Ministry of Defence)

provided a spring board from which the Bomber Offensive, already building up, could be launched. The influx of American servicemen and equipment on Operation Bolero was set to further increase that capability. These improvements were not without cost in both men and materials. And by the end of 1942, as has been demonstrated, airfield construction was reaching crisis point. All departments struggled to complete their assignments whilst being steadily drained of labour through the call of men to arms. It is, however, worth noting at this point that 1942 was the most productive year for airfield construction with a new station being handed over, incredibly, every three days on average. This came on top of sixty-three extensions to existing sites, mainly grass to paved runway work. To give some indication of cost, £145,000,000 was spent just on Air Ministry work in 1942. Kohan expands:

> £145 millions in a year represents approximately £400,000 pounds a day. In 1942 the country's expenditure on the war was stated to be around about £12 millions to £14 million a day. Thus the Air Ministry works expenditure during the peak period represented about one-thirty-second of the total daily expenditure.

1943 was to bring a new expansion period for the Royal Air Force and the continued build up of the USAAF forces in Britain. It was also to see the almost total destruction of every major town and city in the Central European region. The majority of it was caused by air raids launched from east coast airfields. The Airfield Construction Service was to introduce a completely new airfield type onto the British and later European landscape, whilst others were to be involved in some of the most famous campaigns of the war.

# six

# THE SECOND WORLD WAR 1943–45

From 1943 the emphasis changed on the position and type of airfields that were to be constructed as part of the war effort. The Bomber Offensive, set to become Harris's masterpiece, was finally getting into its stride. 1943 was also punctuated by the build-up of American forces and sites to accommodate them. As you might expect, an expansion in the number of airfields was required to accommodate these much increased bomber fleets. However, the speed at which they appear on the landscape fell dramatically. 1943–45 is a period of consolidation, regroup, audacity and final victory.

*Regroup*

The Royal Air Force was destined to experience its fourth and final expansion programme at the beginning of 1943. Secretary of State for Air Archibald Sinclair notified the War Cabinet that three main objectives were to be set. These were new airfields, extensions to existing airfields, and miscellaneous constructional work other than airfields. Basically the same process that had been ongoing throughout 1940–42 and that is what makes this transition period interesting. It would appear that rather than a complete stop to construction, the Cabinet gave the works department a chance in which to consolidate their figures. New projects were still being commissioned in December 1942 and a large number were seeking authority so to suggest a complete cessation is strictly incorrect. It is true, however that some airfields were cancelled, but this was not entirely due to the Cabinet decision. The fact was that some designated sites were just too close to one another. Furthermore the RAF were not the only service demanding new facilities, nor did they hold a monopoly on airfield construction.

In mid-December 1942 the Admiralty had issued its requirements for the expansion of the Fleet Air Arm (FAA). This came at a time when all other considerations were to scale back airfield construction operations. The War Cabinet, on the advice of the Minister of Production, Oliver Lyttelton, had pulled the plug on all new airfield projects from December 1942. Clearly working on insider information the Admiralty informed the Cabinet of its requirements for 1943 on 18 December 1942. The main reason for the cessation of Air Ministry building had been the sudden increase in labour demands for

Bolero. The Ministry of Works were sceptical as to the benefits of purpose-built airfields. Surely if the labour pool was to be used it would be better served extending RAF accommodation for use by the FAA suggested some in Whitehall. Crucially the FAA airfields were estimated to require 2,000 men per project as opposed to half that on Air Ministry stations. It transpired that the figures relating to production in the Air Ministry had been taken from the construction of Bomber bases in the east of England. Many of the resources needed to construct the paved aspects of the airfields were sourced quite locally to the site. Also the entire process by mid-1942 had become quite a mechanised affair with many operators being fully versed in the use of the plant. Those airfields proposed for the FAA were often in areas of poor access, with limited resources and were tarmacadam top surfaces on a hardcore base. Further, the topography of the site often required substantial modification to allow for the runways to be set.

Other options were explored, and the requisition of RAF airfields already built, including Lossiemouth and Kinloss, was requested. The Air Ministry thought otherwise and offered Dallachy instead. Dallachy was originally intended for Coastal Command, but the site was not ideal and had quickly been abandoned. Topographical conditions had dictated that only two runways had been constructed. Initially the Navy moved in establishing the Observer School; however, the low number of runways forced trainee pilots to attempt landings in adverse cross winds and the FAA moved back out. The airfield subsequently became home to a training unit operating Airspeed Oxfords before Coastal Command, the original recipient, moved in with Swordfish and Beaufighters.

All stations, irrespective of whether they were new builds or old RAF stations, were commissioned like a ship. RAF Ludham, Norfolk, became HMS *Flycatcher* in August 1944; Sydenham, Belfast, became HMS *Gadwall*; Stretton, Cheshire – HMS *Blackcap* and Evanton, Ross-shire – HMS *Fieldfare*, and luckily RAF Twatt, Orkney – HMS *Tern*! The largest of all yards was Fleetlands in Hampshire that remains the primary helicopter servicing station today. However, the majority of repair and storage was carried out at the RAF Aircraft Storage Units, many of which by now had maintenance units attached; one such station was RAF Wroughton, Wiltshire. There were a vast number of FAA aircraft that received both major servicing and modification throughout the last few years of the war.

## Casablanca

At the Casablanca conference in January 1943 the British and American Combined Chiefs of Staff Committee decided on around the clock bombardment. Bomber Command and the USAAF now combined their efforts for the devastation of German economic, military, and industrial infrastructure. U-boat construction yards and pens on the occupied west coast of France were targeted in support of the Atlantic campaign, as were major manufacturing complexes within Germany itself. On 5 March the 'Battle of the Ruhr' began with an attack on Krupps steel works, Essen, in an attempt to slow down arms production. Without doubt the most famous of the raids was that undertaken by No.617 Squadron, 'The Dambusters', on 16/17 May 1943, flying from Scampton. The Ruhr very quickly became known in aircrew circles as 'happy valley' due to the heavy losses conflicted by effective radio-controlled flak and searchlights. Between March and July 1943 the campaign cost the lives of 5,600 aircrew.

## Turning Point

By July 1943 American and British aircraft were bombing targets around the clock culminating that month with an attack on Hamburg. 'Operation *Gomorrah*' commenced on the evening of 24 July in one of the hottest periods of the year. Ground defence and night fighter radars were completely saturated with false 'echoes' caused by deploying 'window', tons of aluminium strips or chaff cut to specific lengths. 721 aircraft reached the target area starting major fires in the old town district. Two days later 235 Flying Fortresses bombed strategic targets around the docks area and the following evening 722 RAF aircraft attacked again. Allied aircraft were to visit a further four times in quick succession leaving the city a smoking ruin. 2,353 sorties by Bomber Command alone, dropping 7,196 bombs had left 'a scene of unimaginable devastation', Harris noted later. Nearly 45,000 people died in the attacks, many suffocated or incinerated by the ensuing firestorm. Hamburg, Germany's second largest city, had been removed from the war in a little over three nights; the devastation of Germany was now inevitable.

On 17 August two major targets were hit. During the day over 200 American aircraft bombed the aircraft factory at Regensburg and a ball bearing factory at Schweinfurt. The USAAF were savaged by German fighters, losing thirty-six aircraft. That night the Royal Air Force bombed Peenemünde on the Baltic coast in an attempt to stop the development of the V2, whilst Mosquitoes undertook a diversionary raid on Berlin, drawing off most of the German fighter cover. The 8th Air Force mounted a second attack on ball bearing production at Schweinfurt on 14 October, which rapidly became known as 'Black Thursday'. 291 B-17s took part with 229 bombing the target but sixty were lost. This broke the spirit of the Americans for a while. It was clear such losses, close to 10 per cent per raid, could not be sustained and subsequently deep territory raids without fighter escort were suspended until the beginning of 1944.

## 'Berlin Next'

On the evening of 23 August 1943, the Royal Air Force fired the opening shots (or more accurately dropped the first bombs) in the Battle of Berlin. Overall sixteen major raids were carried out, often hampered by bad weather. Subsequently, reliance on the Pathfinder force, high speed Mosquito aircraft dropping flare markers, became paramount. The first raid comprised 727 aircraft, however numbers throughout the winter fluctuated between 300 and 800. The RAF was to lose over 500 aircraft in its campaign over the city between August 1943 and March 1944, along with nearly 3,000 aircrew. Naturally, raids on Berlin and other cities, coupled with operations across Western Europe night after night required extensive co-ordination, pushing Bomber Command close to a breakdown of control. The problem was that as the Bomber Offensive had grown the chain of command had failed to keep pace. The Command was split into groups each containing squadrons stationed at specific airfields. By late 1943 this had become so large that information was impossible to disseminate quickly across the squadrons, especially if it was a diverse number of attacks, as was so often the case. The answer was to divide the groups into HQ stations, each one carrying a number with two or three subservient stations below them. Reorganisation of the squadrons helps to explain some of the post-1942 airfields constructed in Britain, and is important to our story at this point.

By 1944 the last of the airfields to be constructed for Bomber Command were underway, primarily due to the focus shifting to more pressing work in advance of

RAF Boscombe Down, Wiltshire, 1943. The airfield finally received its first paved surface in 1943, and construction can be seen in the top left of the picture. The process was to continue until 1949. (Courtesy of the Ministry of Defence)

D-Day. If we return to No.1 Group, whose stations we viewed in the preceding chapter, the bomber station numbering system can be explained. The 1942 layout of eight airfields had, by mid-1944, swelled to sixteen of which only four were from the previous No.1 Group layout. The network was further distributed into base organisations, each responsible for an average three stations. No.1 Group comprised No.11 Base RAF Lindholme, Sandtoft & Blyton; No.12 Base RAF Binbrook, Grimsby & Kelstern; No.13 Base RAF Elsham Wolds, Kirmington & North Killingholme; and No.14 Base Ludford Magna, Wickenby & Faldingworth. Meanwhile the HQ, still residing at Bawtry, directly operated Hemswell, Sturgate & Ingham. What is apparent is that the stations remain nucleated within their specific geographical location.

## No.6 Group

This nucleation is best demonstrated by No.6 Group of the Royal Canadian Air Force. No.6 Group was originally designated as a standard RAF Group; however, throughout 1942 the Canadian Air Ministry had been concerned that its airmen were being absorbed into the RAF numbers. Subsequently No.6 Group was reformed in late 1942 as a Royal Canadian Air Force (RCAF) Group; it became operational at 12.01a.m. on 1 January 1943. The numbers of squadrons rose steadily throughout the Bomber Offensive to fourteen by 1945. Aircraft with RCAF crews were involved in a staggering 40,822 sorties, dropping 126,000 tons of ordnance, at the expense of 3,500 personnel killed or missing and 814 aircraft lost. Those figures give some idea of the scale of Bomber Command's undertaking during 1943–45.

The airfields they operated from were all in North Yorkshire with the HQ at the requisitioned Allerton Park, 4 miles east of Knaresborough. The squadrons were dispersed in an arc around the west of the North Yorkshire Moors on stations initially under the command of No.4 Group. The stations' locations left a bit to be desired. They were some of the most northerly bomber

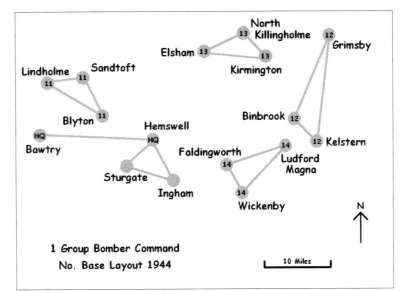

Distribution of Bomber Command No.1 Group in 1944, demonstrating the Station Number System.

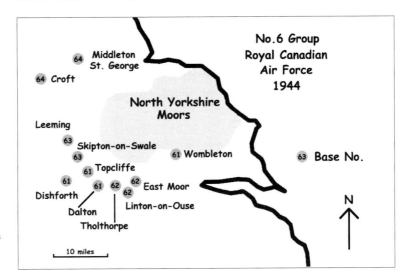

No.6 Group RCAF base distribution around the North Yorkshire Moors in 1944.

bases in the command and subsequently had furthest to travel on the majority of operations; this increased the fatigue on both men and machines. Furthermore, the moors are an unforgiving landscape, prone to rapidly changing weather conditions, and often returning aircraft needed to be diverted or, on a number of occasions, crashed.

F/L WH Egglestone is the Base Press Relations Officer. He states that during the month of June he has been covering RCAF Stations Leeming, Skipton, Croft, Middleton and 1659 Conversion Unit. F/L Egglestone made a new record for himself on Thursday 29th June, by covering three different stations within 20 hours (i.e. RCAF Stations, Leeming, for interrogation, Middleton and Skipton the same night.)'

(Operations Record Book, 30 June 1944 (PRO Air 29/857))

RAF Debach, Suffolk, in 2007. The Norden Bomb Sight Vault built in 1943. This advanced piece of equipment ensured precision bombing, with one drawback – it could only be used during the day. The USAAF suffered heavy losses because of this.

Looking at the distribution of stations in Yorkshire it becomes clear that there is a paucity of locations, especially those in the offensive roles, north of the county border. This is to be expected when considering the bomber bases as distance was a crucial factor if the cities of eastern Germany, especially Berlin, were to be attacked. However, other station types are noticeably lacking, including Fighter and Coastal Command sites. In Durham it would appear that only two major stations were in existence by 1944, Usworth and Middleton St George (now Teeside). Northumberland was better provisioned but had nowhere near the stations of its southerly counterparts. Eight stations were present, the majority housing No.12 Group training bases and one operational night fighter station at Acklington.

The 8th Army Air Force of the United States had a different geographical distribution, predominantly across East Anglia, Sussex and Cambridgeshire. Both fighter and bomber groups were located within this specific region as an attempt to penetrate deeper into enemy territory. It should be remembered at this point that USAAF sorties were carried out in daylight, dictating a critical need for good aerial defence. However, to keep their massive air armada operational a large network of sites had grown up around the United Kingdom – over 300 locations were involved at one time or another. The strain this exerted on civilian construction firms during the build up of Operation Bolero was enormous, culminating in the introduction of American Labour. Those airfields utilised by the 9th Army Air Force tended to be surrendered RAF sites through the West Country or Advanced Landing Grounds constructed in support of the impending invasion of Europe.

Construction in advance of Bolero caused serious problems for the Works and Building Department, eventually forcing the whole airfield construction programme to falter by the end of 1942. One way around this was the employment of American construction teams.

*Right:* RAF Framlingham, Suffolk, in 1945. The early construction can be recognised by the lack of spectacle pans.

*Below:* RAF Welford, Berkshire, in 2005. The original 1943 layout, complete with T2 hangars (left and right) and spectacle pans can still be recognised under this later NATO bomb store.

Interestingly no financial aspect was suggested as the supplied labour was considered to be 'in training'. The advent of the Heavy Bombardment Group in late 1942 dictated that the Class A airfield layout needed some expansion to accommodate these large formations. Initially, it had been thought on both sides of the Atlantic that each group would be dispersed on an HQ station surrounded by a number of satellites. The problem came when the build up outstripped the number of available airfields. In an attempt to counter this British and American construction teams ensured that enough hard standings were available to accommodate an entire group on one station and existing facilities were expanded. Framlingham in Sussex, home of the 95th and later 390th Bomb Group, station was handed over to US forces in early 1943; it comprised fifty hard standings, again allowing us to demonstrate a chronology through expansion. The majority of those were the 'pan handle' variety, and only five were disjointed spectacle types. However, a site visit to existing remains has discovered that the majority of pan handles were extended by an average of 2m on the circumference. Improvements to Horham, Sussex, reveal even more evidence for the extension of aircraft parking. There, the number of hard standings was increased from thirty-six to fifty during the early months of 1943, this time taking three pan handle types and extending them with the addition of a double loop spectacle.

## Stansted

On 8 August 1942 the 817th Engineer Aviation Battalion (EAB) arrived at Renfrew Farm at Stansted Mountfitchet in Essex. In November, having completed the majority of ground work, the 817th EAB moved on. From October a new battalion, the 825th, arrived completing the airfield roads, control tower, fire station and motor transport section, before they too moved on in December 1943. Between May 1943 and April 1944 the 850th arrived to construct the taxiways and runway network. The initial Bombardment Group arrived in February 1944 and flew their first mission on 6 March that same year. The point here is that not only were the Engineer Aviation Battalions instrumental in the construction of one Britain's more well-known airfields, but also that they used different techniques to the indigenous contract teams employed by the Ministry. David Smith, in his work on the construction of wartime sites, estimates that over 17,000 officers and men working in 16 Engineer Aviation Battalions constructed fifteen airfields from scratch including Great Saling, Birch, Boreham, Chipping Ongar, Debach, Eye, Glatton, Gosfield, Great Dunmow, Harrington, Matching, Nuthampstead, Raydon and, as mentioned above, Stansted. The Air Ministry was involved in the construction of a further fifty-four throughout 1943–44 for the bomber groups alone, again concentrated in the south east of Britain.

So what does this indicate? The answer comes from two different directions – geographical location in relation to Europe and aircraft technology. Geographically it is clear that the more remote the landscape from your enemy the less likely attack. Naturally this works both ways and a raid from you on your enemy is also less likely. This becomes even more apparent when we look back to the Battle of Britain. You will remember that raids were launched on the east coast during that period from Norway; however, the Luftwaffe bombers were unescorted, unlike their colleagues flying from France who enjoyed a level of protection, albeit short in duration. The second factor falls to aircraft duration and speed. The closer you are to the enemy target the less distance you need to fly and subsequently the lower the fuel load needed. And the lower the fuel load the

RAF Framlingham, Suffolk, in 2007. One structural type that made a reappearance during the Second World War was the Nissen Hut. Originally designed in 1915, they were prolific by the end of the war. This is a 24ft span.

RAF Framlingham, Suffolk, in 2007. Temporary Brick accommodation blocks were found across the United Kingdom by 1943.

RAF Sculthorpe, Norfolk, in 2006. A 16ft span Nissen hut, they were much quicker to manufacture and erect that their temporary brick counterparts. (Courtesy of Mike Digby)

larger the bomb load. Speed was also a major consideration especially if raids were to be undertaken in the cover of darkness. The further east the aircraft were expected to penetrate the longer they were in the air and naturally the more vulnerable they were. For a night raid numbering in the hundreds the ideal situation was to traverse the enemy held territory in the dark – both ways. Bomber Command lost more aircraft returning from raids than they did over the target. Once the aircraft had crossed the enemy coast line, forward fighter squadrons got two attempts at attack, both in and out, the latter often being more effective. Subsequently raids to cities such as Berlin relied heavily on the longer winter nights to afford the fleet the cover of darkness and so to cut down on the amount of time exposed by daylight; fast aircraft were a must.

The USAAF had no such luxury. Following the principle of precision bombing the aircraft had no alternative but to operate in daylight. The crews trained intensively for this and carried equipment such as the Norden Bomb Sight to ensure pin-point accuracy. However, they were at the mercy of accurate anti-aircraft fire and, on occasion, effective fighter cover. Little could be done about the flak; however, if a protective fighter escort could be provided then hopefully losses would be reduced, hence the intense grouping through East Anglia, Cambridgeshire, Sussex and Essex. This compaction was compounded by the decision to locate entire groups on one airfield rather than spread it across two or three sites. Had the original idea followed the RAF Base Number System introduced during 1943 then the distribution of airbases that housed the American bomber force would presumably have been spread over a much wider area. As it was some bases initially planned were abandoned due to interference with other existing sites.

*Overlord*

Operation Overlord (D-Day) is arguably the most recognisable date of the whole Second World War, eclipsing almost any other event, save possibly the dropping of two atomic weapons on Japan. The British Isles were uniquely placed for this operation and subsequently a number of airfields were constructed for this endeavour. They fall into two broad categories, permanent and temporary and display two radically different levels of airfield construction. One reflected the need to cater for ever increasing aircraft weights, the other intended to introduce enhanced mobility to a tactical airforce designed to give immediate front line support. Geographically they all occur in the southern area of England but that is where the similarity ends. This is also the point where another of those iconic organisations needs to be introduced, a pure product of the changing tide of war – Transport Command.

*Transport Command*

On 11 March 1943 Sir Archibald Sinclair, Secretary of State for Air, announced to the House of Commons his intention to form Royal Air Force Transport Command. This formation signalled a new phase in the war, but was not a new concept. On 25 March Transport Command became operational, encompassing RAF Ferry Command responsible for the delivery of aircraft from the Americas to all parts of the Empire. Eventually the Command would be responsible for the re-supply of the European front and play a major part in some of the most famous endeavours of the war. One point to make is that air transport, not new to the RAF, was nevertheless an extremely low priority at the outbreak of war. Doctrine throughout the 1920s and 1930s had placed the onus on the bomber, and towards the end of the 1930s this had partially expanded to the construction of a credible, effective fighter defence force. Transport issues, however, took a rather insignificant back seat. It is fair to say that the fact the RAF had any capable transport aircraft was mostly due to civilian operators; no military designated transport aircraft had been designed, let alone built by the outbreak of war.

What transport effort that did exist did so by necessity. A network of reinforcement routes, especially across the Atlantic, had developed primarily to ensure aircraft manufactured in

RAF Broadwell, Oxfordshire, 1944. Airfields across the south were to take part in a number of massed airborne assaults in the later stages of the war.

America and Canada were delivered to the UK. At the outbreak of war the RAF had just one transportation squadron (No.24) that was responsible for VIP and mail delivery. To achieve this a bewildering array of aircraft had been requisitioned from civilian airlines. These included de Havilland Rapides, Lockheed Electra, Percival Q6 and a de Havilland Flamingo, used in the early days to fly Churchill around. By 1942 Lend Lease Dakotas were making an impression on the way the services moved men and equipment and were also becoming an integral part of the Army co-operation programme, especially in the training of airborne forces.

Air routes across Allied held territory were quickly formed, usually manned by a small number of dedicated engineers, often dealing with several aircraft types at a time. Nevertheless, it was the changes to the airfield landscape in Britain that were to become building blocks of Transport Command's spectacular rise. Naturally it is also a confusing period as the airfield expansion programme struggled to keep up with the turning tide of the European war. By October 1943 Transport Command comprised No 44 Group with six squadrons in attendance. Three, Nos 24, 510 and 512, were based at Hendon, whilst No.271 was at Doncaster, No.511 Lyneham and No.525 Weston Zoyland.

Hendon had been the home of the RAF's transport effort from the beginning of the war. RAF Doncaster was originally one of the first flying fields in the country – from the outbreak of war it had been home to an Auxiliary Air Force squadron before No.271 Squadron arrived in October 1943. Lyneham was one of the original ASUs but in line with other similar stations had steadily become part of the Maintenance Unit network. Weston Zoyland had been open since the mid-1920s and remained a grass strip until identified as a Class A upgrade, originally for Bomber Command. Work started on paved runways early in 1943 and shortly after completion No.525 Squadron moved in, handing over to squadrons of the 9th Air Force in late June 1944. The point here is that no airfield was specifically constructed for transport; paved runways were by now the norm with the majority still being modified for either bomber force or Bolero aircraft in mind.

The cessation of airfield construction at the end of 1942 had been but one small change in the whole process of war construction and production. Along with re-assessment of airfields the Ministry of Aircraft Production also came under scrutiny. The shadow factory scheme had now been up and running for three years and bore no resemblance to the original plan. Spitfires, for instance, had seen their production spread far and wide after major damage was caused to the Supermarine factory at Southampton in September 1940. Production was moved to purpose built facilities in Trowbridge and Reading. Workshops were also located in Salisbury, primarily in car show rooms at the premises of Wessex Motor Garages in Castle Street and New Street. This ad hoc affair was mirrored across Britain and controlling production had become a near impossibility by mid-1942. A short consolidation period at the end of 1942 enabled the Government to appraise the situation. The MAP would be moved to the Ministry of Works as technically they were responsible for all construction work. A priority scheme was also placed, from A to Z, in an attempt to effectively plan the resource requirements of aircraft production, primarily interlinked with alloy production. This reorganisation led to an increase in production and by early 1943 planning for further airbases was underway.

RAF Lyneham, Wiltshire, 1945. ASU storage and assembly covered gliders as well as powered aircraft. Note the Hamilcar on the left. B2 assembly sheds were erected at Wroughton and Kemble for the process.

## Blakehill Farm

Blakehill Farm, Down Ampney and Broadwell were constructed along the southern edge of the Cotswolds during 1943. Two of the three sites, Blakehill Farm and Down Ampney, were numbered USAAF bases intended for the 9th Air Force and built to Class A standard complete with bomb dumps. However Transport Command finally became the recipients, basing their expanding fleets of Lend Lease Dakotas and assault gliders at the stations. It is worth noting some comments from Blakehill Farm's first Operations Record Book, as it gives a valuable insight into the problems faced up and down the country when commissioning airfields.

The requisition and subsequent construction of RAF Blakehill Farm has recently been researched by the Cricklade Historical Society and that work is worth summarising here. At the end of April 1943 the Air Ministry served requisition notices on two farms in the parish of Cricklade, North Wiltshire. Land from the Church and a number of allotments also came under the proposed 580-acre development. By the beginning of May the primary contractor, George Wimpey, assisted by local firms, had started work removing hedgerows and trees. Down Ampney also started in this same period, causing a massive draw on resources in the area. Subsequently the station was no where near finished when the first personnel arrived:

> RAF Station Blakehill Farm is to be transferred from No. 70 Group ADGB to Transport Command and placed in the newly formed No. 46 Group. The Station which is still in the hands of the Part I contractors is to be opened up and made ready to receive and operate

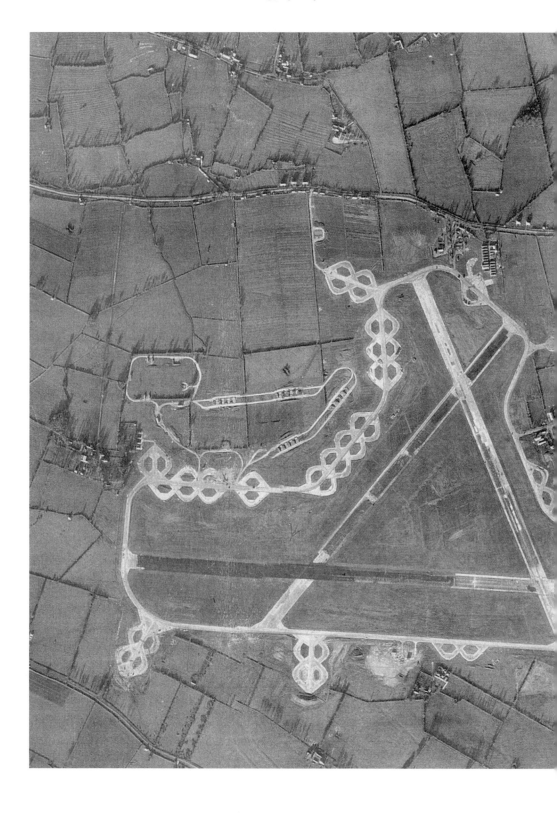

RAF Blakehill Farm, Wiltshire, 1943. Construction teams were still completing areas around the bomb dump in this Class A airfield. Note that by 1943 only spectacle pans have been constructed.

Squadrons which are to engage in Air Support Operations in the forthcoming invasion of Europe.

(Operations Record Book, 6 February 1944 (PRO Air 28/86))

The Opening Up Crew (OUC) was detailed to start work on 9 February 1944. Due to the incompleteness of Blakehill Farm, off-base accommodation was provided at RAF Broadwell, the idea being that they would transit daily whilst commissioning the site. Unfortunately two problems arose. Firstly Broadwell was 21 miles by road, not 11 miles, as the typing error on the orders memo suggested. Not that that would make any difference as there was no motor transport available at Blakehill Farm anyway, and subsequently the OUC moved to Down Ampney, 4 miles distant. Equipment for the station began arriving at the rate of 30 tons per day from 15 February; however, no stores buildings were complete and the crew had to negotiate the use of workmen's huts on No.2 living site as a temporary secure area. It was not until 20 February that six men were dispatched to Esher to collect the first five vehicles for the MT complement. With transportation now available the decision was made to billet the OUC on the new station, unfortunately:

> The opening up party having moved in the sergeants mess which was in the most advanced stage of preparation was opened for use by all ranks, the officers have been messed in one of the changing rooms, all of the ranks using the main dining hall. Arrangements were made for signals and mail to be directed through RAF South Cerney and for NAAFI supplies to be obtained from a main store at Shrivenham. A restricted telephone service was put into operation, this being limited to the times the GPO Engineers were at work, the power for lighting and working the exchange board being obtained from the GPO portable generator.'
> (Operations Record Book, 22 February 1944 (PRO Air 28/86))

From the information stored in the ORB it is clear that the shortage of labour for construction programmes was now causing problems. One way round this was the employment of Irish contract labour and they were brought in, in their thousands. The majority were employed on piece work in an attempt to speed up the construction process; naturally this presented its own problems. Down Ampney had only been open to flying a few weeks when the runway started to break up under aircraft loading. The paving and its taxiways had been constructed using a Cotswold stone foundation, quarried from a site close by, also supplying Broadwell, Fairford and Blakehill Farm, then overlaid with concrete. However, the overlay was too thin and broke up almost immediately. A detachment of the Airfield Construction Service moved in to repair and beef up the areas, often between flights. Contract labour also had other problems attached to it:

> Sqnd./Off. CWA Green, HQ 46 Group, WAAF Staff Officer, visited the station to agree to suggested temporary accommodation for WAAF Personnel. The contractors' camp which had been sited centrally on the two WAAF sites was still occupied by some 300 to 400 labourers chiefly of Irish nationality and it was not considered desirable for the WAAF to be living on the same site.
> (Operations Record Book, 7 March 1944 (PRO Air 28/86))

RAF Blakehill Farm, Wiltshire, in 2007. The 'Technical Latrine' on the airfield side of the dispersed sites. Often these structures are the last surviving remnants of the station infrastructure due to them having services such as water and electricity.

Blakehill Farm displays all the classic identification markers for a Class A airfield. It is dispersed across fourteen sites, making full use of temporary construction only, no permanent structures. It has three paved runways and linking taxiways and no fewer than fifty spectacle dispersals. The only pan handle type was actually a compass swinging pan and not a dispersal. It is clear to see from the vertical photograph of the airfield when nearing completion that it is radically different to the late 1930s expansion period airfield and displays the cutting edge of design, concealment and functionality. It also allows us to confirm the theory that airfields can be given a rudimentary chronological order when the dispersal areas are taken into consideration. Further it demonstrates the economies that were introduced with the 1943 expansion programme, especially when we view the buildings list. There were no educational facilities, gymnasium or squash courts authorised by the Air Ministry, and the anti-gas facility had been converted to a parachute store, demonstrating the diminishing level of threat of a gas attack. As to location, Broadwell, Blakehill Farm and Down Ampney, although not initially for the RAF, were eventually chosen because of their close proximity to other airborne forces and were far enough behind the coast to make the build up of gliders less obvious to the enemy. Stations that performed a similar function included Greenham Common, Membury, Ramsbury, Welford and Brize Norton. As to the chaos experienced in the initial months of RAF Blakehill Farm, it is quite probable that similar events were experienced up and down

*Above:* RAF Ramsbury, Wiltshire, in 2003. Ramsbury was transferred to troop-carrying duties with the 9th USAAF over Christmas 1943, in preparation for D-Day.

*Left:* RAF Grove, Oxfordshire, in late 1945. The later addition spectacle dispersals can be plainly seen here.

RAF Membury, Wiltshire, 1944. Aircraft of the 80th & 81st Troop Carrying Squadrons at Membury.

the country, especially when you consider the constantly changing tide of war. Nevertheless, chaos was not limited to the opening of stations; the massive number of aircraft involved in raids from 1943 could prove to be a headache, especially when aircraft were limping across the coast, rapidly shedding pieces or their parent bases had been closed due to fog.

## Emergency Landing Grounds

As bomber aircraft flew over enemy territory they attracted the attention of defensive fighters and anti-aircraft organisations. Subsequently a percentage of Allied aircraft were lost over their targets or in transit to or from them. Bombers are robust beasts and can take a certain amount of damage, sometimes flying against all the odds, but landing when damaged could be lethal as systems once relied on such as flaps or undercarriages were discovered to be inoperative or non-existent. Each station had a crash crew and fire service of sorts along with a medical centre, often in two linked Nissen huts if a wartime build. Unfortunately, if a wave returned in bad shape these facilities could be quickly overwhelmed. Also, an aircraft in poor shape crashing on the runway could cause a major headache for the airfield staff and possibly close it all together. Then there was the problem of fog – aircraft routinely crashed in it or large amounts of flying hours were lost due to airfields being closed and unfortunately, being on the east coast, this happened quite often during the winter months. In 1943 two new airfields and expansion work on a third started in an attempt to address the problem. They would be fitted with an innovative, if fuel hungry, system that could only be a British invention.

In 1943 two specifically built airfields beyond the proportions of anything seen before were started at Woodbridge, Suffolk and Carnaby, East Yorkshire, whilst the runway at Manston was extended in a similar vane. Each had a singular runway 3,000 yards long by 250 yards wide. A further 75 yards either side was prepared (graded and flat but not paved), as was a 500 yard area beyond both ends. All were aligned basically east–west, the length hopefully allowing an aircraft to come straight in at high-speed with the prevailing wind to still stop on the runway. Woodbridge, the first to open, had its first 'customer' in July 1943 and had seen a steady increase of damaged aircraft, especially B-17s, utilising the strip throughout the winter. Woodbridge's most surprising visitor landed in July 1944 by accident, demonstrating that night flying was still no exact science:

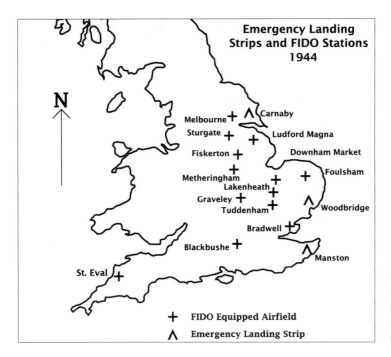

Distribution of FIDO-equipped stations and emergency landing strips, 1944.

By an almost incredible stroke of luck the pilot of a Junkers 88 mistook England for Germany in July 13th and landed with his aircraft quite undamaged on an airfield in England. It was a Junkers 88 of the latest type and it contained two wholly new instruments for detecting aircraft in the dark.

(Sir Arthur Harris, 1947, Bomber Offensive)

## Carnaby

RAF Carnaby was situated a little over a mile from the east coast town of Bridlington and the cliff line facing the North Sea. It was the last of the three airfields to be finished as an emergency runway, taking longer due to labour commitments elsewhere in the east. The site became fully operational from 15 April, although it was capable of accepting aircraft from early February. Its function was simple as were the requirements for use noted in a Headquarters letter to No.4 Group at York:

Operational control is to be exercised as follows:-
Aircraft in distress may use the runway at the pilot's discretion but this right should only be exercised when an immediate landing is imperative or the endurance is insufficient to reach base. Aircraft are to be diverted to Carnaby only after prior permission has been obtained from Central Flying Control, Headquarters Bomber Command.
(BC/s. 27997/13/Air/Flying Control, 16 February 1944 (PRO AIR 14/1610))

Air Traffic Control was still under development in this period and the operation of sites such as Carnaby required a far more complex system of control than that of their Class A neighbours. No hard and fast rules were applied when Woodbridge opened as Bomber

Command had little idea as to how the site would function in times of pressure. The lessons learned at Woodbridge soon spread to the other two sites, helping develop a detailed system of control:

> It is considered that an airfield controller at the East end of the runway cannot control the belly landing area which is 3,000 yards away.
>
> It is considered that the airfield controller cannot search a runway and at the same time fire red Vereys from the end of the runway and that he should, therefore, have at least one assistant.
>
> It is suggested that on nights when aircraft may be expected a stand-by airfield controller be posted at the overshoot area. This could be put into effect without any increase in establishment.
>
> (Air Officer Commanding, No.4 Group, 25 February 1944 (PRO AIR 14/1610))

Both Manston and Woodbridge survive today as airfields and are still prominent landscape features. The location of Carnaby is also recognisable as a landscape feature, preserved due to the number of businesses now aligned the full length of the massive runway. More than 1,400 aircraft used the runway areas during Carnaby's wartime life, often making use of an innovative system known as FIDO.

Naturally all three were situated close to the coast and the weather now played a direct part in the development of an innovative, if unusual, system: Fog Investigation Dispersal Operations, otherwise known as FIDO. Fog dispersal was a problem that had vexed flyers since before the First World War and a certain amount of work had been carried out on the problem at Martlesham Heath and Farnborough between 1937 and 1939. The idea was that if enough heat could be produced it should disperse any fog in the vicinity of the runway. The results proved inconclusive and the idea of a heat generating dispersal system was abandoned.

By 1942 fog dispersal was back on the cards and a series of tests using coke-burning braziers was run in a quarry near Staines. The problem with coke was that, regardless of the lack of smoke, it took forever to get to temperature, each brazier needed constant attention and you could not extinguish it in a hurry. After trials at Graveley, the Pathfinder station, liquid fuel burning FIDO was installed next to a number of paved runways. Tests at the wind tunnel based at Earls Court demonstrated that the burners needed to be 50 yards beyond the edge of the runway and 250 yards beyond either end.

Fifteen stations were eventually equipped with FIDO; three were the Emergency Runways whilst the Coastal Command station at St Eval ensured the Atlantic Operated aircraft had a chance to land whatever the weather. A measure of FIDO's success can be appreciated when considering the following account written by Arthur Hartley in 1948:

> Fido's greatest success was in December 1944, when most of the Pathfinder airfields in the east midlands were fog-bound for several days and the Pathfinder force was enabled to take off and mark targets for the main bomber forces operating from fog-free airfields in other parts of England and to take an effective part in stopping Field Marshal von Runstedt's Ardennes offensive.
>
> (*Civil Engineer at War*, page 148)

## June 1944

By June 1944 Transport Command had expanded into an essential component of the instrument of the liberation of Europe. Airfields and landing grounds across southern Britain had been steadily filling with aircraft ready for the invasion. Glider forces located at No.46 Group's three airfields were complemented by those at Membury, Ramsbury, Welford and a host of other sites. Permanent airfields were fine for the static aspects of war, but they would not be the answer once the enemy had been successfully dislodged from France.

## Advanced Landing Grounds

Throughout the summer of 1942 a number of potential airfield sites had been visited across the south coast and by the end of the year twenty-five areas had been identified as the locations for Advanced Landing Grounds (ALG). The concept was simple: the airfields were to be as temporary and ephemeral as possible, allowing for rapid construction and a bare minimum of resources used. They had one objective: to provide as close an airfield as physically possible to the Normandy landing areas. Allied commanders clearly understood the necessity of at least good air cover, if not total air superiority, and ALGs would be the most direct way of providing that prior to the establishment of the RAF in Normandy. The distribution of sites practically covered the entire south coast from Bournemouth to Ramsgate and used a number of topographies. Their construction necessitated the removal of woodland, especially in the New Forest, and the modification of marshes required substantial drainage, especially around Romney.

The sites comprised two runways paved with metal tracking, perimeter tracks linking the runway ends. Substantial marshalling areas were placed at the end of each runway allowing aircraft to be dispatched in close succession. Other structures normally encountered on more permanent airfields were conspicuous by their absence on ALGs. The best that could be hoped for was often a weatherproof bell tent, but where ever possible existing farm structures were retained and served as billets or messing areas. Only minimal cover was provided for servicing aircraft, usually in the shape of a blister hangar, but more often than not servicing was carried out in the open. As part of the D-Day build-up further land around some ALGs was required for extra aircraft parking.

The landing areas and associated tracks were unlike the normal layout. For a start the fields comprised only two runways laid at 90 degrees to each other, the master one being 4,800ft, the secondary 4,200ft. A perimeter track was laid to just one side of each runway but also linked both together and lying off these at regular intervals were dispersal pads, allowing for servicing without causing obstructions. The by now standard practice of dispersing nucleated sites structures was also undertaken on the ALGs, although they often comprised little more than bomb, fuel and POL stores.

Areas requiring hardcore, especially in marshy locations south of London, utilised tons of rubble brought out from the bombed city. However, the consolidation of the sites was kept to a minimum, thus increasing the speed in which they were constructed. What was the most obvious difference to other airfields was the gratuitous use of temporary tracking. Such steel planking and structure was used in a multitude of ways and now seems an opportune time to discuss it in relation to airfields.

## Temporary Construction

The function of metal track surfacing was best described by Major R.R. West-Grigson in a paper on the subject in 1948:

> To distribute wheel loads over a larger area of ground than the contact area of the tyres, thus assisting aircraft to operate under ground conditions which otherwise might prove difficult or impossible.
>    To delay deterioration of the natural bearing capacity of the soil resulting from abrasion by aircraft and vehicular traffic.

Obviously these were basic requirements; typically the military had a number of specifics, including the fact that track should 'readily lend itself to camouflage treatments' and 'be economical in materials'. The track was further divided into three distinct groups – wire, panel and pierced steel planking (PSP).

## Wire

Wire type tracks were predominantly two patterns. The first of these, the Sommerfeld, came in 25-yard lengths, 10ft 7in wide, and comprised a hexagonal mesh with 3/8 mild

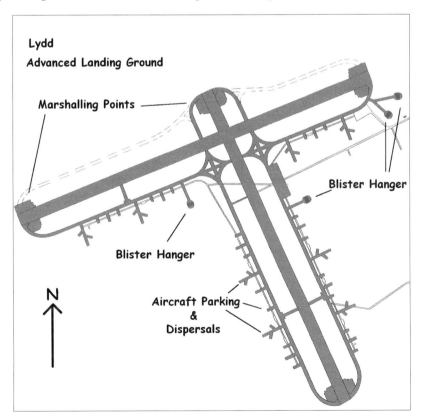

ALG Lydd.
(After Paul
Francis)

steel rods running transversely through it. The type had been used operationally in the desert campaign where it earned the name 'Tin Lino'. The track, once laid, was tensioned by picketing down one side and then stretching using tractors attached to the other side. A development of this early form was the Square Mesh Track. This could be supplied in either panels or rolls and was far easier to fabricate than the Sommerfeld. Square mesh was used throughout late 1944–45 but holds the honour of being the first material used on a French side beach-head landing strip in 1944.

### Panel

Panel track was dominated by three specific types – Channel, Irving Grid and Bar-and-Rod. Both Irving Grid and Bar-and-Rod were of US design and saw limited usage in Europe. The major drawback was their complexity during manufacture, demonstrating their pre-war design. Channel track, however, was supplied in rectangular panels 11ft x 6ft from British factories and was considered the cutting edge of steel planking by the Air Ministry. Channel was predominantly used on the majority of temporary surfaces after January 1945.

### PSP

One further type has, one could argue, become iconic – the Pierced Steel Plank or PSP. PSP was a pre-war American design and had many advantages over its rivals. Production was simple; a ten gauge mild steel blank was cut 10ft long x 1ft 3in wide and was then stamped into shape. Stamping introduced two strengthening ribs into the plank and flanged holes cut into it, increasing strength whilst removing weight and excess material. Also, careful planning of how the track was to be laid allowed for any section to be replaced with minimum of effort, something that was to be a bonus in 1948 during the Berlin Airlift. It was not perfect. As the soil became wet underneath the passage of traffic or aircraft would hydraulic mud up through the holes making the track unusable. And the ends were not tied down making life around the edges hazardous for both personnel and aircraft tyres.

Construction of the ALGs was undertaken by the Royal Engineers, RAF Airfield Construction Service and the USAAF Engineer Aviation Battalion. This was due, in part, to the shortage of civilian manpower and the urgency of the project; however, the crews gained valuable experience for work across the Channel post-D-Day. Advanced Landing Grounds by their very nature were destined to leave little on the landscape. Of the twenty-three built only the occasional blister hangar remains. A great number were laid under protest from the Ministry of Agriculture, who were concerned that valuable, productive agricultural land would be lost at a time when food production was at its most vulnerable. Whilst the Ministry was overruled, it was only a temporary arrangement, and the majority of ALGs were torn up by November 1944. A measure of their superficial nature can be gained by a glance at paperwork concerning Bisterne in Hampshire.

The site was opened on 3 March 1944 with the standard two strip layout and very sparse infrastructure, the majority of station sections being housed in requisitioned farm buildings close to the runway intersection. However, by 27 March the site was being extended for the arrival of 371 Fighter Group, P47 Thunderbolts. The request also hinted at the process of requisition by 1943/44:

RAF Boscombe
Down, Wiltshire.
PSP laid in the war
period and recently
rediscovered during
ground work.
(Boscombe Down
Conservation Group)

Further to the superintending Engineer's letter of the 1ˢᵗ March Ref: A.14/825/L.1A/LO he
is advised that covering authority has been given for the requisition of the two areas of land
– which are required for additional sites for tented camps at the above station.
Regarding the Keepers Copse referred, it is not proposed to derequisition this property until
it is finally ascertained that no further land is required.

(C. Jarrett for Director of Lands & Requisitioning (PRO AIR 2/8533))

The transitory nature of these airfields was demonstrated that same year as Bisterne was
to discover:

I inspected Bisterne ALG on 19/10/44 and append my report on land to be derequisitioned.
The removal of Summerfeld tracking is proceeding quickly and given fine weather it is
probable that the whole will be lifted within the month. The thousands of 5 gall. petrol tins
dumped around the site are also being slowly removed and outside transport and inclement
weather are the two factors which materially affect the clearance. The whole of the pierced
planking has been removed by USA Troops.

(Director of Lands & Requisitioning (PRO AIR 2/8533))

Those ALGs that survived the year had gone by mid-1945, disappearing back under
plough in the majority of cases. Archaeologically what remains of the ALGs is amongst
the most fragile of airfield evidence.

### Total Bomber War

Throughout the winter of 1943–44 Bomber Command intensified its pressure on
German economic targets. From March 1944 sporadic Mosquito and B-17 raids kept
the pressure on the German Air Defence network and population. However, the focus

changed throughout the spring and summer as Bomber Command switched to pinpoint targeting of defensive facilities and transport networks in support of the coming invasion. Economic targets were hit throughout the summer; it was after Christmas before the air assaults restarted against Berlin and other German cities. On Monday 26 February 1945 a pathfinder force marked out Berlin, as usual in thick cloud. Behind them was the biggest force the Allies had yet mustered against the city. Over 1,000 USAAF B-17s and B-24s plus an escort of P-51 Mustangs dropped nearly 3,000 tons of bombs in the central district. Three weeks later a similar force dropped 3,276 tons. The final major air offensive against the city took place to 'celebrate' Hitler's fifty-sixth and last birthday, destroying a number of rail installations.

## Reduction

From early 1945 the frontline was moving steadily east and as it did more enemy aerodromes fell into the hands of the Allies. The expertise gained in the construction of the Advanced Landing Grounds along with expansion construction and modification of existing airfields in the UK now paid dividends. However badly damaged German vacated airfields were the Airfield Construction Service and Engineer Airfield Battalions, along with other Allied organisations, soon had them at least functional. At home the reduction of attacks and changing tactics signalled the beginning of the end for some stations and by May 1945 a number were already just holding sites for demobilisation and repatriation. There is one exception to the rule, the Fleet Air Arm. The FAA was still an expanding force by Victory in Europe Day. The conflict in the east was still to reach its climax and the Royal Navy was to be heavily involved in the support of an amphibious assault on Japan. Subsequently the FAA took over a number of recently vacated USAAF sites in East Anglia and continued the construction of Culdrose whilst a number of RAF stations in the vicinity were being placed in care and maintenance. Then, on 6 August, the world changed forever as the United States dropped the first of two atomic weapons on Japan. By 14 August Japan had collapsed leaving many in a state of limbo.

The final two years of the war had seen a major change in the way airfields had both been constructed and located. Their temporary nature, especially those built for American forces, would mean they were soon abandoned. The use of atomic weapons in the east ushered in a new, more devastating type of warfare, one that would save many airfields around Britain from immediate closure and ensure some survive to this day. That said, from here on in the story of airfields is one of reduction.

RAF Thorpe Abbots, Norfolk, in 2007. Bomber Satellite Tower, now a splendid museum to the 'Bloody Hundredth'. USAAF airfields were concentrated in this small area on England to exploit the distance to the Continent.

RAF Debach, Suffolk, in 2007. The Operations Block. Debach was the last 8th Airforce Base to become operational in 1944. It was built by the 820th Engineer Battalion Aviation.

# seven

# COLD WAR

War, as should be expected, greatly increases the speed at which new weapons and defence systems are developed. Innovative ideas and concepts, especially jet engines, radar and nuclear technologies, all saw a rapid elevation from obscurity to national dependency during the Second World War . These developments continued post-war although the immediate climate was one of political uncertainty. The majority of Europe was either destroyed or bankrupt; this was especially the case for Britain where the termination of Lend Lease had pushed any chance of immediate economic recovery far beyond the reach of the Government. Coupled with this was the added burden of the administration of a quarter of devastated Germany, the growing problems in Greece, Turkey and the disintegration of Britain's remnant Empire. By March 1946 there were 680 surplus aerodromes in the United Kingdom, a vast number of which saw their accommodation blocks housing displaced persons from Europe rather than service personnel. One such site being Ludford Magna in Lincolnshire where Polish families were in residence up to the early 1950s. Nevertheless, a potentially far more dangerous conflict was just over the horizon, one which would shape world political direction for nearly forty years and see some dramatic developments on British airfields. The western Allies had fought a war to prevent Central Europe coming under the influence of one man; unfortunately they did not reckon that Adolf Hitler would be replaced by Joseph Stalin. Subsequently, the Communists filled the Nazi vacuum and dominated Central European politics for the next four decades. To investigate the airfields concerned this section has two main themes – the involvement of the newly formed United States Air Force (USAF) in the United Kingdom and Britain's role in the North Atlantic Treaty Organisation (NATO).

*Reduction*

By May 1945 the Royal Air Force had grown to gigantic proportions. Airbases stretched right around the globe and its personnel strength had risen to 1,079,835 officers and men operating over 55,000 aircraft. The dilemma now was how to reduce both numbers of men and equipment whilst maintaining a credible force. Estimates for proposed effective front-line numbers suggested fifty-one fighter squadrons, forty-two bomber squadrons, forty-two transport squadrons and twelve reserve squadrons, 1,500 aircraft in total. Unfortunately the reduction was far harsher than this. During the first two years of peace no clear political direction had emerged. Whilst internal politics in Greece, Turkey, Yugoslavia, Italy and France suggested communism could still threaten the fragile peace it was estimated it could take up to ten years to reach that point.

## American Drawdown

By 1946 the sizeable American air fleet had all but vanished from Britain. The majority of bomber squadrons had returned to the United States whilst tactical and support wings had moved either into Europe or were now stationed in Japan and the Far East. Many air stations closed within this first year. Looking at just the 1st Air Division of the 8th USAAF, Bassingbourn, Ridgewell, Nuthampstead, Molesworth, Kimbolton, Grafton Underwood, Podington, Chelveston, Thurleigh, Polebrook, Deenethorpe and Glatton had all reverted back to the Royal Air Force by the end of 1945. This situation was mirrored up and down the country; of the sixty-three airfields operated by the 8th at the end of the war, the majority were relinquished by the Americans within the year. Along with the squadron airfield closures came the reduction of support infrastructure including the massive Base Air Depot at Burtonwood, incidentally the last base to close.

The first hint of a reversal in the reduction policy came in the summer of 1946. Whilst visiting airfields on the point of closure, Marshall of the Royal Air Force Lord Tedder and General Carl Spaatz, USAAF, discussed the worsening political situation on the Continent. By now it had become apparent that the Soviets would not be dislodged from their territorial gains. To make matters worse Stalin was increasingly obstructive in any decision regarding the future of Germany. Tedder, at Spaatz's request, agreed to upgrade five airfields, Marham, Lakenheath, Scampton, Bassingbourn and Mildenhall, making them capable of supporting long-range heavy bombers, namely the B-29. Throughout 1947 the airfields received substantial alteration to their runways in both length and strength. Interestingly not many in the Government were told the reasons for the work. One thing stands out about the five airfields chosen – their construction dates: Marham (1937); Lakenheath (1941); Scampton (1936); Bassingbourn (1938); Mildenhall (1934). With the exception of Lakenheath all the others are constructed in permanent brick due to their expansion scheme origins.

## Communists

Such airfield retentions and upgrades were to be the first building blocks towards Britain's involvement in the new world order and subsequently NATO. In defeat Germany had become a new battleground, one in which the West struggled to contain the growing spectre of Communism. This was not confined to Germany; throughout the countries of the war devastated world socialism found perfect conditions for expansion, and it was not confined to the years of peace – Britain had since 1944 been attempting to defeat a communist guerrilla uprising against the Greek royalist government. With the collapse of Germany the Soviet army occupied the majority of central Europe including Czechoslovakia, Rumania, Hungary, Albania, Bulgaria and Yugoslavia, along with the Baltic States, Poland and around East Germany. Regardless of this, the United States began its withdrawal from Europe, intended to be completed by 1947. In Britain, the

United States Army Air Forces rapidly withdrew to their home bases in America, and a similar process began on the Continent. Many in the British government were alarmed by this but it took a voice from the past to shake the world into action. On 5 March 1946 Winston Churchill, whilst on a tour sponsored by President Truman, delivered what has become one of the most famous speeches of the twentieth century:

> From Stettin in the Baltic to Trieste in the Adriatic an Iron Curtain has descended across the continent. Behind that line lie all the capitals of the ancient states of Central and Eastern Europe. Warsaw, Berlin, Prague, Vienna, Budapest, Belgrade, Bucharest and Sophia; all these famous cities and the populations around them lie in what I must call the Soviet sphere, and all are subject, in one form or another, not only to Soviet influence but a very high and in some cases increasing measure of control from Moscow.
>
> (Winston Churchill, Fulton, Missouri, 5 March 1946)

Less than a year later it was clear that Britain could no longer maintain any level of involvement in Greece and it looked increasingly likely that communist elements would infiltrate the governments of France and Italy. On 12 March President Truman went before Congress and demanded financial support for the Greek and Turkish governments. Truman by now understood that leaving both governments to their own devices would only invite major communist advances in both countries. Poverty, one sure breeding ground of communism, clearly had to be eradicated – the problem was how to do this. The President's requests became known as 'The Truman Doctrine', a key component being the containment of communism. On 1 July 1947, US Secretary of State George Marshall sowed the first seeds of the European Recovery Programme subsequently to be known as 'The Marshall Plan'. The scheme was offered to all – 'our policy is directed not against any country or doctrine but against hunger, poverty, desperation and chaos', Marshall explained, clearly offering countries still under Soviet influence the opportunity to sign up. Naturally Stalin, conscious the economic aid would almost certainly spell the end of Russian domination in Central Europe, denounced the plan and forbade any occupied territory from taking advantage. Western Europe on the other hand grasped the Marshall Plan with both hands. The Iron Curtain Churchill had warned about was now firmly in place.

## The Year Everything Changed

By the beginning of 1948 it was clear that the Soviets were shaping eastern Germany in a similar way to other occupied European states. Major concern was access to the Allied-controlled city of Berlin. The city, like Germany itself, had been divided into four control areas at the end of the war. The problem was that Berlin was firmly located in Soviet-controlled eastern Germany. Large amounts of supplies were needed to keep just the garrisons going, never mind 2 million civilians. The majority of supplies came in via road, rail or on the waterways; the western sectors were serviced by two airfields, neither being used at the time as supply depots. Ominously, on 24 January, a British train travelling from Berlin to the west was stopped at the border. When the Allies complained the Soviets stopped more trains and proceeded to interfere with a road transport on the autobahn. By April 1948 Allied flights started to supply their garrisons in Berlin as it had become almost

The Berlin Airlift caused Transport Command a major headache, stripping training to a bare minimum. It did, however, give the ageing RAF Dakota fleet a new lease of life. (Courtesy of Frank Watt)

A rare picture of Stalin at a sports event in the early 1950s. Stalin's territorial gains after the Second World War gave rise to the Cold War and dominated world defence for nearly forty years after his death.

impossible to rely on road and rail transport. This exploded into a full-blown political and military stand-off when the Soviet authorities blocked all road, rail and river access to West Berlin in an attempt to force the Allies to abandon their plans for West Germany.

## A Cut Too Far

In the years leading up to June 1948 the RAF had been steadily running down its vast equipment stockpile; by the time of the blockade the front-line force comprised twenty-five squadrons in Fighter Command, twenty-four in Bomber Command and 160 transport aircraft spread over twenty squadrons. Coastal Command comprised eleven squadrons and thirty-three squadrons were still stationed overseas, especially in the eastern theatre. This was basically half the projected acceptable figures that the Air Ministry had hoped for. However,

RAF Burtonwood, Cheshire, 1956. A C-124 cargo aircraft of the USAF on the Tech Site Ramp. These types were frequent visitors throughout the 1950s and early '60s. (RAF Burtonwood Association)

it was not the reduction of equipment that highlighted the inadequacies of the post-war force. Between 1946–47 manpower strength in the service had been 760,000 with 142,000 on demobilisation leave. The following year this had been dramatically reduced to 375,000, and by the year of the airlift the number had again been reduced to 325,000. Unfortunately demobilisation was not properly managed and subsequently large sections of the Royal Air Forces skills base were decimated. To make matters worse National Service, one wartime aspect that was retained, failed to make good these inadequacies. Whilst the Air Ministry was trying to sort out the manning crisis, especially as it looked like a limited war over Berlin might be on the cards, Ernest Bevin was requesting help. On 16 July 1948 the National Security Council met in Washington to discuss Bevin's request for American aircraft to be stationed in the United Kingdom. The following day the 28th Bomb Group landed at Scampton. Shortly after, a further thirty B-29s landed at Marham and a few weeks later thirty more arrived at Lakenheath, initially on thirty days temporary duty but soon increased to ninety days. The aircraft were known in the press as 'The Atomic Bombers', although none were actually capable of carrying one. However, it served to allow the public to think they could.

## Burtonwood

When it was apparent that the USAF intended to base B-29 aircraft in the United Kingdom a support depot was required. The former Central Repair Depot at Burtonwood, Cheshire, was the obvious choice. RAF Burtonwood opened in 1940 as No.37 Maintenance Unit and Repair Depot. The site received new aircraft from manufacture and prepared them for service forming a part of the Aircraft Storage Unit (ASU) network. On 15 July 1942 the site was handed over to the USAAF as Base Air Depot No.1, becoming an MU for American built aircraft and engines. Situated on England's West Coast, close to major ports, it could readily accept supplies from the United States. In just two years Burtonwood grew into a site of gigantic proportions, employing upwards of 30,000 US and UK staff by late 1944. By 8 May 1945 the site had prepared an incredible 15,575 aircraft and 30,286 radial engines for all theatres of war. After the war the airfield, like so many others in the UK, declined in importance. Burtonwood was headquarters to thirty-four other airfields at its height and was the last US base in Britain to close when handed back on 9 June 1946. From June 1946

RAF Burtonwood, Cheshire, in 1970. Wartime and post-war air traffic controls. Burtonwood saw a revival of fortune due to the Berlin Airlift – it was to become an important USAF station until the 1980s. (RAF Burtonwood Association)

No.37 MU re-occupied RAF Burtonwood, storing hundreds of Mosquitoes, Harvards and Lancasters. No.276 Maintenance Unit (MU) also took up residence at Burtonwood, utilising some of the vast workshop facilities, primarily to scrap surplus aircraft. This role fell to the majority of the ASUs immediately after the war. The airfield at Wroughton in Wiltshire had by the end of 1945 received over 200 Lancasters for disposal. Along with 37 MUs the Master Provision Office also took up residence at Burtonwood, acting as the central supply depot for all parts related to American aircraft in service with the RAF, especially the Douglas Dakota. A few weeks before the arrival of the B-29s, nearly 1,500 technical staff of the USAF moved to Burtonwood to prepare the facilities for bomber support. As the airlift built up pace so did the requirement for aircraft servicing of the USAF's primary transport aircraft, the C-54. Eventually a kilometre-long 'assembly line' was designed that could cope with eight arriving C-54s a day.

## A Divided Europe

On 6 March 1948 the European Foreign Ministers met in London to discuss the possibilities of a West German Government. However the make-up of the conference demonstrated the changing political situation. The Benelux countries (Belgium, Netherlands and Luxemburg) were present, but in a clear snub the Soviets were not. A number of monumental issues were on the agenda including the Marshall Plan and some form of rudimentary alliance. Whilst in session the conference learned of a Red Army coup in Czechoslovakia and Stalin's political advances towards Finland and Norway. With the dangers now apparently obvious, Secretary of State Marshall announced that the United States was ready 'to proceed at once in the joint discussions on the establishment of an Atlantic security system'. The seeds of an iconic Cold War organisation – the North Atlantic Treaty Organisation – were sown and by 17 March the Treaty of Brussels had been signed.

## NATO

The blockade of Berlin demonstrated to the West that an alliance throughout the free world had become inevitable in the face of Soviet aspirations. The formation of the North Atlantic Treaty Organisation (NATO) signalled to Moscow that it would not be able to dominate Europe by political means alone. It was also to shape the majority of decisions regarding the Royal Air Force, United States Air Force and the airfields of Britain for the next thirty-five years.

The 'Brussels Treaty', a basic self-help organisation, helped to polarise public opinion in the United States. It was clear that Marshall Aid would not singularly halt communist expansion and the Europeans would need further help from the US if an alliance was to hold. Portugal, Denmark and Iceland were soon to join as well, and by July 1948 talks between the Brussels signatories and Washington were well under way. The final document was signed on 4 April 1949. An attack on Belgium, Canada, Denmark, France, Iceland, Luxembourg, Holland, Italy, Portugal, Norway, the USA or United Kingdom would now be considered an attack on all. Stalin, who had hoped to dislodge the Americans from Germany, had clearly misread the situation. The United States moved from a reduction policy, aiming to be out of Europe by 1948, to its protector. NATO was formally ratified in the Senate on 21 July 1949. The Cold War proper had begun.

## A New Force for a New War

The growing situation in Central Europe coupled with experiences drawn from the Second World War forced Washington to re-evaluate how its air forces were controlled. Subsequently, on 21 March 1946, the 2nd, 8th and 15th Army Air Forces were formed

RAF Sculthorpe, Norfolk, December 1957. Crews of the 47th. Wing of the 3rd Air Force USAF being briefed as to weather conditions prior to a sortie.

RAF Upper Heyford, Oxfordshire, 1967. By the time of this photograph Upper Heyford had become one of the USAF's most important UK assets. The expansion work that can be seen here was in advance of Phantom RF-4 deployments.

into the Strategic Air Command (SAC). Just over a year later President Truman signed the National Security Act (27 July 1947), effectively laying the foundation for a separate air force. On 16 September 1947 the United States Air Force (USAF) came into being.

After the build-up caused by the Berlin Airlift, it was apparent that Truman's containment policies would need to have a quick armed response capability if it was to be effective. That quick response dictated that aircraft should be stationed within striking distance of Eastern Europe, and subsequently the USAF identified bases throughout the west that could, with minimal work, house American aircraft. In Britain a number of redundant airfields were identified for occupation. Even at this early stage in the proceedings a change occurred in how US assets were to be distributed. The initial deployment of B-29s had been based as close as possible to the front; indeed one group was stationed in what was to become West Germany. Once it was clear that the USAF was here to stay, through agreement cited by NATO, a more permanent, less vulnerable topography was sought. Underpinning this was the fact that Russia had, on 29 August 1949, broken the nuclear monopoly by detonating its own weapon.

Subsequently four airfields were selected by the USAF and RAF, all further west than the B-29 aerodromes. All had been operational during the Second World War, although facilities differed widely. Fairford and Greenham Common possessed very little infrastructure, having been built during 1941–43. Brize Norton dated from 1936 and Upper Heyford, you will remember, was even earlier, being part of the 1920s expansion process. All required substantial work to bring them up to operational readiness. Each needed a runway in excess of 3,000 metres, parking for at least forty-five aircraft, and technical and domestic infrastructure to support long-term detachments. Further airfields were earmarked for upgrade in case reinforcement was needed. These included Elvington,

Yorkshire and Bruntingthorpe, Leicestershire; the Emergency Landing Ground at Carnaby also received some upgrade work. All this complemented the existing bases at Lakenheath, Mildenhall, Sculthorpe and Bassingbourn. Not all were permanently occupied by Strategic Air Command but some clear differences are noticeable on the surviving stations, not least large dispersals intended to allow forty-five aircraft to be held on site. Dispersals could range from the infilling of war time spectacles through to specific expanses of concrete, the most impressive being a single expanse at Elvington of nearly 50 acres.

## RAF

Developments in the late 1940s were dominated by the Berlin crisis. Transport Command was almost overwhelmed by the operation, closing down many of its training routes and flight operations just to keep the air bridge functional. The primary aircraft operated by the Royal Air Force was the war service Dakota, a derivative of the highly successful DC-3. The Dakotas were detached to Germany from parent stations at Waterbeach, Oakington, Broadwell, Fairford, Lyneham and Abingdon. Unfortunately the Dakota could only carry around three tons per trip. Avro Yorks, a development of the Lancaster, carried substantially more but suffered major serviceability problems, as it was not designed for short haul flights at all up weight. The York's home bases were Abingdon, Lyneham and Bassingbourn. However, from November 1948 the air fleet was joined by a brand new transport aircraft – the Handley Page Hastings. This aircraft eventually took the lion's share of the RAF commitment. Hastings were detached from Dishforth and Topcliffe, both Royal Canadian Air Force bomber bases in North Yorkshire, and for the last five months of 1948 Short Sunderlands from Nos 205 and 230 Squadrons, Calshot, flew from Finkenwerder, Hamburg, on to Lake Havel close to the city. Fighter cover was offered in the early days by No.80 Squadron, one of the last to operate Spitfires, detached from RAF Coltishall. The airlift benefited the RAF in a number of ways. It put in place an accurate weather forecasting system that now covered the Atlantic and most of Western Europe. Vast improvements were made to the Air Traffic System, still in its infancy at the end of the war, including a new runway light approach system, developed at Farnborough and still in place today. Improvement of Ground Control Approach (GCA) radars continued, ensuring maximum flying in all but the very worse weather conditions. However, the airlift highlighted some major short comings. The demobilisation of personnel, especially from ground trades, was now beginning to bite. In an effort to stem the flow National Servicemen who were expecting to be demobilised had their release dates cancelled indefinitely. The Ministry could not rectify a shortage of aircraft so easily, though. A number of Dakotas ready for disposal were hurriedly serviced and placed back on a charge but eventually the Foreign Office had to admit defeat and a number of civilian operators were employed.

One major point stands out: the shift of importance between Bomber and Transport Command. Waterbeach, Oakington, Abingdon, Bassingbourn, Dishforth and Topcliffe were all bases originally operating Bomber Command squadrons. From the end of the war most of these had become the home to transport squadrons, ferrying prisoners of war back and forth around the world, bringing troops home from the conflict theatres and reconnecting supply routes with the empire.

Closure of bases after the war was a rapid affair in many cases and it is worth revisiting some of the airfields discussed previously if we are to identify any form of trend with the

A. & A.E.E. BOSCOMBE DOWN.
19TH. FEB. 1949.

0    250    500         1000              2000 YDS.

RAF Boscombe Down, 1949. The second runway construction in 1949, this aerial shot demonstrates the amount of ground disturbance caused. (Courtesy of the Ministry of Defence)

process. No.6 Group Royal Canadian Air Force operated Nos 61, 62, 63 and 64 Base airfields until 1945, covering eleven aerodromes located around the North Yorkshire Moors. Of those eleven bases, six – Dalton, Wombleton, East Moor, Tholthorpe, Skipton-on-Swale and Croft – were closed by 1946. The remainder, Topcliffe, Dishforth, Linton-on-Ouse, Leeming and Middleton St George, remained operational until the late 1960s. Leeming and Linton-on-Ouse remain operational today whilst Middleton St George is now the civilian Teeside Airport. So what decision drove this distribution? The key is in the construction dates, underpinned by the types of structure located on them. The five remaining sites are all expansion period constructions; they span the whole scheme series and have permanent brick infrastructure, especially hangarage, both C and J types being evident. The six quickly disposed of were all standard Class A with very little in the way of permanent structures; the hangars in these cases are T2s and B-Types, all temporary builds that could easily be removed.

To test this further, if we now consider No.1 Group Bomber Command airfields, then the same pattern of closure becomes immediately apparent. The group operated Nos 11, 12, 13 and 14 Base airfields covering thirteen sites, plus No.1 Lancaster Finishing School and two stations as satellites in 1945. Of these, Swinderby, Lindholme, Binbrook and Hemswell remained open and were again expansion period airfields. Added to this list is Kirmington. Opened in 1942, this site became Humberside Airport. Blyton, Sandtoft, Grimsby, Kelstern,

Elsham Wolds, North Killingholme, Ludford Magna, Faldingworth, Wickenby, Sturgate and Ingham, all with austerity construction, were closed within two years. Naturally other site types survived much better, especially as there were so many aircraft to dispose of. The Aircraft Storage Units now became the final resting place for the majority of aircraft from these now defunct stations. Scenes of destruction that would horrify today were played out up and down the country as thousands of aircraft were scrapped. At Burtonwood 354 aircraft were scrapped in September 1945 alone, and at Wroughton in Wiltshire additional field storage areas were needed to park the influx. Eventually over 200 Lancasters, some veterans of over 100 missions, were unceremoniously reduced. The ASUs were valuable assets as they were invariably pre-war or pre-war design, and carried all the infrastructure of a modern heavy base including paved runways and often lots of hard standings.

## Korea

The process of containment was put to the test on 25 June 1950 when Communists supporting North Korea invaded South Korea. This act of aggression immediately diverted political attention from Europe to the Far East. The Korean War dragged on for three long years, forcing the Government to reassess the rearmament programme. Eventually, spending over a three-year period was increased to £4,700 million. Air defence was to be at the top of this spending list and the Government embarked on one of its most ambitious projects to date – the Rotor Programme. Rotor had been in the planning stage since the Cherry Report in 1945, which called for a fully integrated radar system. Naturally during the lean post-war years this had been shelved by the Government, only to be resurrected after the Berlin Crisis. Other weapons systems were also commissioned, especially surface to air missiles. Now, with some in the Government considering Korea as a prelude to a European campaign by the Soviets, air defence became a major priority. This priority became focused as the Soviets detonated their first fission weapon.

## Warsaw Pact

The political and military alliance between the Soviet Union and the East European socialist states, known as the Warsaw Pact, was formed in 1955 as a counter to NATO. Moscow cited the inclusion of West Germany into NATO that same year as the main catalyst for its formation; however, during much of its early existence, the Warsaw Pact essentially functioned as part of the Soviet Ministry of Defence. Its unofficial function was as a primary mechanism for keeping its Eastern European allies under political and military control. Moscow used the pact to present a façade of solidarity, covering its political domination in the internal affairs of its allies. At the same time, the Soviet Union also used the Warsaw Pact to develop the Eastern European socialist armies complementing its security policy, especially in the east–west border regions. It also meant that aircraft carrying nuclear and conventional weapons were far closer to the west and subsequently the response time was severely reduced.

## Air Defence in the Early 1950s

With the advent of the Soviet capability and the fact that they possessed a delivery platform in the shape of the Tu-4, a rivet for rivet copy of the B-29, it became clear that Britain had again moved, theoretically, onto the front line. Throughout the late 1940s to the early 1950s

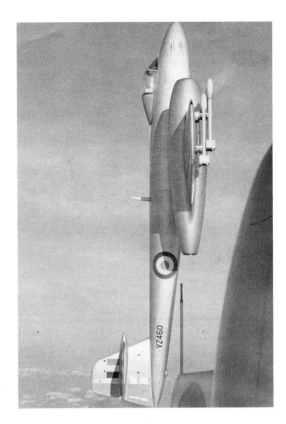

RAF West Raynham, Norfolk, mid-1950s. The advent of the Gloster Meteor and subsequent jet developments dictated a radically different airfield infrastructure, one that was dominated by concrete.

the old system of air defence via gun batteries prevailed. The fledgling radar network, still under construction, over budget and beset with technical problems, struggled to keep up with the pace of avionic advances, as did the concept of how to bring an enemy aircraft down once it was over the United Kingdom. Information from the Rotor sites was filtered through a number of Sector Operations Rooms and then passed on to the RAF at Fighter Command and the Royal Artillery, who operated a network known as the Gun Defended Area (GDA). The GDA was usually a high value industrial area, often connected with defence manufacturing or a large population centre. At the centre of each GDA was an Anti-Aircraft Operations Room (AAOR) that controlled a number of automated gun sites. The GDA was the last line of defence intended to bring down any aircraft that made it through the fighter intercept squadrons. The GDA concept was the last vestige of wartime thinking. By the time the last AAOR was finished in 1955 the entire system had been made obsolete – both sides had tested thermonuclear weapons by 1953, aircraft were now operating far higher than anti-aircraft guns could throw the shells and ballistic missile technology was soon to make even the idea of the lone bomber an archaic concept.

## Fighters

The immediate post-war period was dominated by the quest for speed. During the last years of the war both Britain and Germany had introduced the first rudimentary jet-powered fighters. Both demonstrated their potential and it was unsurprising that upon

Germany's defeat the race was on to find the scientists who had made this possible. Britain had independently developed the jet engine through the efforts of Sir Frank Whittle and in July 1944 No.616 Squadron became the first RAF unit to operate jet fighters. The Gloster Meteor, powered by two Rolls-Royce Welland engines, had a maximum speed of 385mph at sea level and a rate of climb of over 2,000ft per minute.

In 1946 the first two wings of fighter jets for the RAF were formed, operating Meteor F3s with three squadrons at Bentwaters and a further three at Boxted. 1946 also saw the formation of the first wing of de Havilland Vampires at Odiham. Over the next five years a multitude of variants of both aircraft were developed including ground attack, night fighter, interceptor and reconnaissance. The number of airfields concerned with fighter defence dropped dramatically until, by 1951, only eighteen aerodromes were left. Whilst some fighter squadrons still operated final marks of the Spitfire, the majority had become all jet by the end of the decade.

The introduction of new technologies such as jet aircraft had an effect on the layout and facilities provided on airfields. A jet aircraft, unlike its predecessor, is very destructive if operated on grass. The jet efflux quickly burns off any vegetation ensuring that areas where they start, run up engines or stand for any length of time, i.e. the end of the runway, loses the majority of its integrity. Any rain then quickly turns the area into a mud pool. This introduces the second problem. Jet aircraft have a different undercarriage arrangement to piston aircraft. To necessitate better thrust characteristics the aircraft have a nose leg instead of a tail wheel. This makes the aircraft want to dig in, especially when taxiing; if the end of the runway is mud then a potential disaster is on the cards. The third factor is the all-up weight of the aircraft. To demonstrate the point it is worth noting the increase in weight that jet technology brought. A Spitfire Mk V was 5,090lbs when empty and had a maximum all-up weight of 6,770lb at take-off. The Meteor exceeded that when empty (10,684lb) and had an all-up weight at take-off of 19,100lb. When this load is transmitted through the tyres it is clear that only a substantially sound taxiway and runway will be able to cope with the aircraft. Subsequently any airfield used as an operational fighter base, be that training or standby, needed these improved facilities. This spelled the end for many stations that had until now relied on PSP or were operating light aircraft from grass strips. Naturally those bases retained are situated down the east coast of Britain with two, Leuchars and Lossiemouth, protecting the northern approaches.

By the mid-1950s a new series of aircraft were beginning to make their presence felt. Fighter Command was taking delivery of the Hawker Hunter, an advanced, single engine, near supersonic jet fighter, re-equipping Meteor and Sabre squadrons in Britain and Germany with the type. In 1956 the new Gloster Javelin Night Fighter joined the Command, seeing service until 1964, and that same year Fighter Command achieved its greatest strength since the war, operating thirty-five squadrons. The following year policy dramatically changed when the Government accepted the recommendations of the 1957 White Paper, noting:

> The defence of the bomber airfields is an essential part of the deterrent and it is a feasible task.
> A manned fighter force, smaller than at present but adequate for this limited purpose, will be

RAF Binbrook, Lincolnshire, 1966. A English Electric Lightning of No. 5 Squadron Air Defence. The Cold War saw the rise of specialist stations. Binbrook was to become inextricably linked with the Lightning.

maintained and will be equipped with air-to-air guided missile systems. Fighter aircraft will in due course be replaced by a ground-to-air missile system.

(Defence – Outline of Future Policy (PRO AIR 2/14692))

Whilst the concept of a low numbered fighter force struck a chord with the Treasury, those in the Air Ministry were not so happy. In any event the policy was overturned a few years later, but the damage had been done and its legacy was to be felt into the mid-1980s. However, stations still needed to be fit for purpose and the increased all-up-weight of new fighter types dictated a number of expensive changes, especially to runway lengths and surfaces.

Dear Wolfe,

Following Whittuck's letter to Serpell of the 2 August, 1956, five airfields in Fighter Command have been developed to Peace and War standards, namely; Coltishall, Wattisham, Leconfield, Leuchars and Middleton St. George. Another two (probably Binbrook and Leeming) will be required for a Fighter Force of 13 Lightning Squadrons, as envisaged by plan M, but a decision on these two airfields need not be taken for the moment. In general, the work carried out on the lengthening and strengthening of the 7,500' runways at the five developed airfields has proved satisfactory for Hunters and Javelins but some modification will be needed for the Lightnings now coming into service.

(L. Potts, 16 February 1960 (PRO AIR 20/8542))

RAF Lindholme, Yorkshire, in 2006. Lindholme became home to the 'Northern Radar' in the early 1960s, a tracking network for air defence Bloodhounds. A clear legacy of the 1957 Defence White Paper. This is the plinth for the Type 82 'Orange Yeoman' radar.

Two weapons did enter service as a direct consequence of the White Paper – the Bloodhound and Thunderbird surface-to-air missiles. Thunderbird was issued to the Royal Artillery from 1958 and received an upgrade in 1966; however, this was a mobile weapons system and subsequently required little infrastructure. The introduction of the Bloodhound, however, had a profound impact on the RAF and led to some major work being carried out at a number of airfields, again in the east of Britain.

### Bloodhound

The Bloodhound Mk1 was a total air defence system bringing together many different facets of the previous ten years of defence research and development. This included advances in materials, propulsion (both ramjet and solid booster), target illuminating radar and guidance. Four Wings were operational by 1960 with tactical control at North Luffenham, North Coates, Northern Radar (Lindholme) and Watton. Further squadrons were distributed between these sites at Carnaby, Breighton, Misson, Dunholme Lodge, Woodall Spa, Woodfox Lodge, Warboys, Marham and Rattlesden. This distribution was designed to give the maximum coverage to the V-Force bases (discussed further on) and naturally are all focussed in the east of the country. The sites are recognisable by the distinctive layout of the launch control areas. Each station contained two or three 'fire units' of sixteen Bloodhounds each; within this were two flights of eight weapons, 352 could be on standby at any one time. The launch control areas were laid out over the top of the existing airfield layout if they were the only units on the base. On occasion fire units shared the base with other squadrons. Carnaby was also a diversion base for the V-Force and had prior to that been the home of No.150 Squadron's Thor IRBMs. Breighton also had both types of missiles on station throughout the late 1950s early 1960s. The Tactical Control Centres introduced some different types of structure to the airfield layouts, the most visible today being Northern Radar on the opposite side of the road to the main site at Lindholme. Built across the remnants of spectacle dispersals, this large Type 82 radar tracked the incoming aircraft after handover from the early warning stations such as Staxton Wold or Neatishead.

The station distribution changed dramatically with the introduction of the Bloodhound Mk2. During 1964 West Raynham, an expansion period airfield from 1939, was selected to become home to the Bloodhound servicing wing for the entire missile force, whether at home or abroad. Deployments of the missile were at North Coates, Woodall Spa and West Raynham, effectively reusing those sites already employed as missile air defence stations. The replacement of manned fighters with missiles decimated the airfield network. Fighter Command was reduced to eleven squadrons comprising 140 aircraft by 1962. It was to be a major shift in British and NATO policy that was to go some way to rectifying the situation.

### Bomber Force

By 1947 the Royal Air Force's formidable bomber fleet had all but been destroyed with the majority of aircraft, especially the heavy types, meeting a swift end at one of the ASUs around the country. Thought had been given to a replacement for the Lancaster and since 1944 Avro had been developing a long range aircraft intended to operate in the Far East. The Avro Lincoln could fly further and higher than the Lancaster and deliver a heavier payload; nonetheless, it was too late to see active service. Derivatives of the type did see service in limited numbers and the airframe provided the basis of the Shackleton and Tudor aircraft. However, Bomber Command's future lay in jet aircraft, especially one that also had its origins in 1944 – the English Electric Canberra.

The Canberra entered service in late 1951 and was, within three years, stationed at a number of airfields across Britain and Germany. Binbrook was home to the first Canberra wing with five squadrons in attendance. Further wings took up residence at Hemswell, Wyton, Scampton, Coningsby, Wittering, Marham, Watton and Honington. Again a pattern emerges once placed on the map; the stations are located in two groups, one around Lincoln, the other between Cambridge and Norwich. Naturally these bases are well placed for flights into Europe if so required. Also, they are all pre-war expansion period bomber bases which have substantial bomb dump facilities. The only exception to this is Wittering, which had been primarily an advanced fighter training unit until the arrival of the Canberra.

Unfortunately the Canberra was a light to medium bomber which carried around 10,000lb of ordnance and by 1950 the Lincoln, the RAF's aging heavy bomber, was proving to be increasingly dated and in dire need of replacement. During 1946 a requirement for a high-level multi-engine jet bomber was issued as Operational Requirement 229. Eventually this encouraged a number of designs from British manufacturers which culminated in the creation of the legendary V-force – Valiant, Victor and Vulcan. All three

RAF Marham, Norfolk, October 1950. Seventy Washington B1s were utilised by the RAF to fill the very heavy bomber gap caused by the design and production of the V-Force. This crew is reading for the day's sortie on 'Exercise Emperor', testing the UK's air defence network.

No.57 Squadron Handley Page Victor at RAF Marham in 1973. The Victor went on to dominate the NATO strategic tanker force after a twenty-year career in the deterrent force.

aircraft were revolutionary and subsequently took a substantial amount of time to design, test and produce. To cover this, seventy B-29s were loaned by the United States to plug the gap. Known as the Washington, they served with Bomber Command until 1954, although a small number were on charge until 1959.

## Nuclear Deterrent

The nuclear capability of the RAF began with the issuing of Blue Danube in 1953, a fairly crude low yield weapon that was based on the implosion principle applied at Nagasaki. The weapon itself was unwieldy; it took the first of the V-Force, the Vickers Valiant, to carry the 10,000lb, 24ft-long bomb. Joining the nuclear club demanded some major re-working of airfields, not least the storage of the weapons. Up until now the majority of ordnance had been stored at the airfield or in centralised stores often underground, such as Chilmark in Wiltshire. Unfortunately nuclear weapons are rather more temperamental than their 'dumb' predecessors and subsequently two specific storage sites, Faldingworth and Barnham, were constructed as Permanent Ammunition Depots (PAD). The first Valiants flew into RAF Gaydon in 1955 whilst the Avro Vulcans arrived at RAF Waddington in February 1957, with the Handley Page Victor appearing at Gaydon in November that same year.

RAF Greenham Common, Berkshire, in 2005. A Gaydon Hangar. Whilst construction work on airfields slowed in the post-war period design of facilities did not. This is a new type of structure first erected at RAF Gaydon (hence the name) for the V-Force.

## V-Force Restructure

With the introduction of such a radically new series of aircraft came the realisation that very few airfields were adequately equipped to operate them correctly. Subsequently a massive investment programme was initiated to bring a number of airfields up to the required standard. Ten stations were modified as parent bases for the V-force, Finningley, Scampton, Waddington, Coningsby, Cottesmore, Wittering, Wyton, Marham, and Honington, whilst training was undertaken at Gaydon. Again, the distribution of these bases centred on the east coast running in a line from Doncaster down to Cambridge; the two nuclear storage depots are at either end of this diffused line. Designated 'Class One' airfields, the most noticeable development was the construction of a singular 9,000ft runway capable of carrying aircraft weighing around 90 tons. New briefing rooms and flight simulators are also a feature of the upgrades as are new workshop facilities for avionic equipment servicing and increased dispersal capacity. Sites also saw a new type of purpose-built hangar, capable of taking the new aircraft. The first, built at Gaydon in 1954 by Laing Construction, was the first of a number that appeared on the V-force stations. Subsequently they became known as Gaydon Hangars after that original build. On top of this the main runway was provided with an Operational Readiness Platform (ORP) with a direct link to the end of the strip. The bomb storage site on station was also redesigned. The unarmed nuclear weapon was brought by road from the PAD to the station where it was taken to the Unit Store, as the bomb dump was now named, and armed.

Naturally the modifications for the heavier aircraft were going to be expensive, and for a cash-strapped Government some prioritising would be needed. By the mid-1950s another consideration had to be considered: public opposition.

> Prime Minister
>
> You will remember that the Lord Privy Seal is concerned about the proposal to develop Scampton Airfield, near Lincoln, for use by modern bombers. When the Cabinet considered this matter on March 17 they agreed to look at it again when the Secretary of State for Air had carried out the normal consultations with the Departments and local interests affected. This process has now been completed, but the local opposition to the project is still strongly maintained.
>
> (Harris, Air Ministry, 4 September 1954 (PRO CAB 21/3182))

Other stations had been considered for the V-force; in fact quite a number were still on the Air Ministry's inventory, the majority either utilised as training bases or in an advanced stage of 'Care and Maintenance'. Further, with money being spent in other areas it had become apparent that the Air Ministry could not afford to keep all this development 'in house':

> It was during the course of 1951 that the Air Ministry first authorised the expenditure of considerable sums of money at Sturgate. By September 1953 when, so far as I can trace, we received the first objections to the development of Scampton, we were committed to spend about £400,000 at Sturgate and had in fact spent the greater part of this sum.
>
> (C. Davis, Private Secretary, 2 October 1954 (PRO CAB 21/3182))

The problems arose when it was discovered that Hemswell, a first choice site, especially since it was further away from a major population centre, would need a substantial amount of groundwork before a runway capable of taking the Vulcan could be built. Scampton was, the Air Ministry assured, the best location in the area. Actually, if finance had not been directed to Sturgate for the USAF the cost would have been no problem. Subsequently, the matter was decided by the Home Secretary:

> The Home Secretary, the Minister of Labour and the President of the Board of Trade have completed within the fortnight prescribed by the Cabinet their examination of the relative costs of developing Scampton and Hemswell as a medium bomber base. Their conclusions support the view of the Secretary of State for Air that Scampton must be preferred to Hemswell because the latter's development would – cost £1.63 millions more; involve abandonment of the American base at Sturgate on which £½ million has already been spent.
>
> Subject to any further points which the Lord Privy Seal may wish to raise, the way seems to be clear for the Cabinet finally to approve development of Scampton.
>
> (Home Secretary's Office, 4 October 1954 (PRO CAB 21/3182))

During the closing stages of the Second World War Germany had hinted at the shape of warfare to come in the shape of the V weapons. The V1 was the first of the cruise missiles but the V2 was something far more sinister to which there was no known antidote, and the concept was not lost on the USA, Soviet Union or Britain. After the war all three Governments were engaged in the development of rocket technology; however, it was the Soviets who first demonstrated, in August 1957, a vehicle capable of striking the United States from Central Europe. The spectre of a pre-emptive strike on the west spurred the American Government on and by the end of 1957 it had successfully tested an Intermediate Range Ballistic Missile (ICBM) capable of carrying a 1.4 megaton warhead a maximum distance of 1,500 miles. To make the weapon system effective, the US had to station Thor close to the Soviet Union; Britain had already signed a bilateral agreement to accept the missile as a stopgap. Its own developments, the Medium Range Ballistic Missile (MRBM), Blue Streak and the V-force stand-off vehicle Blue Steel were some way off, leaving the country vulnerable with only a manned deterrent.

## Thor

Twenty bases were utilised as part of this change in policy, driven by the Defence White Paper of 1957. In it Duncan Sandys, recently appointed Minister for Defence, initiated major cost-saving cuts by demonstrating that missile technology made the role of the fighter/interceptor obsolete and that the high-flying bomber could be replaced by the ICBM. He also forced the many aircraft manufacturers still in Britain to merge, most recognisably under the British Aircraft Corporation umbrella. In a stroke the direction of the air force changed. Now the policy was officially one of a strong deterrent, coupled with the end of National Service by 1960 and the reduction of Britain's overseas commitments. Thor was also seen by the Government as an attempt to win back favour with Washington after the disastrous Suez campaign – America had failed to support the venture whilst the Soviets had used the situation to mask the put down of the Hungarian Uprising. Harold Macmillan agreed to accept the missile system at the Bermuda Conference in March 1957. The following February (1958) the Government signed a joint agreement starting Project Emily; sixty Thor IRBMs would be stationed in eastern Britain, allowing RAF servicemen to gain valuable experience in the handling of both rocket and nuclear technology.

Four stations were chosen to host the missiles and each was responsible for four satellite bases. The four parent stations, Driffield, North Luffenham, Feltwell and Hemswell, were all expansion period bases offering permanent hangars with substantial single-messing arrangements and married accommodation. Each station was provided with a secure launch compound, often on the other side of the airfield to the technical site. Contained within this were three launch pads connected to all the required services, including power, light, liquid oxygen and fuel. Naturally these missiles were stationed at sites away from the intended V-force. However, to be effective they needed to be as close to the coast as was physically possible. The distribution of all Thor bases, both HQ and satellite, demonstrate this. Subsequently they run in an arc from East Yorkshire through to East Anglia. This was the case at Carnaby and Breighton, both satellites of Driffield. The first missiles were deployed at Feltwell, Norfolk, in September 1958 with No.77 Squadron, whilst the last squadron (No.144) stood down in August 1963 from North Luffenham.

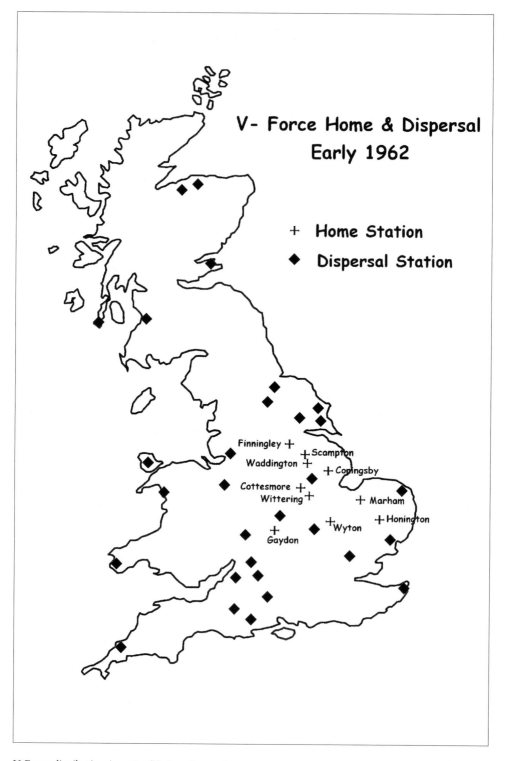

V-Force distribution in 1962. (Various Sources)

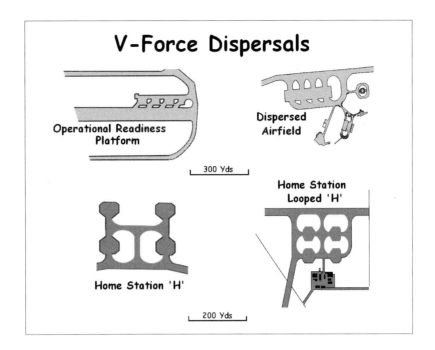

V-Force
dispersals in
the United
Kingdom.

## *Dispersal*

In an attempt to counter the impact of a pre-emptive strike, a series of dispersal airfields were identified around the British Isles, to which the V-force could be dispatched at times of international tension. The choice of airfields is again dominated by those airfields containing permanent pre-war constructions, but their distribution mirrors the concerns clearly felt within the Air Ministry. The fleet was to be scattered across a further thirty-two airfields plus those that remained at one of the ten parent bases and this time the distribution was country wide. Airfields across Britain were to become hosts to either two or four aircraft. To support this Operational Readiness Platforms (ORP) were constructed and provided with rudimentary service buildings. In the West Country, Kemble, Lyneham, Filton, Boscombe Down, St Mawgan, Tarrant Rushton and Yeovilton were all designated dispersed sites. Others could be dispatched to Kinloss, Lossiemouth, Leuchars, Prestwick or Machrihanish in Scotland, Ballykelly or Aldergrove in Northern Ireland, Brawdy, Llanbedr or Valley in Wales. Whilst in the North and Midlands Middleton St George, Leeming, Carnaby, Elvington, Leconfield, Burtonwood, Cranwell, Shawbury, Bruntingthorpe, Pershore, Coltishall, Stansted, Wattisham, Bedford and Manston were to be used. It would appear that the only criterion for the choice of airfield is that it had a long enough runway to facilitate the take-off and landing of the aircraft. Some airfields such as Shawbury, Boscombe Down, Leconfield, Pershore and Leeming were provided with a specific ORP which allows the aircraft to taxi straight in and back out again without the aid of a tug. Other sites utilised existing facilities. No distinction is made as to the primary function of the base concerned; dispersals occur on training, fighter, transport and bomber stations demonstrating the initial difficulties faced by the investigator.

*Above:* RAF Boscombe Down, 1957. By now Boscombe Down had a complete mixture of architectural types. The six seen here date from the expansion, wartime and Cold War periods. (Courtesy of the Ministry of Defence)

*Left:* A line up of nine Avro Vulcan B2s at RAF Scampton in 1961. The Vulcan is probably one of most iconic aircraft of the Cold War period. Its deployment throughout the 1960s ensured the survival of over thirty RAF stations.

## MAD

Throughout the 1950s the entire doctrine of defence, culminating in the 1957 Defence White Paper, was concerned with the aptly titled Mutually Assured Destruction (MAD). Any form of aggression would bring about the annihilation of the perpetrator; naturally both east and west supported this. The role of the RAF was to support MAD by having V-force aircraft in the air and on the way to their targets within four minutes. To ensure this occurred the airfields, and in the late 1950s this included the twenty Thor bases, were protected by Bloodhound and a limited fighter response framework. By 1967 it was clear that if conflict was to erupt it was more likely to involve conventional weapons, at least from the outset. Subsequently NATO adopted 'Flexible Response', basically meeting like with like. This change of policy also had an element of American self-preservation. A limited nuclear war in Europe would be costly but the effects on the United States would hopefully not be too bad, however by the mid-1960s the Soviets had produced enough Intercontinental Ballistic Missiles (ICBM) to hit the US hard. Clearly now Moscow could not be threatened without global ramifications; subsequently NATO, whose biggest funding nation was the US, changed its policy.

Whilst these monumental changes to defence policy were being pushed through, the airfield estate was being slowly reduced. Britain still contained thousands of acres of redundant land, some being leased out by the Government. Two radically different stations serve to demonstrate this.

### Skellingthorpe

Immediate post-war disposals took some time to organise, especially since other Government departments might be interested. One such base was Skellingthorpe, a few miles to the west of Lincoln. The airfield was opened to flying in October 1941 but was not fully completed until 1942. It was home to a number of Bomber Command squadrons flying Hampdens, Manchesters and Lancasters under the command of No.53 Base Station at Waddington. After the war the site was handed over to No.58 Maintenance Unit who set about reducing aircraft to scrap, and by 1952 the airfield was deserted:

> Note
> This airfield was considered by the US of S. Working Party on Inactive airfields (fourth meeting) and it was subsequently agreed that so far as the Air Ministry is concerned it could be disposed of.
>
> (E.R.Bevan, 9 December 1955 (PRO AIR 2/17807))

As with so much land that had been requisitioned over the war, the next course of action should have been to offer the land back to those who had lost it in the first place. However, the site was offered around to other Government departments first:

> Please see Encl.2A in which MAFF say that there are no agricultural grounds for the purchase of the requisitioned land at Skellingthorpe. No bids have been received from other Government departments to take transfer of this airfield. Perhaps you will arrange for us to be informed of the de-requisitioning date eventually decided.
>
> (R.L. Bridger, 27 March 1956 (PRO AIR 2/17807))

By June 1956 the buildings on site, especially the hangars, were up for sale and shortly afterwards removed along with some other structures. Unfortunately an electricity conduit was still surviving across the land and for some reason the Government wanted it removed before the land could be derequisitioned. Other facilities were also causing interest, especially for the Ministry of Housing and Local Government, who were on the lookout for building land:

> It is noted that the City of Lincoln proposes, inter alia, to include Skellingthorpe Airfield within the Borough boundaries and we can see no objection to this course, in fact we view the proposal very favourably. With respect to the sewage disposal works, these are on requisitioned land, the requisition being transferred outright to the Ministry of Health in 1946.
>
> (N.N. Forster, 14 October 1957 (PRO AIR 2/17807))

The boundary change was effective from 1 April 1959, although the Ministry still made no move to derequisition the land. On 4 August 1960 a letter set out what was holding up the process:

> Unfortunately the sale back has not yet been commenced. The delay is because the purchaser of the cable conduit cannot remove it until the barley crop on the whole of the land involved has been harvested.
>
> (PRO AIR 2/17807)

By December it looked like the cable had been removed but bad weather was delaying the refill of the site. In 1962 the land eventually reverted back to the owner, who promptly sold it for building. Very little survives today as the entire area is covered with substantial housing development. The point is this protracted process was nothing new and was being played out up and down the country irrespective of size or volume of disposal land.

### Alton Barnes

Alton Barnes had been a grass field strip, open since 1935 and eventually became the satellite for No.29 Elementary Flying Training School at Clyffe Pypard. The majority of the land reverted, as did that forming the flying field at Clyffe Pypard, back to agriculture during 1945. However the land covering the few temporary brick structures and three blister hangars remained in Ministry hands until the mid-1960s.

In May 1968 2.3 acres were sold back to New College, Oxford, by the Defence Land Agent based at Durrington, South Wiltshire, for £250. The college had had the land requisitioned when the site was expanded in 1940. The land, situated next to the road through the village, became the location for the offices, a link trainer building and a few air raid shelters. Local landowner Captain Lane also had land taken. The problems started when the Ministry of Defence, in existence since 1964, came to dispose of the site. What follows serves to demonstrate the complexities of returning land back to its original owner, especially if they take matters into their own hands.

Wherever possible the Ministry tried to hand back land with the original boundaries, and in the majority of cases this was possible. The problem with Alton Barnes was that the land taken from Oxford and Lane (originally a fence stood between the two) had been used for buildings. One structure straddled the boundary, making it impossible to return the original boundary whilst it still stood. Subsequently the boundary had been changed and Oxford benefited. Captain Lane was having none of it and took matters into his own hands:

> Captain Lane has changed his mind on several occasions during negotiations, and has arranged for the demolition of the buildings on the land that is to be conveyed to him without permission. In the circumstances MOD cannot be held responsible for his having cleared the building or a section of the building on the land [boundary]. Irrespective of what Captain Lane says I feel that it was the intention of the parties to convey the land he formally owned excluding the triangle due to the boundary difficulty caused by the presence of the building.
>
> (A. Lodge, Lands 2a, 17 September 1968 (PRO DEFE 51/1))

The Estates Office at Durrington was not very impressed. When the land had been re-surveyed it had been made clear that the boundary was different. Basically if Captain Lane did not accept the terms then the land was to be offered for auction. Clearly about to lose out, Lane accepted the conditions on 22 November. To put this in perspective, 444 airfields were built or extended during the Second World War so it is no wonder land disputes were rattling up and down the country for the next thirty years. The situation had been brought to a head in 1954 with the Crichel Down Affair, claiming the head of Government Minister Sir Thomas Dugdale. The Air Ministry had requisitioned 725 acres of land for £12,000 in 1938 to use as a bombing range. When it came to dispose of the area the Air Ministry transferred it to the Ministry of Agriculture who promptly inflated the value to way beyond what it was worth. The original owner could not afford the hike. Subsequently the Ministry rented the land out as a going concern. The situation forced a public inquiry and it found in favour of the original owner. From then on in, land had to be offered back to its rightful owner, and only after they were consulted could it be disposed of by auction.

## Second Fiddle

The story of the Royal Navy controlling the deterrent through Polaris is complex. The 1950s V-force was armed with a myriad of freefall nuclear weapons including Blue Danube, Red Beard, Violet Club and the aptly named Yellow Sun. Throughout the 1950s an ambitious scheme to develop a joint Medium Range Ballistic Missile to complement the Americans' Atlas ICBM was proposed. Unfortunately Washington legislated against the exchange of nuclear technologies through the McMahon Act; undeterred the British persevered. Operational Requirement (OR) 1139 issued in 1955 laid down two primary objectives – a missile that could strike Moscow and do it with a thermonuclear warhead. At the time Britain could do neither. A large number of civilian aerospace firms were drafted in to the development of Blue Streak, causing major logistical headaches, and as if that was not bad enough, the Air Ministry amended OR 1139 to include underground silos, again an unknown quantity at this time. By 1960 the project had cost £60 million

Disarmament talks at the United Nations in November 1968. Diplomacy was a constant tool against conflict throughout the Cold War period.

and was projected to eventually run to £450 million. The Treasury looked for a way out, as did the Air Ministry, and they found it in Skybolt, an American standoff missile.

Skybolt was Strategic Air Command's weapon of choice for the B52H platform. A stand-off weapon, designed to be air launched outside Soviet territory, it carried a thermonuclear warhead around 1,000 miles. The Treasury liked the idea as Avro was in the process of designing a similar weapon, Blue Steel, to be carried by the Victor and Vulcan. Acquiring Skybolt would allow that to be cancelled. Unfortunately disaster struck when the US Government unceremoniously cancelled the project, leaving the Air Ministry with nothing – except Blue Steel. The first rounds were issued to No.617 Squadron in October 1962. Unfortunately the delivery technique, launching at high level, was now obsolete, as demonstrated in 1960 when a Soviet SAM brought down a U2 over their territory. Through the early 1960s low-level flying tactics were developed but the possibility of success carrying Blue Steel was considered negligible. By 1970 Blue Steel was decommissioned, the Victor had been reassigned to the tanker role and the Vulcan fleet was being reduced. Royal Navy Polaris submarines, through an agreement between Macmillan and Kennedy, in the wake of the Skybolt affair, took over the deterrent in mid-1969 with patrols initially by HMS *Resolution*. This did not mean the end for the RAF's nuclear capability – indeed, WE-177, a freefall device in operation from 1966, was the primary tactical weapon until 1995.

From the 1970s the story of British airfields is one of accelerated reduction. The increasing role of the RAF within NATO streamlined some operations down to bare limits and this, coupled with ever-decreasing commitments overseas, allowed the Treasury to make swathing cuts to the Ministry of Defence estate. The effects of the 1960s cancellations and Defence White Papers began to bite hard into the airfield inventory throughout the 1970s. Reductions in the Army and Navy flying commitments also saw the reduction of stations controlled by them. That said, the disposal of airfields was limited as the majority were to be placed in care and maintenance – just in case.

## Realignment

At the end of the 1960s it had become apparent that the Royal Air Force had been reduced to a size that did not warrant the Four Command structure. Subsequently two iconic names, Fighter and Bomber Command, were merged into a new organisation – Strike Command. By 1972 Transport and Coastal Command had also gone. Strike Command had responsibility for all home and overseas operations, bar RAF Germany. It had four main objectives, to protect the United Kingdom against all air attack; provide a combat ready air force for direction by NATO; to participate in NATO directed nuclear programmes, and support NATO General Defence Plan. Strike Command was by the mid-1970s reduced to four groups in the United Kingdom, Nos 1, 11, 18 and 38, with a fifth covering Cyprus.

This initiated a further round of station closures. Colerne and Thorney Island, both home at the time to Hercules aircraft, were closed in 1976; however, both received a reprieve a few years later when the army took over. A similar fate awaited Leconfield, Driffield and Rufforth. These initial takeovers were as much to do with escaping the, by now, inadequate Victorian facilities most Army camps endured as anything else. The Army

Protection against chemical attack or nuclear fallout became a preoccupation for the services from the late 1950s. The emphasis was on personal protection, very little was done to modify airfield structures in case of either. Subsequently evidence is difficult to find.

reoccupying airfield locations was to become a reoccurring theme throughout the late 1980s and early 1990s, but for a different reason. Then it was to house battalions returning from Germany as part of 'Options for Change'. Throughout the 1970s the aircraft fleet also saw a reduction in types operated, as first the de Havilland Comet, then Bristol Britannia, and finally the very capable Short Belfast, were all disposed of. More was to come with the reduction of Andovers, Lightnings and a number of other obsolete types. With this and organisational realignment it is now possible to describe both the groups and note the operational stations as they stood in 1980.

## No.1 Group

No.1 Group's main function was to control strike, attack, reconnaissance and tanker force operation and training requirements. Strike aircraft were based at Honington, Lossiemouth, Marham, Waddington, Wyton and Brize Norton. These six widespread airfields contained a bewildering array of aircraft spanning three decades including Buccaneers, Vulcans, Hunters, Nimrods, Andovers, Victors and VC10s. In the event of war the whole of the group would be committed to NATO, conducting conventional and nuclear strikes as directed by Supreme Air Commander Europe (SACEUR).

Panavia Tornado. The Tornado became the mainstay of the RAF throughout the 1980s and '90s; only now are they being replaced by the long-overdue Typhoon.

### No.11 Group

No.11 Group's primary concern was the air defence of the British Isles. Beyond the domestic commitment No.11 Group were also an integral part of the NATO air defence network. As with other groups, a bewildering array of aircraft was employed for the task including Lightnings, Phantoms, and Hunters, and at the beginning of the 1980s, the Air Defence Variant (ADV) Tornado. Up to the end of the Cold War, Bloodhound was also under No.11 Group control. The network was controlled through a series of Sector Operations Centres that received information from sources all over Europe. By the mid-1970s the primary interceptor was the Phantom, slowly taking over from the fuel thirsty, if effective, Lightning. Air Defence stations were Binbrook, Lossiemouth, Coningsby, Leuchars and Wattisham. These were complemented by the introduction of Hawks in 1976 based at Brawdy and Chivenor.

### No.18 Group

The primary function of No.18 Group was maritime defence. Naturally with over 1,000 miles of coastline and substantial territorial waters, specialist equipment was needed. This came in the form of squadrons comprising the Nimrod, based at St Mawgan and Kinloss, and from the early 1980s Buccaneer in the anti-shipping role from Lossiemouth. No.18 Group also operated a number of launches from around Britain's coastline as well as the

RAF Colerne, Wiltshire, 1966. A Handley Page Hastings next to an expansion period C-Type hangar. By 1976 the RAF Transport fleet had been concentrated at Lyneham and Brize Norton, initiating the closure of many stations, including this one.

air-sea rescue aspect of pilot rescue. Helicopters utilised were stationed at airfields close to the coast such as St Mawgan and Leconfield, and through the years included Whirlwind, Wessex and Seaking.

## No. 38 Group

No. 38 Group can trace its roots back to the Army Co-operation Squadrons of the early expansion period; indeed, the HQ was until the mid-1980s located at Upavon. Battlefield support was offered through a number of different media – Harriers from Wittering and Jaguars based at Coltishall from the 1970s being the most potent. Wessex at Aldergrove, Pumas from Odiham and Chinooks from November 1980 performed battlefield support roles and equipment transport. To facilitate theatre movements Andovers, Hercules, Belfasts, VC10s and from the early 1980s Tristars operated from Brize Norton, Lyneham, Northolt and Benson. No. 38 also operated the Queen's Flight from Benson.

What is really striking here is the rapid reduction in airfields fully operational in an offensive or defensive role by the early 1980s. Naturally the position of these stations has as much to do with the perceived threat as anything else. Aldergrove continued to be active due to the troubles throughout the previous two decades, with No. 38 Group helicopters in the ground support role as well as Army Air Corps Lynx and Gazelle. By 1980 the reduction was such that stations became the sole homes to many specific

Harrier Hide. With the introduction of the Harrier the services became less reliant on fixed airfield structures. Note this aircraft is parked on PSP.

types. One station, Lyneham, perhaps demonstrates this better than most. Often referred to in the press as 'home to the giant Hercules transport aircraft', the Hercules had until 1976 resided at Thorney Island and Colerne as well, both incidentally early expansion period stations. The Hercules moved to Lyneham from these two bases on closure whilst a further squadron arrived from Akrotiri after unrest in Cyprus. Other such bases in a similar situation were Wittering with the Harrier and Coltishall with the Jaguar.

The Soviet air threat continued to develop during the late 1960s, driving the RAF to increase its fighter defence with No.11 Group and introduce Airborne Early Warning (AEW) aircraft as an attempt to detect intruders earlier. With nothing contemporary in the pipeline the MOD fell back on an old type – the Shackleton. Designated AEW.2, a number were serviced and then fitted with chin-mounted AN/APS 20 radars taken from scrapped Fleet Air Arm Gannets. They were subsequently stationed at Lossiemouth, the closest base to the perceived threat. Most alarming in the Soviets' arsenal was the TU-95 Bear, the fastest turbo-prop to enter service with any airforce. This formidable weapons platform had the ability to launch up to ten standoff and later cruise missiles at the United Kingdom. This was complemented in the mid-1970s by the TU-22 Backfire, a swing wing bomber, again with potent potential. To counter this threat, fighter defence was mounted from Leuchars and Lossiemouth, along with a more general air defence network already described in No.11 Group above.

No.53 Field Support Squadron (Airfields) at Waterbeach Barracks, Cambridge, 1975. The legacy of the Airfield Construction Service and Works Repair Depots, Field Support Squadrons were deployed around the world. (Courtesy of Nick Rayner)

RAF Church Fenton, Yorkshire, late 1970s. A Mk3 Jet Provost on the apron. A number of Bomber Command bases were utilised for the operation of the Jet Provost, including Linton-on-Ouse, Leeming, Topcliffe and Dishforth.

RAF Upper Heyford, Oxfordshire, in 2005. The hardening up of airfields changed the landscape on a number of airfields across Britain and was the final large-scale construction programme of airfield histories.

## Training

By the 1970s a comprehensive aircrew training programme formed the backbone of the RAF's all-through jet training. The primary aircraft had become, by 1970, the Jet Provost and it was stationed across a number of airfields, especially those located in Yorkshire. In 1980 these included Leeming, Topcliffe, Dishforth, Church Fenton, and Linton-on-Ouse. The type was also found at Brawdy, Finningley, Cranwell and a number of other stations in support roles for weapons training and navigation. Advanced jet training was undertaken at Valley, Chivenor and Brawdy, the last two also being Tactical Weapons Training. Rotary wing based at Shawbury was complemented by conversion units around the UK. All these stations were well appointed, making use of the extensive hangarage to house fleets of aircraft, sometimes fifty strong.

## Hardened

One development that was to have a major impact on Britain's landscape was the introduction of the hardened airfield. Already a feature of RAF Germany, now added protection appeared on a number of sites on the mainland. Their addition was the result of events in the Middle East in 1967 when the Israeli Air Force effectively destroyed the majority of Egypt's aircraft on the ground. This was not the first time the luckless Egyptians were taken by surprise; during the Suez Crisis the RAF had carried out the same mission, again reducing the number of serviceable aircraft to next to nothing. However, it was the lightning war that was to change the face of the British airfield landscape. Throughout

RAF Greenham Common, Berkshire, in 2005. The Cruise Missile Control Centre. Note the sunken bunker on the right-hand end of the structure. From the late 1970s airfield use became increasingly more specialised.

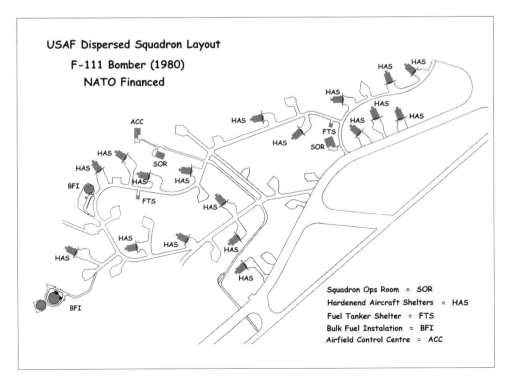

A typical hardened airfield layout.

RAF Upper Heyford, Oxfordshire, in 2005. Quick Reaction Area including temporary covers to hide armed aircraft from both the English weather and spy satellites.

the 1970s the practice of Quick Reaction Alert dictated that at least two fighter aircraft were ready for immediate take off at each air defence base. In a similar vein aircraft, by now armed with free fall WE177s, were also on standby. In an attempt to keep the aircraft serviceable for longer they were often parked under rudimentary shelters to keep the weather off; however, by the mid-1970s the spy satellite phenomena had reached maturity and the shelters helped conceal what type of aircraft, how many and, on occasion, what armament they were carrying from prying eyes. Whilst these shelters covered the aircraft they afforded no physical protection from attack, and the aircraft could conceivably be knocked out with little effort.

The realisation that a pre-emptive strike could give the enemy the tactical advantage had been recognised for a decade; however, NATO's chief financier, Washington, had been spending the majority of its defence budget on the Vietnam War. Subsequently it was not until the late 1970s that the first Hardened Aircraft Shelters (HAS) appeared in Britain. The hardening up of airfields was without doubt the last major work carried out on a national scale. Subsequently, the numerous structures encountered with this process nicely date the airfields that were considered important assets during the late 1970s through to the mid-1980s. The first thing to note is the reversion to dispersed sites. Post-war the trend, excluding the V-force, was towards lining aircraft up on the pan in front of the technical site. This had as much to do with the type of airfield retained as anything else. By the mid-1970s the vast majority of stations with temporary buildings had been disposed of and after 1976 this had started to include those with permanent architecture.

Leonid Brezhnev addressing troops in 1964. His death on 10 November 1982 proved to be the catalyst for the collapse of the Soviet Union.

Solidarity in Gdansk, Poland, 1981. Poland was the political catalyst for the mass migrations seen across Europe in the late 1980s and indirectly led to the demilitarisation of Eastern Europe.

Those that remained had become more centralised in both aircraft types and the roles they performed. Surprisingly, in most cases these stations suffered the legacy of the First World War Training Depot Stations. At the time, held up as innovative, the construction of technical and domestic sites in two distinct areas had been continued by the designers of the late 1930s expansion period. Now with the retention of these stations at the expense of the dispersed sites from the war, aircraft were clearly easy targets. The programme of construction started in 1977 with work at Bentwaters, Woodbridge and slightly later Lakenheath. Alconbury, Upper Heyford and Boscombe Down saw construction start in 1979. Furthermore, other stations received HAS including Honington, Marham and Wattisham and the final completion of RAF Leeming, designated an Air Defence Station, in the mid-1980s.

Naturally the architecture is distinctive. HAS were laid out across the airfield and a number of other important structures were hardened. In a return to the dispersal of assets a number of HAS, usually enough to contain a squadron, were built at one specific location. Each was furnished with a protected squadron HQ, structures for bowsers and electrical generation. A number of other buildings were provided, including a station HQ to control both aircraft and airfield security, a telephone exchange, a bomb store and bulk fuel installations. Specialist structures such as the avionics centre at Upper Heyford also made an appearance at this time signalling the end of standard airfield construction in favour of specifically designed buildings. Probably the most contentious issue throughout the early 1980s was the introduction of Cruise missiles in Britain and across Western Europe. One airfield in particular, Greenham Common, became synonymous with both the weapon and protests against them; however other stations benefited from their arrival. As a precaution against air attack Washington financed the formation of three Rapier squadrons, stationed at Brize Norton, West Raynham and Honington. Weston-on-the-Green became home to No. 19 Squadron, who used the station for exercise. However, air attack, or indeed any attack, never materialised as by 1984 the Soviet leadership was in crisis.

Events in the east, especially through the success of 'Solidarity' in Poland and the resurgence of democracy in Hungary, sent shock waves through the Warsaw Pact countries. By early 1989, Mikhail Gorbachev had announced his intention to remove over 50,000 troops from client regime territories. On 9 November 1989 the Berlin Wall was breached and less than two years later the Soviet one-party system lay in tatters. On the 25 December 1991 the Soviet Union was relegated to the history books as the red flag was lowered over the Kremlin for the last time. A reduction of defence spending around the world was now inevitable. Strangely, some British airfields were initially to benefit from this reduction.

eight

# OPTIONS FOR CHANGE
# AND THE FUTURE

With the end of the Cold War the United Kingdom, like many other nations, sought to position itself in the 'New World Order'. It was to find that position in the deserts of Iraq, ironically the very place Trenchard had demonstrated the worth of an independent air force some seventy years before. Reduction of the number of airfields in Britain has gathered pace since 1991 and many in Government openly questioned the wisdom of such swathing cuts in national defence. With the Royal Air Force having just sixty-three sites on its books at present (2007), and that includes all non-flying stations, the critics may well be right. However, we are not here to debate defence policy, only use it as an instrument to interpret. It is customary in books of this type to demand action, cite lost examples and point the finger at the impotence of both Government and Heritage bodies, but however tempting it may be to do so, it would simply not be justified. A vast amount of work has been carried out in the last decade to ensure representative sites do survive. Here then is the final chapter in the story of our airfields, covering the rapid reduction of the aerodromes coupled with renewed interest from conservation groups.

*Drawdown*
The first major effect the collapse of the Soviet Union had was the reduction of American forces committed to Europe. By the mid-1980s US principle airfields in Britain included Alconbury, Bentwaters, Fairford, Greenham Common, Lakenheath, Mildenhall, Molesworth, Upper Heyford and Woodbridge. Sculthorpe, Wethersfield and Boscombe Down were designated reserve stations and sites such as Filton and Kemble were involved in the maintenance of F-111 and A-10 respectively. As it became clear that a major NATO force in Europe would no longer be required, these stations began 'draw down'. The reduction was quick, especially since a number of USAF squadrons were quickly deployed to the Gulf and stood down from there. The MOD also took the opportunity to start clearing out some stations that were surplus or deemed to become so in the near future. Cardington, Hendon, Lee-on-Solent, Binbrook, Watton, Tranwell, and Bicester, along with acres of married quarters, were placed on the disposals list in mid-1990.

By 1990 it was clear that the Soviet system was on the point of collapse; what lay ahead was an unclear future for millions.

Boris Yeltsin at a press conference in late 1991. Yeltsin oversaw the collapse of the Soviet system leading to the 'Options for Change' legislation of the mid-1990s. Recently his time in office has been called 'catastroika'!

The end came swiftly for many stations. Archie Hamilton, junior in the Ministry of Defence, reiterated a number of closures:

> It was announced in the statement on the Defence estimates that RAF Abingdon would close by May 1993. We now plan closure on 31 July 1992. The flying units from Abingdon, which comprise the Oxford and London university air squadrons and No. 6 Air Experience Flight will move to RAF Benson in July. Following the announced withdrawal of the USAF from RAF Kemble it will no longer be economic to maintain the RAF maintenance tasks at the base. It is proposed that airfield operations should end on 31 March 1992 – when US flying will also cease – and that the RAF will withdraw by 31 July 1992. In the meantime the Army will use RAF Kemble for vehicle storage on a temporary basis, while reviewing its longer term requirement for such a facility.
>
> All flying training at RAF Brawdy will cease on 31 August 1992 as part of the general reorganisation of advanced flying and tactical weapons training which will be concentrated at RAF Valley and RAF Chivenor. RAF Brawdy will remain open and possible alternative uses will be explored.
>
> (Rt Hon. Archie Hamilton, House of Commons Written Answers for
> 24 January 1992, column 378)

RAF Kemble, Wiltshire, in 2007. The emphasis is now on re-use rather than clearance on some airfields. At Kemble, the Historic Environment is being enhanced by the sympathetic refurbishment of expansion period structures for business use.

Finningley survived for a while as a new course for navigators was introduced utilising Bulldog, Dominies, Tucanos and Hawk, much the same as the South Yorkshire station had already been covering from the late 1970s. However, this did not last long:

> The closure of RAF Finningley has been proposed following a thorough review of all flying training in the RAF. That review sought to identify the most cost-effective utilisation of the RAF training estate as a whole.
>
> (Rt Hon. Nicolas Soames, House of Commons Written Answers for
> 23 February 1995, column 334)

Incidentally, Finningley was placed on 'care and maintenance' after it was closed on 31 March 1996. It was sold in 1999 to a private firm and is now Robin Hood Airport. Even care and maintenance had its price — in the years between closure and sale the station cost the tax payer £803,633! Just two weeks later (5 March 1996) there were more closures as Soames informed Parliament that the following RAF stations were in the course of disposal: Greenham Common, Upper Heyford, Elvington, Bentwaters, Alconbury and Burtonwood. West Raynham, Swinderby, Binbrook, Medmenham and Kenley were also to go, and if that was not enough, he warned that:

Additionally, there are a number of other stations currently under consideration for alternative defence use and which may ultimately be passed for disposal, and others where some land is surplus to requirements and is either in disposal or may be passed for disposal.

Quite a number of airfields, especially close to Salisbury Plain, were retained and continue to survive due to the draw down of forces in Germany. Troops there had been used to modern facilities and now with their impending return required accommodation. The problem was the majority of barracks in the United Kingdom were built in the Victorian period and had facilities to match. Subsequently RAF stations became the natural choice. In the majority they dated from the 1930s, although married quarters could be 1960s or on occasion later.

Obviously, our first requirement when we remove a particular RAF unit from, say, an RAF base is to find an alternative defence use for it. If a use could not be found, we would negotiate with local councils and planning authorities as to the best use for the site. I assure the hon. Gentleman that where we use an RAF base for which there is no longer a Royal Air Force need, say, to accommodate an Army battalion, we do so merely because otherwise we should have to put that battalion in a place that might be more expensive or build new accommodation. The problem arises particularly with the draw-down of forces from Germany, Belize and Hong Kong. There has been a great need, particularly with the draw-down from Germany, to find alternative accommodation. Therefore, RAF bases, with their excellent accommodation and housing, have been used fairly regularly. I assure the hon. Gentleman that we seek to use the estate efficiently and effectively. Our policy is that, if there is no defence need, we sell the site to the broader community.

(Rt Hon. J. Hanley, House of Commons Written Answers for
27 January 1994, column 443)

In this way, Colerne, South Cerney, Hullavington, Upavon, Netheravon, Driffield and Bassingbourn were all saved from disposal. Others have not faired so well. Burtonwood was quickly cleared. Cardington has only two structures left on it – the massive airship sheds. Swinderby is in the process of being reduced for housing and business development, as has been the camp at Filton. Newton, closed in 2004, is under a planning proposal for housing and others must surely be ready to go the same way. If we look into the future, things look uncertain for Cosford, Halton, Lyneham and Chivenor.

The ironic thing is that we have been here before. The effects of the end of the Cold War and subsequent 'Options for Change' can be mirrored in the run down of all airfields across the United Kingdom after the First World War. If you remember, the argument in the 1920s was that we had no need for national air defence, especially one undertaken by an independent air force. What seems clear is that the RAF and the airfields that remain may once again owe their continued survival to a war fought in Iraq, just like the Aerial Policing that demonstrated the young forces' worth in the 1920s. But what of those 'historic' remains? This is, after all, an archaeology of airfields, so the question must be should we consider anything for preservation, especially since everything is less than 100 years old and connected with that most contentious of modern issues, warfare?

## Revere or Remove

Put in its simplest terms we would be lacking in judgement if we didn't consider such sites worthy of protection. Airfields, like any other archaeological resources, are finite. Remember the Government has not built a new one since 1945 but has continued to reduce their number from that date. It is worth exploring the preservation already experienced on a number of sites to demonstrate that, contrary to popular belief, statutory protection is available for aerodromes.

Our first military airfield site was Larkhill, closely followed by Netheravon and Upavon. Surprisingly the latter two airfields survive almost complete, demonstrating the development of airfield structures across a sixty-year period. Without doubt the key to their survival is their location on Salisbury Plain, the primary reason for their initial construction. Larkhill has lost the majority of its buildings; however, the British and Colonial Aircraft Company (BCAC) sheds are now listed. A similar situation can be found at both Upavon and Netheravon.

Since 1994 English Heritage has been working on the problem of how best to protect military remains, and have been in close contact with the Ministry of Defence, Central and Local Government, and the owners of the former Defence Estate. The Thematic Listing Programme, as the name implies, has been, in this case, concerned with military aviation sites and structures across the country. Due to the MOD's initial reluctance to give up any airfields, no matter how tenuous the argument for retention, English Heritage has got a good head start. There are some points to consider here. An airfield is a massive area, often in excess of 500 acres. Often the structures concerned are so specialist as to make the cost of converting them prohibitive. In the case of wartime buildings their very construction can render them unsafe unless they have been consistently maintained from new. Maintenance has to be carried out sympathetically, and if the roofing and windows have been replaced with something not in keeping, or if inappropriate additions have been made, the chance of protection is reduced. And most importantly, who pays?

In April 2000 a team headed by Jeremy Lake at English Heritage published the *Survey of Military Aviation Sites and Structures; Summary Report*. In this, English Heritage took a step back from the traditional 'listing buildings by type' process and investigated the wider picture. Over 200 recommendations were made, this time from a landscape perspective. From this pivotal moment on, all of us who work on airfields have been able to demonstrate that the conservation effort should not be centred on just the building.

## The Defence of Britain Project

The Defence of Britain Project ran from April 1995 to March 2002 under direction of the Council for British Archaeology. In an indication of the enormity of the task the initial finish date had to be extended by two years. In that time, nearly 20,000 twentieth-century military sites in the United Kingdom were recorded by over 600 volunteers. This project, probably more than any other, engaged the public at all levels. Schools ran local surveys, as did historical and archaeological societies. But, much more than that, County Archaeologists became involved, elevating the position of the data. The knock on effect is that military remains now receive the same consideration in planning issues as any other environmental aspect. For airfields this has been an important step.

RAF Yatesbury, Wiltshire, 2005.
Unfortunately legislation can lead to
stagnancy in restoration. This Aircraft
Repair Section shed was listed as Grade
II★. Subsequent differences in the direction
the owner should take, caused by too many
parties expressing an interest, have led to its
collapse.

On 2 December 2005 the Department for Culture, Media and Sport proudly proclaimed, 'Chocks away! David Lammy secures a future for the aviation sites that protected our past.' The Culture Minister, under direction from the far-reaching Thematic Listing Programme conducted by English Heritage, recommended a number of sites be listed. The airfields concerned were: Bicester, Biggin Hill, Calshot, Catterick, Cosford, Cranwell, Debden, Duxford, East Kirkby, Elvington, Filton, Halton, Henlow, Hullavington, Kemble, Larkhill, Little Staughton, Little Walden, Ludham, Manby, Netheravon, Northolt, North Weald, Old Sarum, Rougham, Scampton, Spitalgate, Swanton, Morley, Upavon and Uxbridge. I make no apologies for listing these here as they serve to demonstrate the wide ranging implications of work to date, and it does not stop at the Second World War.

The Cold War brought about its own unique monuments and architecture, especially through the development of airfields. Stations that were retained after the Second World War invariably originated pre-war. Subsequently they now possess a multitude of structures, on occasion demonstrating practically every phase of aviation development. Two sites, Upper Heyford and Boscombe Down, serve to demonstrate this point. As introduced earlier, Upper Heyford was re-purchased in 1924 and became the first of Trenchard's 'Class A' aerodromes. It had earlier beginnings; however, the structures had been cleared at the end of the First World War. The setting of the hangar layout was to drive airfield construction for over a decade, yet it is Upper Heyford's post-Second World

RAF Upper Heyford, Oxfordshire, in 2005. Detailed discussion has secured large areas of the former USAF base for nature and architectural conservation. Meanwhile the site has 'earned its keep' by becoming one of the biggest car storage facilities in the country.

War structures that make it interesting. The air base contains architecture from the 1950s, '60s, '70s and '80s. Certain aspects have been identified as nationally important and as such will remain. Moreover, we are in the almost unique position to preserve the majority of the site, all 1,000 acres. This is certainly the view of a number of local pressure groups and probably the majority of aviation enthusiasts, but is it the right view? It is now ten years since the airfield was sold (1997) to the North Oxfordshire Consortium and since then they, English Heritage and Cherwell District Council, have worked intensively together to ensure the appropriate outcome for all interested parties.

5.7 In 2005, the Council, English Heritage and the North Oxfordshire Consortium jointly commissioned the production of a Conservation Plan to identify the historic significance of the site (excluding the mainly domestic and technical areas of the site to the south of the main airfield) and what is necessary to retain the significance of the main airbase as a monument and landscape when balanced against other requirements for the site, beyond those relating to its survival as a monument to the Cold War. Subsequently, a Conservation Area Appraisal was undertaken and in April 2006, following public consultation, the Council designated the whole of the airbase as a Conservation Area.

(Final Sustainability Appraisal Report (March 2007), Former RAF Upper Heyford Supplementary Planning Document, Cherwell District Council)

*Above:* RAF Greenham Common, Berkshire, in 2005. The GAMA site was the focus of much media and civil attention during the 1980s. Subsequently the site has been designated a Scheduled Ancient Monument, primarily due to its place in British social history.

*Left:* RAF Greenham Common, Berkshire, in 2005. In a classic piece of environmental recycling the runway and hard standings of this contentious site were removed and used as aggregate for the Newbury bypass in the 1990s. The airfield has subsequently been returned to its former common appearance.

The plan is ambitious and has already seen the scheduling of the Special Weapons Store as a Scheduled Ancient Monument. But does it go far enough? With all such projects it is a matter of trade-off. The secret is to balance the upkeep of those nationally important structures with both the conservation effort and proposed development. Ideally, if the development goes ahead then there should be more impetus to maintain those monuments, although whilst the debate drags on the structures are deteriorating. Only time will tell if all parties make the right choices.

Boscombe Down, just north of Salisbury, has a similar pedigree to Upper Heyford. It was opened as a Training Depot Station before spending a few years in private hands. then the Government re-purchased the site in 1925 as part of the Wessex Bombing Area initiative. A series of construction phases can be readily recognised, covering every decade from the 1920s through to the 1980s, and defence orientated construction is still ongoing. So what makes the site different from Upper Heyford? Simply, it is still operational. Boscombe Down is one of the post-war 'Ministry' airfields utilised by the Aircraft & Armament Experimental Establishment (A&AEE). Through a series of major cuts it has become the last of its kind. Today Boscombe Down is home to the QinetiQ fleet, a number of aircraft that, like the airfield, span the entire post-war period. Various trials on military orientated flight equipment are carried out and the Empire Test Pilots School (ETPS) operates its world famous training course from the station. The aerodrome is very close to the ranges on Salisbury Plain and the coast, enabling the majority of test flying to be carried out in the local area. Interestingly this was the main reason its sister airfields at Bedford and Farnborough were closed and the main reason for the TDS eighty years previously. Granted, some small-scale demolition has occurred over the years but generally all the main aspects are present. Boscombe Down is, however, substantially different from those sites already disposed of. The station still forms part of the Ministry of Defence estate.

Conservation is not the preserve of the last ten years; much earlier, aerodrome-wide initiatives have been in evidence over the years. One such site is RAF Hullavington. The Aircraft Storage Unit is often cited as a triumph of expansion period construction. The majority of the airfield structures were designed in consultation with the Royal Fine Arts Commission and Council for the Protection of Rural England, leading to the facing of all buildings with Cotswold Stone. On 15 September 1992 North Wiltshire District Council, recognising the importance of the station, designated the entire airfield a conservation area. This placed a further obstacle in the way of any proposed development and forced the MOD to consider alternative, sustainable uses for the site. Post-2005, the majority of the station is now protected. However, this situation is neither unique, nor is it the earliest example of conservation on an airfield. One station that has had its fair share of close shaves with the developer is RAF Duxford. It is worth describing some of the aerodrome's history and how it has become one of the most famous aviation museums in the world. I make no apologies for the following as it serves to demonstrate the historical complexities of the station.

Duxford was first used by flying machines during the manoeuvres of 1912; however, it was as No.35 Training Depot Station, opening in 1918, that aircraft were first permanently stationed there. Duxford was one of the few sites to be retained after the First World

Building 62: The Guardhouse. Built in 1932 this structure is now protected through listing, demonstrating the far-reaching effects of work by English Heritage and the Imperial War Museum.

War, continuing as a training establishment and, from April 1923, as a fighter station as part of the Fighting Area defending London. During this period a number of structures synonymous with 1920s airfield designs were built including the Station HQ, Operations Block and Guardhouse. In 1938 the resident squadron (No.19) took delivery of the Royal Air Force's first Spitfire, an aircraft that the station was to become inextricably linked with over the next few years. Duxford played a pivotal role in the Battle of Britain. The station was part of No.12 Group, responsible for the protection of Eastern England and the Midlands and being the most southerly base in the group it was well placed to support No.11 Group on the south coast. It was from here that Squadron Leader Douglas Bader led into battle what was to be known as the 'Duxford' or 'Big Wing', eventually five squadrons' strong. In 1941 the Air Fighting Development Unit took up residence, flying captured German aircraft for tactical evaluation, and by April 1943 this and the RAF had been replaced by the 78th Fighter Group of the USAAF.

After the war the station was handed back to the Royal Air Force. Luckily the USAAF laid a substantial amount of PSP in the latter stages of the war thus allowing Gloster Meteors to be stationed there from 1947. A singular paved surface was completed in 1951 with an operational readiness platform at each end and, in 1961, the final jet fighters to operate out of Duxford, the Gloster Javelins, left the station. After that, debate as to how the site was to be utilised rolled on for a number of years. Ideas spanned a possible sports centre or even a prison; the accommodation, especially married quarters, was subsequently handed over to families from RAF Stradishall, a situation that prevailed into the early 1970s. The airfield side of the station was destined for greater things.

In 1965 the seeds were sown for one of the epic films of the latter twentieth century – *The Battle of Britain*. Its producer, Ben S. Fisz, quickly ascertained that the Air Ministry would support such a film, possibly with facilities and aircraft. By 1967 a dedicated company, Spitfire Productions Ltd, had been set up to create the required 'air forces' for the film:

> Further to our discussion earlier today, I would like to reiterate the needs of my client – Spitfire Productions Ltd. – for technical assistance during the forthcoming film production 'THE BATTLE OF BRITAIN'.
>
> It was outlined that the main Battle Fleet would consist of some 33 Spitfires (11 to fly and 6 to taxi), 7 Hurricanes (5 to fly and 2 to taxi) and 27 Me 109s, (18 to fly and 6 to taxi). The latter can be discounted since they will be serviced by Spanish Air Force personnel in Spain early in 1968 and later in the U.K.
>
> (Hamish Mahaddie to Air Cmdre A.L. Winskill, 31 October 1967 (Air 2/18162))

Naturally the 32nd largest airforce in the world, as it later swelled to, needed stations to park-up. Henlow was to be used as the company's MU; it was there that the majority of the aircraft needed were refurbished, some to flying conditions. West Malling and Hawkinge were pressed back into service, as was North Weald. However, it was Duxford that became the centre for filming the majority of the flying scenes.

> Duxford – The Company said this airfield was vital to the film, and was required from now until September 1st 1968. Accommodation would be required for 250 people, plus a Wing of Spitfires and a Wing of Messerschmitts etc. The Company will wish to refurbish, at their own expense, some of the airfield buildings, but not the accommodation.
>
> (Meeting held on 8 November 1967 (Air 2/18162)).

The airfield subsequently played three different stations in the film – a French airfield, complete with replica château, the South Downs Flying Club, and Duxford itself. The centre-piece of the ground-filmed sequences was the bombing of the airfield, the situations around which has since become the stuff of legend. Discussion rages today as to whether the production company actually had permission to demolish, through explosion, the general repair shed as part of the scene. Leonard Mosley in his history of the film in 1969 suggests not. In a letter to David Haft, the producers' assistant, John Palmer stated:

> I have not seen any specific document giving us permission to destroy certain parts of Hangar No.3… I am particularly anxious to have sight of our Ministry of Defence permits for this sequence and at the same time do not wish to open a can of beans.

Not deterred by the lack of paperwork, the production crew 'bombed' the airfield, including the general repair shed. Incidentally, it took two attempts to fully demolish it!

By 1970 discussions had resurfaced regarding the disposal of the site. In mid-June 1970 proposals were towards a regional sports centre 'to include flying, gliding and parachuting among the recreational activities.' In an indication of what was to come, redevelopment could include 'the occasional use of the main runway (reduced to two thirds its existing length) by aircraft being flown into an aero-museum which would be set up in one of the existing hangars'. A public enquiry in 1976, in the face of proposed motorway construction over the airfield, was supported by Douglas Bader, amongst others. Consequently only the eastern extremities of the site were affected, ensuring Duxford retained a usable length of runway. Subsequently the Imperial War Museum has used the site as a location for its large object collection prior to the purchase of the site by Duxford Aviation Society, IWM and Cambridgeshire County Council in 1977. The Thematic Listing Programme requested the site be made a conservation area in 1999 and in 2005 thirty-four structures were listed or had their existing protection risen. Incidentally, the use of airfields as overspills for large museum collections is not unique to Duxford. Wroughton is utilised by the National Museum of Science and Industry, whilst at RAF St Athan the National Museum of Wales stores some of its arts treasures.

## 'Defence is our Nature is in our Defence'

The Ministry of Defence has a very active conservation and environmental operation. Operated through the Defence Estates network, the team manages over 670 listed buildings and 1,100 scheduled monuments. From a central office DE(Cons) supports a large number of conservation groups located on major sites, and these include airfields. In 1973 the Nugent Report recommended the establishment of the post of MOD Conservation Officer to help target and co-ordinate the MOD's conservation efforts. The post remains the principal link between the MOD and statutory bodies (English Heritage, English Nature and so on). A team of dedicated MOD conservationists has evolved, with over 100 conservation estate managers to advise on sensitive management of the land used by MOD in the UK and overseas:

> MOD conservation policy takes account of all relevant UK and International legislation. Under this policy, it is mandatory to establish a Conservation Group wherever there are nationally protected sites on MOD land, or significant conservation value. The groups contain a broad range of interest groups, from both military and civilian backgrounds. The Commanding Officer or Head of Establishment is usually the Chairman, and the group consists of representatives from Defence Estates, the relevant statutory bodies (English Nature, Scottish Natural Heritage, Countryside Council for Wales and the Environment and Heritage Service (NI)) and other experts in wildlife, geology and archaeology, most of whom are volunteers. There is an army of over 5000 volunteers that take part in MOD Conservation projects in the UK and on the land our military uses overseas.
>
> (Defence Estates Conservation, 2006)

## How does it all fit together?

I said at the beginning of this work that I ask different questions of airfields to my colleagues and I hope this has come across here. Throughout the myriad of constructional techniques and political posturing that has driven so much of the British landscape, is it possible to recognise patterns? The answer is a clear yes; I trust you agree. Airfields are not very mobile (unless you consider the Advanced Landing Grounds of the Second World War or the Harrier Hide) and subsequently their position in the landscape has been the subject of many meetings, surveying and planning. This position is driven by two factors – who the threat is from, and the aircraft technology. This explains the positions of RNAS stations, especially the airships, countering the U-boat threat. It also explains: the location of the Training Depot Stations (TDS) in areas clear of enemy attack; the opening of the bomber bases in the late 1920s in the Wessex region when France was considered a problem; the positioning of the Aircraft Storage Units in the western areas of Britain, around the major aircraft manufacturers, and as far away as possible from the European threat; and the subsequent location and structure of the dispersed bomber airfields, with their temporarily constructed buildings of the Second World War.

From here there is regression. The dispersed, temporary sites were the first to be abandoned in favour of the permanent architecture of the inter-war aerodromes. The inter-war aerodromes conform to the same rigid layout as the TDS – Hangars, Technical, Domestic – all next to each other. By the mid-1950s this arrangement is considered vulnerable and dispersal becomes relevant again. However, cost dictates that only the aircraft benefit from this and the nuclear force is subsequently dispersed around the United Kingdom. It is not until the late 1970s that dispersal appears back on airfields, this time in the shape of the Hardened Aircraft Shelter. The location of sites from the 1950s makes little sense to the landscape historian, as the increased performance of first jet powered aircraft and subsequently ballistic and cruise missiles renders geographic location obsolete. From the late 1970s, the airfields still operational in the United Kingdom owe their existence as much to luck as judgement. By the end of the Cold War only specialist bases, often holding the aircraft type Operational Conversion Unit, appear safe. With the turn of the century only sixty-three military airfields are still operational, many housing a multitude of types. Clearly the emphasise here is cost effectiveness rather than tactical consideration.

The one luxury the twentieth-century archaeologist has over his earlier period colleagues is a good, if incomplete, set of records. However, when I started the research for this book, little did I know how fragmented the coverage could be. Granted, English Heritage has heightened awareness of all periods, but overall the coverage is noticeably bias towards the Second World War. If I have achieved anything in this work, it has to be to demonstrate that continuity, especially of ideas, is the key behind these large landscape features. It is this continuity more than any other that has driven the landscape we see today. In the coming decades airfields will undergo more change and more difficult choices will need to be made, yet I consider we are better placed now than ever before to make the right choices.

# BIBLIOGRAPHY

Betts, A., 1995 *Royal Air Force airfield construction service 1939 to 46*, Airfield Research Publishing.

Campbell, L., *Netheravon Airfield Camp 1913: From Royal Flying Corps to Army Air Corps*, private publication.

Clarke, B., 2005 *Four Minute Warning: Britain's Cold War*, Tempus Publishing, Stroud.

Clarke, B., 2007 *Ten Tons for Tempelhof: The Berlin Airlift*, Tempus Publishing, Stroud.

Cooksley, P.G., 2000 *The RFC/RNAS Handbook 1914–18*, Sutton Publishing, Stroud.

Cruddas, C., 1994 *In Cobhams' Company: Sixty Years of Flight Refuelling Limited*, Cobham plc, Wimborne.

Dye, P.J., 2001 Logistics and the Battle of Britain, *Air Force Journal & Logistics*, Vol.XXIV, No.4, page 33–42.

Francis, P., 1996 *British Military Airfield Architecture: From Airships to the Jet Age*, Patrick Stephens Limited, Somerset.

HMSO 1952 *Military Engineering, Volume 5 – Roads and Airfields, part two. Soil mechanics in road & airfield construction*

Higham, R., 1998 *Bases of Air Strategy: Building Airfields for the RAF 1914–1945*, Airlift Publishing, Shrewsbury.

Hilling, J.B., 1995 *Strike Hard: a bomber airfield at war, RAF Downham Market and its squadrons 1942 to 46*, Alan Sutton Publishing Ltd.

James, N.D.G., 1983 *Gunners at Larkhill: A History of the Royal School of Artillery*, Gresham Books, Oxfordshire.

Kohan, C.M., 1952 *Works and Buildings: History of the Second World War*, United Kingdom Civil Series, HMSO.

Longoria, M., 1992 *A Historical View of Air Policing Doctrine: Lessons from the British Experience between the Wars, 1919–1939*, unpublished Thesis, School of Advanced Air Power Studies, Maxwell Air Force Base, Alabama.

Mowthorpe, C., 1998 *Battlebags: British Airships of the First World War*, Wrens Park, Stroud.

Osborne, M., 2004 *Defending Britain: Twentieth-Century Military Structures in the Landscape*, Tempus Publishing, Stroud.

Parsons, M., 2006 *Cricklade Revealed: Social Life During the Second World War*, part 6, Parson Creative.

Raper, B.J., 1972 *White Rose Base*, Aero Litho Company, Lincoln.

Saunders, H. St G., *1944 Per Ardua: The Rise of British Airpower 1911–1939*, Oxford University Press, London.

Simmons, G. & Abraham, B., 2001 *Strong Foundations: Driffield's Aerodrome from 1917 to 2000,*
    Hutton Press Ltd, Beverley.
Steel, N. & Hart, P., 1997 *Tumult in the Clouds: The British Experience of the War in the Air, 1914–*
    *1918,* Hodder & Stoughton, London.
Wessex Archaeology, 1998 *Stonehenge Military Installations: A Desk Based Study,* unpublished Client
    Report 444411, Wessex Archaeology.
Wynn, H., 1996, *Forged in War: a History of RAF Transport Command 1943 to 1967,* Air Historical
    Branch, Ministry of Defence, the Stationery Office.

## Public Record Office Documents

Air 2/294 ASSOCIATIONS, CLUBS, SOCIETIES: etc: Named (CODE A, 57/6): Dance at
    Catterick Aerodrome and infringement of Copyright of Performing Right Society. (1926-
    1931)
Air 1/72/15/9/140 Aerodrome Constructional Company – correspondence re establishment.
    (1918)
Air 1/2558 Proposed air stations at Scarborough, Redcar and Hornsea (19 June 1915)
Air 1/2310/217 Resume of the Central Flying School, Upavon (1913)
Air 2/254 ACCOMMODATION: LAND (CODE A, 2/9): Re acquisition of land at Boscombe
    Down. (1924-1925)
Air 2/258 ACCOMMODATION: Buildings (CODE A, 2/3): Arrangements for possession of
    Hendon Aerodrome and certain buildings with the Receiver (1924-1925)
PRO 30/69/620E Defence White Paper March 1935.
Air 2/18884 RAF operational capability (1970–74)
CAB 21/3182 Scampton Airfield: proposal to develop aerodrome (March–October 1954)
Air 14/1610 Emergency runway: Carnaby Yorks (1943 May–1944 March).
DEFE 51/1 Pewsey, Wilts: disposal of former airfield camp at Alton Barnes (1962–1968)
Air 5/335 Sites for new aerodromes in Oxfordshire and Gloucestershire (1923–1924)
Air 29/622 No. 29 Clyffe Pypard, Wiltshire. (September 1941–October 1947)
Air 28/440 RAF Lossiemouth Operational Record Book (July 1945–April 1946)
Air 2/8533 Air Ministry; Lands (Code B, 7/4) Bisterne, Hampshire, Acquisition of land for
    advanced operational site (1942–1947)
Air 20/8542 RAF Stations (Code 67/36) Lands; Accommodation RAF Coltishall (1938–1970)
Air 28/86 RAF Blakehill Farm (February 1944–January 1946)
Air 29/857 No.63 RAF Base Leeming (June 1944–August 1945)
Air 8/237 RAF Expansion Scheme 'L' (1938)
Air 2/4293 Aerodromes (Code B,3); Site for new aerodrome at Finningley, Yorks (1935)
T 161/846 Land Drainage; Methwold and Feltwell Drainage Board (August 1937–March 1938)
AVIA 2/1450 Aerodrome Licences; East Heslerton, Yorks (1939–1940)
Air 2/343 Personal Accounts and Claims: General (Code A, 28/2); Claim for compensation by
    Mrs Atkinson for depreciation of property near Tangmere Aerodrome (1928–1929)
Air 20/8539 Aerodrome (Code 3) Lands and Accommodation; Finance Matters RAF Dishforth
    (1935–1961)
Air 5/515 Defence of Aerodromes (Home Defence) against low flying attack (1925–1926)
Air 2/17807 Disposal of Airfield at Skellingthorpe (1956–1965)

# INDEX

If you are interested in purchasing other books published by The History Press,
or in case you have difficulty finding any of our books in your local bookshop,
you can also place orders directly through our website

**www.thehistorypress.co.uk**